The Playworker's
HANDBOOK

The Playworker's
HANDBOOK

Teena Kamen

Hodder Arnold

A MEMBER OF THE HODDER HEADLINE GROUP

Dedication

To my son, Tom Jennings, with love and affection.

Orders: please contact Bookpoint Ltd, 130 Milton Park, Abingdon, Oxon OX14 4SB. Telephone: 44 (0)1235 827720. Fax: 44 (0)1235 400454. Lines are open from 9.00–6.00, Monday to Saturday, with a 24-hour message answering service. You can also order through our website, www.hoddereducation.co.uk

If you have any comments to make about this, or any of our other titles, please send them to educationenquiries@hodder.co.uk

British Library Cataloguing in Publication Data
A catalogue record for this title is available from the British Library

ISBN-10: 0 340 88545 9
ISBN-13: 978 0 340 885 451

First Edition Published 2005
Impression number 10 9 8 7 6 5 4 3 2 1
Year 2009 2008 2007 2006 2005

Typeset by Pantek Arts Ltd, Maidstone, Kent.
Printed in Italy for Hodder Arnold, an imprint of Hodder Education, a member of the Hodder Headline Group, 338 Euston Road, London NW1 3BH.

Contents

Acknowledgements   vi

Introduction   1

How to use this book   2

1 So you want to be a playworker?   3

2 The play environment   30

3 Play and child development   52

4 Planning and supporting play   74

5 Health and safety in the play setting   95

6 Child protection   117

7 Children's health and well-being   137

8 Promoting positive relationships and behaviour   155

9 Working with parents and carers   181

10 Professional practice   190

11 Managing a play setting   220

12 Promoting play services   249

Appendix A: A–Z of useful contacts and information   263

Appendix B: Record of key tasks   271

Glossary   276

References   279

Index   284

Acknowledgements

Many thanks to the children and staff at the Badger's Sett Playscheme and the St Thomas Rainbow Guides with whom I gained my experience of providing play opportunities in an informal setting.

Thanks also to the pupils and staff at Rood End Primary School and Withymoor Primary School where I gained much of my experience of working with children.

Special thanks to Chris Helm and Karl Doughty for their technical support during the writing of this book.

The author and publishers would like to thank the following for permission to reproduce material in this book:

Pages 5, 62, John Birdsall Photography; pages 13, 23, 113, 156, 245, John Walmsley; pages 42, 68, 160, 188, Paul Doyle/Photofusion; pages 60, 76, 77, 88, 148, Alamy Images; page 66, Richard Smith/Masterfile/Zefa; page 143, Zelick Nagel/Getty Images; page 169, Richard Alton/Photofusion; page 207, Lauren Shear/Science Photo Library.

Every effort has been made to obtain necessary permission with reference to copyright material. The publishers apologise if inadvertently any sources remain unacknowledged and will be glad to make the necessary arrangements at the earliest opportunity.

Introduction

The Playworker's Handbook is a comprehensive guide to all aspects of working with children and young people in a variety of play settings including after-school clubs, breakfast clubs, hospital children's wards, adventure playgrounds, play centres, playbuses, sport/leisure centres, holiday play schemes and community projects. This book covers practical considerations such as:

* ✯ organising the play environment
* ✯ maintaining children's health, safety and security
* ✯ promoting positive working relationships
* ✯ developing professional practice
* ✯ planning and supporting self-directed play.

This book clearly links theory and practice by exploring different *theoretical* aspects of play and child development. It demonstrates how these aspects relate to providing *practical* support for children's play in the play environment. It explains complex theoretical issues in ways that can easily be understood, but is sufficiently challenging to assist students in developing a sound knowledge base to complement their practical skills.

There is particular emphasis on the role of the playworker in supporting self-directed play, with detailed information on planning for play opportunities that meet children's and young people's (including those with disabilities) needs and rights. The book also includes exercises to develop the playworker's professional skills as well as key tasks (linked to the current NVQ Level 2 in Playwork and the new NVQ Level 3 in Playwork), which may be used to contribute towards a portfolio of evidence.

This book is of particular use to students (and their tutors/assessors) on playwork courses and provides the background knowledge relevant to the requirements of providing appropriate play opportunities for children and young people aged 4 to 16 years in a variety of play settings.

How to use this book

This book contains the knowledge requirements for a range of topics related to playwork. The book includes practical ideas for linking knowledge and understanding with meeting the national standards for playwork, and is suitable for students on a wide range of playwork courses, especially NVQ/SVQ Levels 2 and 3 in Playwork. It may also be of interest to experienced playworkers who are updating their current practice as part of their Continuing Professional Development.

The headings in each section are related to NVQ Levels 2 and 3 for ease of reference. Read the relevant chapter for the topic you are currently studying and do the exercises/key tasks as specified. The key tasks can be done in any order, as appropriate to your college and/or play setting's requirements, and can contribute to your formal assessment (for example, as part of your portfolio of evidence). However, it is suggested that you read Chapter 4, 'Planning and supporting play', *before* you start planning and implementing your own play opportunities for children and young people. *Do* remember to follow your play setting/college guidelines.

The chart in Appendix B at the back of the book will help you to keep a record of the key tasks as you complete them.

1 So you want to be a playworker?

Key points

- ✿ What is a playworker?
- ✿ Why be a playworker?
- ✿ Types of playworker
- ✿ The role of the playworker
- ✿ Personal qualities, skills and attitudes
- ✿ Experience of working with children
- ✿ Playwork training and qualifications
- ✿ How to apply for a job as a playworker
- ✿ Finding employment as a playworker
- ✿ Advantages and disadvantages of working as a playworker
- ✿ Considering other types of work with children

What is a playworker?

A playworker plans, organises and supervises a range of play opportunities for children and young people aged 4 to 16 years or for one particular age group. Playworkers aim to encourage children and young people to:

- ★ learn and understand about themselves and others
- ★ experiment with a variety of play materials and equipment
- ★ explore the world around them
- ★ express themselves through play
- ★ develop co-operative and team-building skills
- ★ develop their imaginative and creative skills.

Playworkers are involved in planning and supporting appropriate play opportunities for the children and young people they work with. These include providing relevant and readily accessible play activities for males and females, children and young people with disabilities, or from ethnic minority communities or low-income families. Play opportunities may include organising team games and sports, arranging drama, music and other entertainments, supervising art and craft activities, taking children on day trips and outings, such as a visit to an adventure playground, an animal sanctuary, a country park or the seaside.

Playworkers are also responsible for supervising the children at all times, ensuring that safety procedures are followed, encouraging positive behaviour and dealing with challenging behaviour.

A qualified and/or experienced playworker can:

- ★ look after children and young people aged 4 to 16 years
- ★ provide high-quality and convenient childcare (e.g. in out-of-school clubs or at holiday play schemes)
- ★ provide plenty of fun learning opportunities within a safe play environment
- ★ ensure the children are safe, well cared for and happy
- ★ provide opportunities for self-directed play
- ★ meet each child's physical, emotional, social and intellectual needs
- ★ have special playwork skills with a clear understanding of children's play.

Why be a playworker?

It is estimated that 180,000 new childcare and playwork jobs will be required as part of the expected expansion to provide 250,000 new childcare places by 2006 (Early Years National Training Organisation, 2003). There is a nationwide shortage of playworkers, and thousands of people are needed to work with children and young people aged 4 to 16 years. Playwork is an ideal career for people who want to work with children and young people in a variety of play settings, including out-of-school clubs and holiday play schemes.

Ten possible reasons for wanting to be a playworker
1. You have a genuine love of children and young people.
2. You enjoy the company of children and young people.
3. You enjoy working with children and young people.
4. You enjoy assisting with the all-round development of children and young people.
5. You want to help children and young people to develop social skills for adult life.
6. You prefer working with groups of children and young people in an informal setting.
7. You want a rewarding and fulfilling career working with children and young people.
8. You want to make a real difference to the lives of children and young people.
9. You want to provide a positive role model.
10. You want a career that fits in with your own family commitments.

It can be a rewarding and enjoyable profession. Playwork skills and experience can also be useful for people who need an understanding of children and young people for related occupations such as nursery nursing, teaching, psychology, social work, and so on. Playwork experience and qualifications can also be used to move into other types of work with children and young people, including early years care and education or youth work.

> EXERCISE: List your own reasons for wanting to work as a playworker.

Types of playworker

Some playworkers work directly with children and young people by providing play opportunities ranging from sporting activities to art and crafts. Others (such as senior playworkers or playwork managers) have less direct contact with children and young people; their work may involve planning, supervising, dealing with paperwork and organising play projects.

Most playwork provision is required outside school hours (in the evenings, at weekends and during school holidays, say). However, some playwork provision is needed during the day (such as playwork with the under-5s and hospital playwork). Some playworkers work in play settings during term time only (for instance, in out-of-school clubs). Others work during school holidays only (for example, at holiday play schemes). Some work at holiday play schemes provided for a specific group of children and young people (for example, children with special needs or children from refugee families). Some play provision is available all year round (in day care settings, say). Some playworkers may work away from home (perhaps at a summer camp). Some may work full-time (about 35–39 hours per week) and some part-time (up to 16 hours per week).

Playworkers may work in a wide range of play environments, such as adventure playgrounds, community centres or church halls, day care settings, holiday play schemes, hospital playroom/children's wards, leisure centres, out-of-school clubs, playbuses, play centres and youth clubs.

Playworker working in an out-of-school club.

The role of the playworker

The role of the playworker includes planning play activities for each day. They should also involve the children in planning what they are going to do. The playworker supervises the children at all times, ensuring that all appropriate safety procedures are followed and giving first aid if required. They should encourage children's positive behaviour and deal with any challenging behaviour.

A playworker's role also involves setting up and putting away equipment, as well as encouraging the children to help with these tasks as appropriate to their ages and levels of development. At the end of each day, a playworker evaluates the day's play activities and keeps any necessary records. They may talk to parents/carers, colleagues and other professionals about the children (remembering to follow the setting's confidentiality policy). They must also follow the correct child protection procedures if they suspect a child is being abused.

A playworker's exact duties depend on the type of playwork provision, the location of the setting and the ages of the children or young people. Examples of typical duties include:

- ✮ planning stimulating play activities for children to choose themselves
- ✮ preparing the play space before the children arrive (e.g. getting materials ready)
- ✮ checking that all play equipment is working properly and safely
- ✮ welcoming children and their parents/carers
- ✮ talking with the children about the play activities they would like to do
- ✮ establishing ground rules and ensuring that all the children know what these are
- ✮ organising and participating in art and craft activities, day trips, outdoor activities, sports, storytelling, team games, and so on

---

The role of the playworker

The role of the playworker includes:

1. enabling children to learn and discover more about themselves and their world
2. providing play materials for the children to choose from and use to devise their own activities
3. suggesting play activities, but leaving the final choice to the children themselves
4. ensuring that all the children can play how they want to without being bullied
5. supporting children in resolving disagreements between themselves
6. encouraging play activities that develop social skills and help children to make friends
7. ensuring all children have play opportunities regardless of ethnic origin, sex or disability
8. enhancing children's play through positive and sensitive involvement in their activities
9. developing positive working relationships with children, staff and parents/carers
10. working effectively with other staff members as part of a team.

- ★ encouraging all the children to participate in activities
- ★ supervising play and ensuring the safety of the children at all times
- ★ tidying away and cleaning up after activities
- ★ administering basic first aid, if necessary
- ★ supervising more junior playworkers, volunteers and students
- ★ dealing with basic administration including record-keeping and controlling petty cash.

Personal qualities, skills and attitudes

Although their experience and qualifications will be varied, all playworkers should have a genuine interest in and respect for children and young people as individuals. All playworkers are unique individuals with their own distinct characteristics. However, to provide sensitive and effective support for children and their families, a playworker should possess the following personal qualities:

- ★ cheerful and friendly disposition
- ★ good sense of humour
- ★ reliability and stability
- ★ patience and tolerance
- ★ kindness and a caring manner
- ★ honesty and discretion
- ★ flexibility and versatility
- ★ confidence
- ★ enthusiasm
- ★ independence
- ★ physical fitness, stamina and energy.

A successful playworker should also possess the following personal skills and attitudes:

- ★ enjoyment of children's and young people's company
- ★ an understanding of the needs of children and young people aged 5 to 15 years
- ★ a knowledge and understanding of the importance of play
- ★ an ability to create a safe, fun and enjoyable play environment for children
- ★ an ability to listen to children and take what they say seriously
- ★ good verbal and written communication skills
- ★ resourcefulness and effective organisational skills
- ★ a responsible attitude
- ★ an ability to build positive relationships with children, staff and parents/carers

- ⭐ a calm approach to life
- ⭐ alert and observant
- ⭐ able to deal with children in an emergency or crisis
- ⭐ an ability to use creative ideas to stimulate children's imagination
- ⭐ able to gain children's and young people's respect
- ⭐ awareness of equal opportunities issues and the ability to be a positive role model
- ⭐ able to work well as part of a team.

EXERCISE: Make a list of your own personal qualities, skills and attitudes.

Experience of working with children

To find out if you have the necessary personal qualities, skills and attitudes to work as a playworker, you should spend time with children in a structured setting – for example, doing voluntary work in a school, playgroup or after-school club. Not only will this help you to decide if working with children is for you, it will also be useful preparation for a playwork course.

To start work as an assistant playworker you do not need any academic qualifications, but some experience of working with children is an advantage and may be required by some play settings or colleges offering playwork courses. Any experience of working with children will also help you to develop your knowledge, understanding and skills regarding the developmental needs of children and young people. The more experience you have of working with children, the more prepared you will be to deal with the demands of being a playworker, and this will give you a distinct advantage when applying for jobs as many employers value a playworker's experience as much as their qualifications.

Examples of experience of working with children include:

- ⭐ looking after children in your own family or friends' families (e.g. babysitting)
- ⭐ work experience in a school, nursery, etc.
- ⭐ leadership involvement in guide or scout activities
- ⭐ voluntary work (e.g. at playgroups or parent and toddler groups)
- ⭐ voluntary work for charities (e.g. children with special needs)
- ⭐ other jobs working with children (e.g. childminder, nursery nurse, youth worker).

If you have little or no experience of working with children, you may be able to gain some work experience by:

- ★ contacting local organisations and charities to find out about opportunities to work with children and/or young people as a volunteer
- ★ contacting your local council to find out about the work experience opportunities it has to offer
- ★ doing an introductory-level playwork course that includes a practical work placement.

Playwork training and qualifications

It is possible to work with children and young people aged 4 to 16 years without having any qualifications. Many people get into playwork by working as volunteers and, once they have some experience, move into paid part-time or full-time work. Some people combine voluntary work in a play setting with studying an introductory-level playwork course or Level 2 playwork qualification (see below).

However, since the introduction of the National Daycare Standards in September 2001, at least 50 per cent of staff working in a play setting must have an appropriate Level 2 qualification and the person in charge of the setting must have a relevant Level 3 qualification.

If you are thinking of becoming a playworker you could start by taking an informal 15-hour course called 'Making Choices', which looks at different aspects of working with children and young people. The aim of this course is to help you decide whether working with children and young people is the right career for you. The course is free and is run by a variety of organisations, including colleges, local councils, training providers and voluntary bodies. As part of the Making Choices course you will meet local people who work with children and young people, discuss childcare careers with local employers, look at different types of jobs in childcare, education and playwork, find out about relevant qualifications and training, look (briefly) at relevant legislation including health and safety, and gain a certificate for attending the course.

Introductory-level playwork courses

Since the introduction of the National Daycare Standards, all staff working with children must have appropriate induction training, relevant qualifications and appropriate experience of working with children. The Playwork Induction Standard (introduced in 2003) ensures that an introductory training course covers a specified range of relevant topics and is recognised by Ofsted.

The Playwork Induction Standard includes the key aspects of working with children and young people in a wide range of settings. The Playwork Induction Standard covers (SkillsActive, 2004c):

1. Play and Playwork
2. Supporting Children's Play
3. Teamwork
4. Health and Safety
5. Child Protection
6. Building Relationships.

Once you have completed a Playwork Induction Standard introductory training course you will receive a certificate with the SkillsActive national endorsement logo and you will then be recognised as working towards a Level 2 playwork qualification. The certificate is valid for a full year from the date of issue. To receive the certificate, you must:

☆ attend and actively participate in 80 per cent of the course
☆ work with children/young people as a paid employee or volunteer
☆ complete a Reflective Practice Sheet after at least ten hours of practical experience.

There are currently four courses that meet the Playwork Induction Standard criteria:

☆ Introducing Playwork (The Playwork Unit at SkillsActive)
☆ Playwork Basics Plus (Common Threads)
☆ Take Five for Play (Playwork Partnerships)
☆ Time to Play (Brighton and Hove Play Service).

There will be more nationally recognised introductory courses in the future; for an up-to-date list see the website at www.playwork.org.uk.

Level 2 playwork qualifications

Level 2 qualifications are for people working under supervision (such as assistant playworkers). Playworkers may have a Level 2 playwork qualification such as:

☆ CACHE Level 2 Certificate in Playwork
☆ CACHE Level 2 Certificate in Supporting Playwork Practice
☆ City & Guilds Level 2 Progression Award in Playwork
☆ NCFE Intermediate Certificate in Playwork
☆ NCFE Intermediate Certificate in Developing Skills for Working with Children and Young People

- ★ NOCN Intermediate Certificate in Playwork
- ★ NVQ Level 2 in Playwork (England, Wales and Northern Ireland)
- ★ SVQ Level 2 in Playwork (Scotland).

Studying for a Level 2 playwork qualification can be a useful starting point for a career working with children and young people, especially if you have limited experience of working with children or young people, are uncertain which aspects of working with children appeal to you or lack the academic skills or entry requirements for a Level 3 course (see below).

Having successfully completed a Level 2 playwork qualification you could:

- ★ continue your studies with a Level 3 playwork qualification
- ★ move directly into employment (working as a holiday scheme playworker, say)
- ★ study for an S/NVQ Level 3 qualification while working as an assistant playworker
- ★ study for a Level 3 playwork qualification at a later date.

Level 3 playwork qualifications

Level 3 qualifications are for people who plan and organise their own work as well as supervise the work of others within the setting. Examples of Level 3 playwork qualifications include:

- ★ CACHE Level 3 Certificate of Professional Development in Work with Children and Young People
- ★ CACHE Level 3 Certificate in Work with Children
- ★ CACHE Level 3 Diploma in Playwork
- ★ CACHE Level 3 Diploma in Supporting Playwork Practice
- ★ City & Guilds Level 3 Certificate in Work with Children
- ★ Edexcel Level 3 Certificate in Work with Children
- ★ NCFE Advanced Certificate in Playwork
- ★ NOCN Level 3 Certificate in Work with Children
- ★ NVQ Level 3 in Playwork (England, Wales and Northern Ireland)
- ★ SVQ Level 3 in Playwork (Scotland)
- ★ NVQ Level 3 Certificate in Work with Children APEL (Accreditation of Prior Experience and Learning).

Studying for a Level 3 playwork qualification can be a useful way to develop your career working with children and young people, especially if you have lots of experience of working with children or young people, have regular contact with children/young people in a playwork setting, possess a Level 2 playwork qualification, have a satisfactory level of general education (e.g. GCSEs at grade C or above) or want to progress to a supervisory role in a playwork setting.

Having successfully completed a Level 3 playwork qualification you could:

★ continue your studies by doing a Level 4 qualification
★ work as a senior playworker or play scheme leader
★ study for an S/NVQ Level 4 qualification while working as a senior playworker
★ study for a Level 4 qualification at a later date.

Level 4 playwork qualifications

Level 4 qualifications are for experienced practitioners who manage large or multiple settings across an area. Examples of Level 4 playwork qualifications include:

★ NVQ Level 4 in Playwork (England, Wales and Northern Ireland)
★ SVQ Level 4 in Playwork (Scotland)
★ BTEC Higher National Diploma (HND)
★ Diploma in Higher Education (DipHE) in Playwork
★ Foundation Degree in Playwork.

Studying for a Level 4 playwork qualification can be a useful way to further develop your career working with children and young people, especially if you have lots of experience of working with children or young people, have plenty of supervisory experience in a play setting, possess a Level 3 playwork qualification, have a higher level of general education (e.g. A levels/H grades) or want to progress to a managerial role in a playwork setting.

Having successfully completed a Level 4 playwork qualification you could:

★ extend your DipHE to a degree-level qualification
★ continue your studies with a degree-level qualification (e.g. BA (Hons) Professional Studies in Playwork)
★ work as a playwork manager or playwork development officer
★ study for a degree-level qualification at a later date.

> EXERCISE: What playwork qualifications and/or experience do you have already? What playwork qualification(s) are you currently studying or would like to study?

Entry requirements for playwork courses

Entry requirements can vary, but may include five GCSEs (A–C)/S grades (1–3) and two A levels/three H grades, or equivalent. An Access to Higher Education qualification may also be accepted for entry to certain courses. If experienced in a related field, you may be able to gain recognition of skills through Accredited Prior Learning (APL). You will need to check with colleges or universities for exact entry requirements.

The entry requirements on any playwork course may be waived for mature applicants with appropriate experience of working with children (e.g. working in a playgroup or as a childminder) as long as they have a satisfactory interview.

S/NVQ courses involve assessment in the workplace and students have their performance assessed against the National Occupational Standards for Playwork. Such courses usually have no formal entry requirements as there are no assignments or examinations. However, if you decide to pursue an NVQ qualification, do not underestimate the demands of the course as there will still be some written work, such as writing and evaluating activity plans.

Whatever the entry requirements for a particular course, you will need to attend an interview, where you should show that you have a genuine interest in working with children/young people and that you can meet the demands of the course.

Qualified playworkers will usually have followed a course that covers various aspects of working with children and young people aged 4 to 16 years in a playwork setting, including:

- ☆ understanding the roles and responsibilities of the playworker
- ☆ promoting equal opportunities and anti-discriminatory practice
- ☆ promoting children's development through play
- ☆ planning and supporting play
- ☆ maintaining children's health and safety (including first aid)
- ☆ promoting children's health and well-being
- ☆ contributing to child protection
- ☆ responding to children's behaviour in play settings
- ☆ developing positive relationships with children, parents and other staff
- ☆ working as part of a team
- ☆ being a reflective practitioner
- ☆ promoting play services.

Student at work placement in a playwork setting.

In addition, a college course includes written assignments and practical assessments in a variety of playwork settings including play schemes, out-of-school clubs and sports centres.

You can find out the latest information about playwork qualifications from the Qualifications and Curriculum Authority (England, Wales and Northern Ireland), the Scottish Qualifications Authority, playwork websites, national examining/awarding bodies and local colleges that run playwork courses in your area. (For further details of where to look, see Appendix A, 'A–Z of useful contacts and information', at the end of this book.)

> **EXERCISE:** Find out what playwork training opportunities are available in your local area.

Disclosures

All playworkers – including paid employees, volunteers and students – must be checked by the police before they can work with children or young people. The term 'police check' is now obsolete in the UK; the correct terminology is now disclosure.

A disclosure from the Criminal Records Bureau (CRB) is a legal requirement for anyone with regular, continuous and close access to children, including volunteers and students working in schools, nurseries and play settings. If you work directly with children and young people you will need an enhanced disclosure, especially if you have unsupervised contact with them. (For further information, see Chapter 11.)

Finding employment as a playworker

As a result of the National Childcare Strategy, the number of job opportunities for playworkers is growing rapidly. Positions are available with local authorities, NHS hospital trusts, voluntary organisations and private companies including holiday operators and the leisure industry. There are some full-time jobs for playworkers but most are part-time. Some jobs are seasonal (for example, play schemes in the school holidays). Some playworkers may be self-employed or work as play consultants.

There are many places you can look for employment. Details of job vacancies can be found in newspapers or specialist magazines, local colleges, local councils, local networks and on the Internet. You could try looking at:

- ★ local council jobs bulletins (available from libraries, community centres, town halls and council personnel departments)
- ★ local council websites
- ★ the official recruitment website for local government (www.lgjobs.com)
- ★ community libraries and college noticeboards
- ★ job sections in local newspapers
- ★ national newspapers (the *Guardian*, for instance, includes job advertisements for vacancies in the public sector in its Wednesday edition)
- ★ the Playwork Jobs website (www.playworkjobs.co.uk)
- ★ the Playwork Unit website (www.playwork.org.uk)
- ★ professional journals and magazines (e.g. *Children Now, Nursery World, The Times Educational Supplement, Young People Now*).

For more information about employment as a playworker you could also contact:

- ★ the childcare recruitment team at your local authority
- ★ the JobCentre or JobCentre Plus in your local area
- ★ the local Careers Service for adults
- ★ the local Connexions Service for 13–19 year olds
- ★ local employers (e.g. nurseries, pre-schools, playgroups, play schemes)
- ★ local out-of-school clubs or play centres
- ★ local colleges offering playwork courses, to see if they have details of any suitable vacancies.

EXERCISE: Have a look at the jobs available for playworkers in your area. For example:
- visit your local library or community centre to find information about job vacancies for playworkers
- look in the local newspaper or specialist magazines
- check your college noticeboard or contact the local college
- take a look at some playworker vacancies on the Internet.

Pay levels for playworkers are set locally rather than nationally and salaries vary from region to region. Your salary as a playworker will also depend on:

- ★ the type of play setting
- ★ the number of hours you work
- ★ your training and qualifications
- ★ your experience of working with children/young people
- ★ your level of responsibility.

Salaries for playworkers start at between £8652 and £15,240 per year. An experienced playworker can earn from £11,115. The top salary for a senior playworker can be about £20,364 (www.connexions.gov.uk).

With experience, playworkers can become supervisors or managers. There are opportunities to become self-employed, and set up and manage an out-of-school club. With relevant qualifications, a playworker could specialise in a specific area of playwork, such as:

- ✫ adventure playworker
- ✫ play equipment designer
- ✫ play therapist
- ✫ playwork consultant
- ✫ playwork development officer
- ✫ playwork trainer/assessor
- ✫ special needs playworker.

There are also opportunities to move into related jobs such as working as a nursery nurse, teaching assistant or youth worker.

How to apply for a job as a playworker

Once you have found a job vacancy that meets your requirements, you need to apply for it. You need to make your application as interesting, neat and concise as possible so that the potential employer will decide to invite you for an interview. The employer will use written applications to assess which applicants best match their requirements for a playworker. From their assessments they will then prepare a shortlist of people to interview. The objective of your initial application is to get an interview. Making an application for a job can involve:

- ✫ completing an application form
- ✫ writing a covering letter (emphasising your suitability for this particular job)
- ✫ preparing a standard employment history, or curriculum vitae (CV).

Completing an application form

Employers will often make judgements about prospective playworkers based on the way they complete their application forms. An employer will not be impressed by an application form that is incomplete, difficult to read, vague, unconvincing or that appears to have been completed without careful thought and attention.

When completing an application form remember the following important points

1. Read carefully all the information/questions on the form and make sure you understand what is required.
2. Photocopy the blank application form so you can draft your answers in rough first. When you are satisfied you can copy them onto the original.
3. Fill in the right information in the right place.
4. Use every space on the form effectively; a neat layout creates a good impression.
5. Write clearly and legibly.
6. Check your spelling and grammar.
7. Answer any questions on what you do in your spare time by giving a brief description of your main hobbies and interests rather than just making a long list.
8. Be concise and to the point.
9. Make sure you give details of referees, with their addresses and telephone numbers.
10. Enclose a short covering letter highlighting any points that are especially relevant to your employment as a playworker.
11. Include any copies of certificates of qualification, references or testimonials that you hold. Never send an original certificate or diploma to anyone as, if lost, it may be impossible to replace. Take originals of certificates and any written references with you to the interview so that copies may be made from them.
12. Keep a copy of your application form so that you can refer to if you are invited for an interview.

Writing a covering letter

When replying to advertisements you may be asked to apply in writing, enclosing your CV. The important points for completing application forms are also relevant when applying for a job by letter. Your letter should be neatly handwritten rather than word-processed, as many employers prefer to get a sense of a prospective employee's personality by looking at their handwriting. A handwritten letter also shows a potential employer that you have taken the trouble to respond personally to their advertisement rather than simply printing out duplicate applications.

EXERCISE: Select one of the job advertisements that you found earlier. Write a letter in reply to the advertisement, highlighting why you are interested in the job and giving details of your qualifications and/or relevant experience.

Preparing your CV

A CV is a summary of your employment history. It can be copied and used each time you make a job application. To create a positive impression for future employers, make sure your CV:

- ✮ is neat, legible and clearly presented
- ✮ is typed or word-processed so that it may be faxed and photocopied
- ✮ is a maximum of two pages
- ✮ is up to date (add new jobs and references as necessary)
- ✮ is factual, positive and concise
- ✮ includes all your qualifications
- ✮ includes details of any relevant practical experience.

EXERCISE: Prepare (or update) your CV.

References

Employers will usually ask you for at least two references. One reference should be from your current or last employer. If you are a student straight from college, you should supply a reference from your college tutor and another reference from your final work placement. Remember to ask prior permission of anyone you wish to list as a referee.

A potential employer will contact your referees and ask them about:

- ✮ your work when they employed you as a playworker
- ✮ how they rate your care of the children
- ✮ why you left their employment
- ✮ what your strengths and weaknesses are
- ✮ any difficulties they think you might have if working unsupervised
- ✮ any health problems and sick leave you had during your employment
- ✮ whether they would consider re-employing you.

(DfES, 2004)

Your professional portfolio

You should prepare and organise a professional portfolio. If you put together a well-presented professional portfolio in advance, with all the relevant documents that will be required when you are invited for interview, it will save time when you apply for jobs. Having a well-presented portfolio will demonstrate to potential employers that you are well organised and have a professional attitude towards your career as a playworker. Your professional portfolio may include:

- ✮ school examination certificates (originals)
- ✮ college certificate or diploma (original)
- ✮ first aid certificate (ensure that this is up to date)
- ✮ basic food hygiene certificate
- ✮ CV

- ★ written references
- ★ statement of your play philosophy
- ★ examples of previous work with children and/or young people
- ★ relevant college assignments
- ★ an enhanced disclosure from the Criminal Records Bureau (if you have one).

Remember to update your CV and references as you gain more work experience and/or further qualifications. You could also include examples of previous work with children/young people, or details of relevant college assignments. You may wish to use a display or presentation album with plastic pockets to organise your portfolio.

EXERCISE: Compile a professional portfolio if you do not already have one.

Preparing for interviews

When you succeed in getting an interview do not waste the opportunity. The employer is interested in your skills, qualifications and potential commitment to the job. The interview is an opportunity for the employer to test your suitability for the job in relation to other people who are also being interviewed. The interview is also your chance to meet the potential employer and to find out more about the job. View an interview as an opportunity for an exchange of information.

Find out as much as you can about the job beforehand. Refresh your memory by looking at the advertisement again. Think about the following questions.

- ★ What are the main duties and responsibilities of the job?
- ★ What qualities and skills can you offer?
- ★ Have you got the necessary qualifications and/or experience?
- ★ Why are you applying?
- ★ Are you clear about the aims of the setting?
- ★ How will you present this information at the interview?

It can be helpful and build confidence to rehearse or practise mock interviews. Remember that you will be competing against other people who have also been selected for an interview for this particular job. The way you present yourself at the interview is very important. Dress professionally and appropriately by wearing something smart but comfortable. Look alert and interested. Do not yawn or look bored. Do not sit or stand with your arms folded. Smile, look relaxed and shake hands. Look at the interviewer and show an interest in what is being said.

What to do and say at interviews to get the job you want

Arrive in plenty of time for the interview; not only is this courteous but it also demonstrates that you are punctual – an essential quality for a reliable and professional playworker.

Remember these important points

1. The first two or three minutes of an interview are important for creating a good first impression. Try to develop a friendly approach and address the interviewer by name.
2. Listen carefully to each question. Take a moment to think about it before answering. Speak clearly and not too quickly.
3. Avoid using slang or unprofessional speech (e.g. always say 'children' not 'kids').
4. Be natural and honest. Do not claim to have more knowledge and experience than you really have. Be positive, and concentrate on the achievements and relevant experience you do have.
5. Do not answer questions with just a 'yes' or 'no'; use examples and give reasons for your opinions, but remember to stick to the point.
6. Show enthusiasm but do not be aggressive or pushy.
7. Be ready to ask questions. Prepare some before you go to the interview.
8. Ask (politely) how long you are likely to have to wait for a decision.

EXERCISE: Make a list of questions you might like to ask at an interview.

Questions you might be asked at interview

It is a good idea to think about how you will answer the sorts of questions employers might ask you. Some of the questions you might be asked are listed below.

- ★ How long have you been a playworker?
- ★ What ages of children/young people have you worked with?
- ★ Why do you enjoy working with children/young people?
- ★ What are your particular strengths when working with children/young people?
- ★ What playwork training and qualifications do you have?
- ★ What special skills or creative talents do you have (e.g. arts and crafts, drama, playing a musical instrument, sports)?
- ★ Which aspects of this particular job do you think you will enjoy?
- ★ What play opportunities would you provide for children or young people?
- ★ What difficulties have you experienced as a playworker and how were they resolved?
- ★ What would you do if a child/young person had an accident while in your care?

★ How would you deal with a child's difficult behaviour (e.g. an emotional outburst)?

★ How many days have you had off sick in the last 12 months?

★ Why did you leave your last job or why will you be leaving your present position?

(DfES, 2004)

Important issues to discuss at interview

The interview should be a two-way process. You should be offered the chance to ask your own questions. Make sure that you discuss the following important issues if they have not already been raised in the interview:

★ salary details, including how payment will be made (e.g. weekly or monthly, by cheque or directly into a bank account)

★ the hours and exact duties of the job

★ when you would be expected to start if offered the job

★ holiday entitlement

★ length of any probationary period

★ positive discipline strategies – a professional playworker *never* uses physical punishment as a form of discipline.

(DfES, 2004)

EXERCISE: Consider any other important issues you might like to discuss at an interview.

After the interview

While it is fresh in your mind, think about how the interview went and make a note of any points you weren't prepared for or any questions you found difficult to answer.

Applying for jobs is almost a full time job in itself! You will need to organise your job applications in a businesslike way. Establish your own record-keeping and filing system (e.g. a separate document wallet for each job application) so that you can:

★ make a note of which jobs you have applied for (with dates)

★ keep job advertisements

★ store copies of your application forms and/or covering letters

★ list further developments (e.g. second interview)

★ store any correspondence (e.g. rejection letters and job offers).

EXERCISE: Organise your job applications. Establish your own record-keeping and filing system for these.

What to do if you do not get the job

If you are unsuccessful after a job interview you may feel some anxiety or even depression, especially if you are finding it difficult to get a job. How you handle rejection will depend on your own expectations of how easy or difficult it is to get a job, how much effort and planning you put in, your anticipation of any possible difficulties, your personality (whether you tend to be pessimistic or optimistic), and any other areas of stress in your life (worries about money, relationships, and so on).

If you are feeling anxious, depressed or resentful about not getting a particular job, you should talk to your family or close friends about it. They should be able to help you keep things in perspective – just because you did not get this job does not mean you will never get a job. Try to learn from the experience and take positive action towards being more successful next time.

* Build on your experience with each interview so that you become more confident and knowledgeable.
* Be positive by focusing on your achievements so far.
* Identify and improve on any problem areas (for example, by developing better communication skills).
* Improve your interview technique by practising with a friend.
* Consider studying for (additional) qualifications.
* If you are currently unemployed, consider doing voluntary work to gain more experience.

Remember that there are plenty of playwork opportunities and there is currently a nationwide shortage of experienced and qualified playworkers. Try not to take rejection too personally. The other applicants may have had better qualifications or more experience. Keep trying! You *will* get the job that is just right for you and your particular skills.

What to do if you are offered the job

When you receive an offer, respond as quickly as possible. Usually you will have your answer ready. If you need time to make up your mind (or if you are waiting for the results of other interviews) you should ask the employer if you may have until a given date before sending a firm reply.

Even if you feel it might be the perfect job for you, do not make a hasty decision. Take your time to consider whether you would feel happy working in the particular setting. If there are areas that you feel could lead to potential problems or serious conflicts then you should not take the job. If you decide to accept the new job, do not hand in your notice at your current workplace until you have received written confirmation that the new job is yours.

Advantages and disadvantages of working as a playworker

The demand for quality childcare and play opportunities for children and young people means that there has never been a better time to work as a playworker. It is a challenging career. You can make a real difference to the lives of children and young people by providing play opportunities that will help them to develop their skills and increase their confidence in a safe, stimulating play environment.

Advantages of working as a playworker

The advantages of working as a playworker include:

- ☆ a highly rewarding career
- ☆ working with children and young people can be fun and entertaining
- ☆ an outlet for your own artistic or creative skills
- ☆ satisfaction in helping children progress to their next level of development
- ☆ varied and interesting work
- ☆ helping children and young people to make better use of their free time
- ☆ helping children and young people to gain new interests
- ☆ working as part of a team
- ☆ work to suit your own family commitments
- ☆ opportunities for personal and professional development.

A playworker working at a holiday playscheme.

Disadvantages of working as a playworker

The disadvantages of working as a playworker include:

★ working with children and young people is demanding

★ children can be messy, noisy and unco-operative

★ it can be exhausting, both physically and emotionally

★ there may be conflicting demands (e.g. between what your training has taught you and parents' wishes)

★ working with children and young people can be stressful.

Considering other types of work with children

You may be considering other types of work with children and/or young people such as: art therapist, childminder, children's nurse, hospital play specialist, nursery nurse/nursery assistant, play therapist, social worker, teacher, teaching assistant or youth and community worker.

Art therapist

Art therapists use art materials like paint, paper and clay to encourage people to 'unblock' their emotions, to express themselves and to become more positive. They work with individuals and groups who may have mental health problems, behavioural difficulties or learning disabilities. They work closely with other health professionals and may also work with a client's family or carers to help them understand the client's problems. At therapists usually work 9 am to 5 pm Monday to Friday, but may work in the evenings or at weekends, especially if they have private clients. The NHS, social services departments, local education authorities, prisons and voluntary organisations employ art therapists. Some have their own private practices. Art therapists need a recognised postgraduate qualification in art therapy. There is no maximum age to begin training; however, trainees should be mature with experience of working in the health service, education or community before commencing a postgraduate course. For further information contact the British Association of Art Therapists (see www.baat.org).

Childminder

A childminder is self-employed and looks after children in his or her own home. To look after children under the age of 8 a childminder must be registered with and have been inspected by the Office for Standards in

Education (Ofsted). They need to complete an introductory childminding course and first aid training before starting work as a childminder or within six months of registration. Specific qualifications include the CACHE Level 3 Certificate in Childminding Practice and courses run by local authorities. The exact terms and conditions of employment are negotiated between the childminder and the children's parents. A childminder should provide physical care and intellectual stimulation, including play opportunities, to assist children's development and learning. They may also take children to and from playgroup, nursery class or school. Most childminders have children of their own. Contact your local social services department or your local council's childcare information service (if it has one) to find out about becoming a childminder in your area. For further information contact the National Childminding Association (see www.ncma.org.uk).

Children's nurse

A children's nurse cares for sick children and provides support to their families. Normal entry requirements are a minimum age of 17½ years and five GCSE passes (or equivalent) at grade C or above in English language or literature and a science subject. The NHS welcomes people with alternative academic and vocational qualifications – for example, the CACHE Level 3 Diploma in Child Care and Education or the Edexcel Level 3 BTEC National Certificate or Diploma in Early Years. For more information contact the Nursing and Midwifery Admissions Service (see www.nmas.ac.uk).

Hospital play specialist

A hospital play specialist organises play activities and uses play as a therapeutic tool, but is not a play therapist or play leader. Working as part of a multi-disciplinary team, hospital play specialists provide play opportunities in the hospital playroom or on the children's ward to help children achieve their developmental goals and to encourage peer-group friendships. They help children of all ages to cope with anxieties and feelings about their stay in hospital and use play to prepare children for hospital procedures. They also contribute to clinical judgements through play-based observations of the children, and provide support for their families. The NHS employs most hospital play specialists, although work is also available in children's hospices, day centres and children's own homes. Hospital play specialists work either full- or part-time and may be expected to work weekends and even bank holidays. Applicants for training must be at least 20. The recommended qualification is the Edexcel Professional Development Certificate/Hospital Play Specialism. Further study is also available with the Edexcel Professional Development Diploma/Hospital Play Specialism. To train as a hospital play specialist you need recent and relevant experience of working with children and an appropriate qualification in, for example, childcare, art, drama or music therapy, nursing, psychology, occupational therapy, social work or teaching. For mature applicants, relevant work experience with children is accepted instead of formal qualifications. For further information contact the National Association of Hospital Play Staff (see www.nahps.org.uk).

Nursery nurse/nursery assistant

Nursery nurses provide care and education for children aged from 0 to 8 years. They plan and supervise play and early-learning activities to help young children's development and learning. They may work in a nursery school, primary school, special school, day nursery or hospital. They may work in a day nursery run by a voluntary or community group, local authority, private company or employer with a nursery for the children of staff members. Day nurseries usually provide full day care and education for young children up to the age of 5 years with usual opening hours of 8 am to 6 pm Monday to Friday. In a managerial role (e.g. nursery manager or nursery officer), as well as planning and supervising activities for the children, you would also be responsible for supervising staff and business administration. There are several recognised qualifications, which can be studied full- or part-time or at work, including the CACHE Level 3 Diploma in Child Care and Education, Edexcel Level 3 BTEC National Certificate or Diploma in Early Years, S/NVQ Level 3 in Early Years Care and Education. Nursery assistant jobs are for people with Level 2 childcare and education qualifications and for childcare professionals working under supervision. For more information contact your local council, local education department or the National Day Nurseries Association (see www.ndna.org.uk).

Play therapist

A play therapist works with children aged from 3 to 11 years (and occasionally adolescents) that have psychological difficulties or have had difficult life experiences. Psychological difficulties may include anxiety, depression, learning difficulties or ADHD. Difficult life experiences may include abuse, bereavement, domestic violence or family breakdown. Play therapists observe, listen to and support the child during play activities to enable the child to explore their feelings, make sense of what has happened and feel more positive about themselves. They work closely with the child's parents/carers and may occasionally be involved in parent–child relationship interventions. Play therapists work in health, education and social work sectors as well as for charities and voluntary organisations. They often work part-time or on a freelance basis. Most therapy sessions take place in the child's home, school, clinic or family centre. Trainees in play therapy are usually over 25 years old. They need a first degree in a related field, followed by at least two years' experience of working with children. For further information contact the British Association of Play Therapists (see www.bapt.info).

Social worker

To find employment as a social worker requires a professional qualification. There are a variety of ways to enter the social work profession, depending on your age and previous experience. Many people enter social work as a second or third career. Your previous experience may be taken into account as well as any formal academic qualifications when considering your eligibility to join a degree course. The degree can be studied through full-time, part-time and distance learning programmes. Where appropriate, previous academic experience may be taken into account and some form of credit given. Most social workers work with a range of different client groups during their working life. After graduation you can choose to specialise in work with children and families. For further information see the Social Work Recruitment Campaign website at www.socialworkcareers.co.uk.

Teacher

Teaching is an excellent opportunity for working with children and can be an ideal career for those who enjoy working with them. Teaching in a primary school involves working with children aged 3 to 11 years. A teacher in a primary school teaches all the subjects of the National Curriculum. Teaching in secondary schools involves working with children/young people aged 11 to 16 years (or 18 if there is a sixth form). A teacher in a secondary school specialises in teaching one or two subjects of the National Curriculum. There are two main routes into teacher training:

1. studying for a first degree that includes a teaching qualification (e.g. Bachelor of Education degree); applicants normally need at least two A levels and three GCSEs (grade C or above) in other subjects
2. studying for a first degree, then taking a one-year full-time teacher training course, such as the Post Graduate Certificate in Education (PGCE).

You may also be able to gain entry to a teacher training course with one of the following:

- ✩ CACHE Advanced Diploma in Child Care and Education
- ✩ BTEC Higher National Certificate or Diploma in Early Years Care and Education
- ✩ NVQ Level 4 in Early Years Care and Education or Playwork (England, Wales and Northern Ireland)
- ✩ SVQ Level 4 in Early Years Care and Education or Playwork (Scotland)
- ✩ Foundation Degree in Early Childhood Studies or Playwork.

All applicants for teacher training *must* have GCSEs in English language and mathematics at grade C or above. Applicants born on or after 1 September 1979 who enter primary teacher training also need to achieve a GCSE grade C (or equivalent) in a science subject. There is no upper age limit for entry to teacher training and mature applicants are encouraged. For further information contact the Teacher Training Agency (see www.useyourheadteach.gov.uk).

Teaching assistant

A teaching assistant works in a school and assists teachers in the provision of appropriate learning experiences for children. They are based in primary, secondary or special schools. In primary and special schools, they may be responsible for supporting one child or a small group of children with special needs, or they may be assigned to work with a particular class. In secondary schools, a teaching assistant usually works with one particular child across all curriculum subjects. There is a range of qualifications available for teaching assistants. Personal qualities, previous relevant experience and appropriate skills are often more important than any specific qualifications. For further information about training as a teaching assistant see www.teachernet.gov.uk.

Youth and community worker

Youth workers work mainly with young people, while community workers work with other groups too. Many youth workers are employed in youth clubs or community centres where they organise sports, drama and other activities for young people. They may also be involved in projects providing informal education and guidance to young people, including health education, study support, young offenders, youth volunteering, community regeneration or homelessness. Some youth and community workers offer group discussions or individual counselling. There may be contact with other professionals such as the police, probation officers, social workers and teachers. Full-time youth and community workers usually work 35–37 hours per week; part-time work is also available. They may work in youth clubs, community centres, schools, further education colleges, Connexions centres or neighbourhood offices. Most jobs involve working in more than one location. Local authorities, the Connexions Service, local community organisations and voluntary organisations such as the YMCA or Barnardo's employ youth and community workers. People usually need to do a professional training course (e.g. a DipHE in Community Youth Work) to become full-time youth and community workers. Entry requirements vary, but applicants under 21 may need A levels/H grades or equivalent qualifications as well as relevant experience of working with children and young people. For further information contact the National Youth Agency (see www.nya.org.uk).

> **EXERCISE:** Find out about other job opportunities for working with children and young people in your area.

Further reading

Amos, J. (2003) *Writing a Winning CV: Essential CV Writing Skills That Will Get You The Job You Want.* How To Books.

Brown, F. (ed.) (2002) *Playwork: Theory and Practice.* Open University Press.

Davy, A. (2001) *Playwork: Play and Care for Children 5–15* (3rd edn). Thomson Learning.

Early Years National Training Organisation (2003) *Wanting to Work in Early Years Education, Childcare and Playwork* and *Get That Job in Early Education, Childcare and Playwork.* Both available from the Early Years NTO website at www.early-years-nto.org.uk/.

Hobart, C. and Frankel, J. (1996) *Practical Guide to Childcare Employment.* Nelson Thornes.

Humphries, J. (2000) *Careers Working with Children and Young People.* Kogan Page.

Kamen, T. (2003) *Teaching Assistant's Handbook.* Hodder Arnold.

Lifetime Careers (1998) *Working with Children and Young People.* Hodder & Stoughton.

Marten, S. (1997) *Careers in Child Care: Your Questions and Answers.* Trotman.

Parkinson, M. (2002) *Your Job Search Made Easy: Everything you Need to Know About Applications, Interviews and Tests.* Kogan Page.

Petrie, P. (1996) *Communicating with Children and Adults: Interpersonal Skills for Early Years and Play Work* (2nd edn). Hodder Arnold.

2 The play environment

Key points

- ✪ Organising the play environment
- ✪ The processes of play
- ✪ Playwork assumptions and values
- ✪ Playwork Principles
- ✪ The United Nations Convention on the Rights of the Child
- ✪ National legislation on the rights of children and young people
- ✪ Policies and procedures reflecting children's and young people's rights
- ✪ Promoting and advocating children's and young people's rights
- ✪ Encouraging children and young people to understand and assert their rights
- ✪ Consulting and involving children and young people in decision-making
- ✪ Developing and implementing play setting policies and procedures

Organising the play environment

It is important that the play environment is welcoming and user-friendly. This includes taking account of cultural differences by providing displays and notices that reflect the cultural diversity of the play setting and local community. The play environment should be free from clutter and easily accessible to all children and young people, including those with physical disabilities or sensory impairment. (See the information on equal opportunities in Chapter 10.)

Central to the creation of an appropriate play environment is the provision of space, time and resources appropriate to the needs of all the children and young people who use it. Flexibility is also important to allow for special events, outings or visitors to the setting, such as a theatre or dance group. Working as a team, playworkers should decide how best to use the resources allocated to their setting. This includes 'adult resources' such as the playworkers and any parent helpers, as well as equipment and materials. The senior playworker or playwork manager should ensure that these adults are used to their full potential in order to respond appropriately to the needs of all children and young people, stimulate their learning through play, supervise their activities and safeguard their welfare.

Here are some general guidelines about organising room space.

★ Fire exits must not be obstructed, locked or hidden from view.
★ Chairs, tables and play equipment must be the correct size and height for the ages/levels of development of the children and young people.
★ Books, jigsaws, computers, and art and design materials need to be used in areas with a good source of light, if possible near a source of natural light.
★ Water, sand, art and design activities need to be provided in areas with appropriate floor surfaces, with washing facilities nearby.
★ Any large or heavy play equipment that has to be moved regularly for use should be used close to where it is stored.

The precise way the play environment is organised depends on:

★ the type of play setting
★ the resources for particular play activities
★ the play needs of the children.

(See Chapters 3 and 4.)

Effective organisation is also influenced by the general quality of the play environment. The play environment should have the following.

1. **Adequate floor space** for the age, size and needs of the children and young people. Children with physical disabilities may require additional floor space for wheelchairs and other specialised equipment or furniture.
2. **Appropriate sources of heating, lighting and ventilation.** Children and young people should be able to play in an environment that is neither too hot nor too cold. The heating source must be safe and fitted/maintained to the required legal standards. There should be good sources of both natural and artificial light.
3. **Appropriate acoustic conditions**, to enable children and young people to listen during essential discussions and to help reduce noise levels. Carpeted floor areas, sound-absorbent screens, displays, drapes and curtains all help to absorb reverberation.
4. **Adequate storage space** for materials and play equipment.

Involving children and young people in getting out and putting away play equipment helps them to develop a sense of responsibility for caring for *their* play environment. They will also gain confidence and independence if they are involved in setting out and clearing away play materials as appropriate to their ages/levels of development and safety requirements. Store and display play materials and equipment in ways that will enable children to choose, use and return them easily. Ensure, though, that they help in ways that are in line with the play setting's health and safety policies.

Children and young people have the right to be protected from harm. They must never have access to dangerous materials such as bleach or use very hot water for cleaning, and they should not carry large, heavy or awkward objects due to the risk of serious injury. You must ensure their physical health and safety as well as their emotional well-being. (For more detailed information see Chapter 5, 'Health and safety in the play setting', Chapter 6, 'Child protection', and Chapter 7, 'Children's health and well-being'.)

The processes of play

It is helpful for you to know and understand the processes of play so that you can provide quality play opportunities and appropriate support for all young people within the play setting.

The processes of playwork

1. **Communication process:** talking and listening with children and young people and their parents/carers, including empathising skills and sharing information.
2. **Relationship process:** developing mutually 'respectful' relationships, developing co-operation and 'power sharing' with children and young people.
3. **Play process:** facilitating the play process by creating a play environment in which children and young people are motivated to develop their own play opportunities.
4. **Observation process:** developing approaches to observing children in their play and making informed assessment of children's needs, progress, play signals, and so on.
5. **Intervention process:** making use of appropriate intervention/non-intervention to maintain children's playfulness and sense of acceptance within the play environment.
6. **Evaluation process:** using professional values to make judgements about the quality of play provision and involving children in reviewing their play experiences.
7. **Creative process:** developing a reflective approach to playwork – for example, analysing experience, problem-solving and supporting the limitless potential of the play process.
8. **Organisational process:** ensuring the most effective use of all available resources (including human resources) to promote a positive play environment.
9. **Safety process:** maintaining children's physical, social and emotional safety within the play environment, while promoting appropriate opportunities for risk-taking and challenging play.

(Stuart Lester, on www.playwork.org.uk)

Playwork assumptions and values

As a playworker, you must know and understand the assumptions and values of playwork. Playwork is based on a number of assumptions and values that underpin good practice in the play setting.

Assumptions

These are the current assumptions:

★ The first assumption is that children's play is freely chosen, personally directed behaviour and motivated from within. Through play children are able to explore the world, and their relationship with it, elaborating all the while a flexible range of responses to the challenges they encounter. By playing, children learn and develop as individuals.

★ The second assumption is that whereas children may play without encouragement or help, adults can, through the provision of an appropriate human and physical environment, significantly enhance opportunities for children to play creatively and thus develop through play.

In this way, the competent playworker always aims to provide opportunities for the individual child to achieve his or her full potential, while being careful not to control the child's direction or choice.

Values

These are the current values:

1. Play opportunities are provided in a number of settings (e.g. Local Authority, voluntary and commercial) for children with a variety of needs. Competent playwork always has the following underlying values regardless of social and cultural diversity.

2. The child must be at the centre of the process, and the opportunities provided and the organisation that supports, co-ordinates and manages these, should always start with the child's needs and offer sufficient flexibility to meet these.

3. Play should empower children, affirm and support their right to make choices and discover their own solutions, and allow them to develop at their own pace and in their own way.

4. Whereas play may sometimes be enriched by the playworker's participation, adults should always be sensitive to children's needs and never try to control a child's play so long as it remains within safe and acceptable boundaries.

5. Every child has a right to a stimulating play environment which provides opportunities for risk, challenge and the growth of confidence and self-esteem.

6. The environment in which many children grow up does not lend itself to safe and creative play. All children have the right to a play environment which is free from hazard and ensures physical and personal safety and a setting within which the child feels physically and personally safe.

7. Every child is an individual and has the right to be respected as such. Each child should feel confident that the adults who work and play with them value individuality and diversity.

8. A considerate and caring attitude to individual children and their families is essential to competent playwork and should be displayed at all times.

9. Prejudice against people with disabilities, or who suffer social or economic disadvantage, racism or sexism, has no place in an environment which seeks to enhance development through play. Adults involved in play should always promote equality of opportunity and access for all children and seek to develop anti-discriminatory practice and positive attitudes to those who are disadvantaged.

10. Play should offer children opportunities to extend their exploration and understanding of the wider world and consequently the physical, social and cultural settings beyond their immediate experience.

11. Play is essentially a co-operative activity for children, both individually and in groups. Playworkers should always encourage children to be sensitive to the needs of others. In providing play opportunities, they should always seek to work together with children, parents, colleagues and other professionals, and where possible to make their own expertise available to the wider community.

12. Play opportunities should always be provided within the current legislative framework relevant to children's rights, health, safety and well-being.

13. Every child has a right to an environment for play, and such environments must be made accessible to children.

(www.playwales.org.uk/values)

Playwork Principles

The assumptions and values of playwork have been reviewed and a new professional framework has been established called the Playwork Principles. The Playwork Principles have yet to be adopted by the SkillsActive Playwork Unit and the playwork sector still needs to decide if the Playwork Principles will replace the current assumptions and values, or will be used alongside them.

The Playwork Principles place children at the centre of playwork. The Playwork Principles 'make a clear distinction between playwork as the facilitation of children's play, and playwork that deals with adult agendas (for example, play provision management, legislation and politics)' (*Playtoday*, 42, May/June 2004, p.3).

The Playwork Principles

1. All children and young people need to play. The impulse to play is innate. Play is a biological, psychological and social necessity, and is fundamental to the healthy development and well-being of individuals and communities.

2. Play is a process that is freely chosen, personally directed and intrinsically motivated. That is, children and young people determine and control the content and the intent of their play, by following their own instincts, ideas and interests, in their own way and for their own reasons.

3. The prime focus and essence of playwork is to support and facilitate the play process and this should inform the development of play policy, strategy, training and education.

4. For playworkers, the play process takes precedence and playworkers act as advocates for play when engaging with adult-led agendas.
5. The role of the playworker is to support all children and young people in the creation of a space in which they can play.
6. The playworker's response to children and young people playing is based on sound up-to-date knowledge of the play process, and reflective practice.
7. Playworkers recognise their own impact on the play space and also the impact of children's and young people's play on the playworker.
8. Playworkers choose an intervention style that enables children and young people to extend their play. All playworker intervention must balance risk with the developmental benefit and well-being of children.

(Playtoday, 48, May/June 2005, p.6)

A clear understanding of the principles and values of play will enable you to:

- ☆ ensure that children are at the centre of the play process
- ☆ empower children and young people through play
- ☆ remember that play should not be controlled by adults
- ☆ provide a stimulating and challenging play environment
- ☆ ensure children's physical and personal safety within the play environment
- ☆ respect every child as an individual
- ☆ demonstrate a considerate and caring attitude towards children and their families
- ☆ provide a play environment that is accessible to all children
- ☆ provide play opportunities that extend children's understanding of the wider world
- ☆ encourage co-operation between children, parents and colleagues
- ☆ provide play opportunities within the current legislative framework (see below).

The United Nations Convention on the Rights of the Child

You must know and understand the basic requirements of the United Nations Convention on the Rights of the Child. These rights are for children and young people (up to the age of 18 years). The United Nations (UN) approved the Convention on the Rights of the Child on 20 November 1989. Countries that have ratified (agreed to uphold) the Convention are legally bound to do what it states.

The UK Government ratified the UN Convention on the Rights of the Child on 16 December 1991. This means that it has to ensure that every child has all the rights in the Convention by making all laws, policy and practice compatible with the Convention. The only two countries in the world that have not signed the Convention are the USA and Somalia.

There are 54 articles in the UN Convention on the Rights of the Child. The articles cover four different groupings of rights: survival, protection, development and participation. Each article outlines a different right. A summary of the articles most relevant to playwork is listed in the accompanying box.

Summary of the articles most relevant to playwork

- **Article 1**: Everyone under 18 years of age has all the rights in this Convention.
- **Article 2**: The Convention applies to everyone whatever their race, religion, abilities, whatever they think or say, whatever type of family they come from.
- **Article 3**: All organisations concerned with children should work towards what is best for each child.
- **Article 4**: Governments should make these rights available to children.
- **Article 12**: Children have the right to say what they think should happen, when adults are making decisions that affect them, and to have their opinions taken into account.
- **Article 13**: Children have the right to get and to share information as long as the information is not damaging to them or to others.
- **Article 14**: Children have the right to think and believe what they want and to practise their religion, as long as they are not stopping other people from enjoying their rights. Parents should guide their children on these matters.
- **Article 15**: Children have the right to meet together and to enjoy groups and organisations, as long as this does not stop other people from enjoying their rights.
- **Article 23**: Children who have any kind of disability should have special care and support so that they can lead full and independent lives.
- **Article 31**: All children have a right to relax and play, and to join in a wide range of activities.

('What Rights?' leaflet, UNICEF)

All professionals working with children and young people should know about the Convention. Children and young people's groups and organisations (including play settings) have an important role to play in raising awareness about the Convention, and referring to the Convention whenever making decisions that affect children and young people.

You can find out more about the UN Convention on the Rights of the Child from UNICEF and Save the Children. The Children's Rights Alliance for England also has information for young people and adults on the Convention. If you want to know about young people's right to participate in decisions, you can contact the young people's organisation called Article 12. (See the 'Further reading' section at the end of this chapter and Appendix A.)

KEY TASK

1. Find out more about the UN Convention on the Rights of the Child.
2. Check whether copies of the Convention and related materials are available in your play setting and/or the college library.
3. Design a poster or leaflet outlining the articles most relevant to playwork (e.g. Articles: 1–4, 12–15, 23 and 31). You could encourage the children and young people in your setting to design their own posters/leaflets about these rights.

NVQ links – Level 3: PW6.1

Example of child's poster about children's rights.

National legislation on the rights of children and young people

You must know and understand the basic requirements of national legislation on the rights of children and young people. You also need to know and understand how to carry out research on children's and young people's rights, and identify the implications for your setting.

The Children Act 1989

The Children Act 1989 provided a step towards implementing the articles of the UN Convention on the Rights of the Child within the UK. The Act came into force on 14 October 1991 and is concerned with families and the care of children, local authority support for children and their families, fostering, childminding and day care provision. The Children Act 1989 is particularly important because it emphasises the importance of putting the child first. In summary, the Act states that:

- ✰ what is best for the child must always be the first consideration
- ✰ whenever possible, children should be brought up in their own family
- ✰ unless the child is at risk of harm, they should not be taken away from their family without the family's agreement
- ✰ local authorities must help families with children in need
- ✰ local authorities must work with parents and children
- ✰ courts must put children first when making decisions
- ✰ children being looked after by local authorities have rights, as do their parents.

The Children (Scotland) Act 1995

The Children (Scotland) Act 1995 centres on the needs of children and young people and their families. The Act defines parental responsibilities and rights in relation to children and young people. It sets out the duties and powers available to public authorities in relation to children, including provisions to protect children and young people from abuse and neglect through measures such as providing appropriate accommodation and services for children and young people. The main principles of the Act are:

* ★ all children and young people have the right to be treated as individuals
* ★ every child and young person has the right to express her/his own views or wishes on matters affecting her/him (if able to do so)
* ★ the upbringing of children and young people should usually be the shared responsibility of both parents
* ★ all children and young people have the right to be protected from all forms of abuse, neglect or exploitation
* ★ children and young people should be brought up by their own families as long as this is consistent with their safety and well-being
* ★ intervention by public authorities must be properly justified and supported by services from all relevant agencies working together.

(Scottish Executive, 2003)

The Children Act 2004

The Children Act 2004 provides the legislative framework for whole-system reform to support the UK Government's long-term plans to improve the lives of children, young people and their families.

Summary of the Children Act 2004

The following is a brief outline of the key parts of the Act relevant to playwork.

Part 1: Children's Commissioner

* A Children's Commissioner for England will be established.
* The Children's Commissioner will work closely with the already established Children's Commissioners in Wales, Scotland and Northern Ireland.
* The Children's Commissioner will raise awareness of the best interests of children and young people.
* The Children's Commissioner will investigate how the government and organisations in the public and private sectors listen to children and young people.
* The Children's Commissioner will identify failures in complaints procedures and recommend improvements.
* The Children's Commissioner will advise the Secretary of State on the views and interests of children.

Part 1 of the Children Act 2004 came into force on 15 November 2004, and the first Children's Commissioner for England was appointed in March 2005. England's children are the last in the UK to have a Children's Commissioner. The general function of the Children's Commissioner is limited: 'promoting awareness of the views and interests of children in England' (Section 2.1). Children's Commissioners in the other countries of the UK are each required by law to promote and safeguard the rights of children. The Children's Commissioner for England's general function is the weakest in Europe and does not comply with international standards (Children's Rights Alliance for England, November 2004).

The national framework for children's services

The Children Act 2004, together with *Every Child Matters: Change for Children*, published in December 2004 by the Department for Education and Skills (DfES), sets out the government's direction for 150 local programmes of change to be led by local authorities and their key partners. Many local areas have already started their local change programmes, which bring together local authority, health and criminal justice services, voluntary and community organisations and other local partners to deliver improved services for children and young people.

Every Child Matters: Change for Children sets out the national framework of outcomes for all children and young people, to protect them, to promote their well-being and to support the development of their full potential. The document sets out the action needed locally and the ways in which the government will work with and support local authorities and their partners (DfES, 2004b).

This national framework will enable organisations providing services to children and young people (including hospitals, schools, the police and voluntary groups) to access the same information and work together to protect children and young people from harm, and help them achieve what they want and need. Children and young people will have a greater say about the issues that affect them both as individuals and collectively.

What the outcomes mean

1. Be healthy
- Physically healthy
- Mentally and emotionally healthy
- Sexually healthy
- Healthy lifestyles
- Choose not to take illegal drugs

2. Stay safe
- Safe from maltreatment, neglect, violence and sexual exploitation
- Safe from accidental injury and death
- Safe from bullying and discrimination
- Safe from crime and anti-social behaviour in and out of school
- Have security, stability and be cared for

3. Enjoy and achieve
- Be ready for school
- Attend and enjoy school
- Achieve stretching national educational standards at primary school
- Achieve personal and social development and enjoy recreation
- Achieve stretching national educational standards at secondary school

4. Make a positive contribution
- Engage in decision-making and support the community and environment
- Engage in law-abiding and positive behaviour in and out of school
- Develop positive relationships and choose not to bully or discriminate
- Develop self-confidence and successfully deal with significant life changes and challenges
- Develop enterprising behaviour

5. Achieve economic well-being
- Engage in further education, employment or training on leaving school
- Ready for employment
- Live in decent homes and sustainable communities
- Access to transport and material goods
- Live in households free from low incomes

(DfES, 2004b)

EXERCISE: Highlight those outcomes listed in the accompanying box that are most relevant to the children and young people in your play setting.

Voluntary and community organisations

Voluntary and community organisations have a vital role to play in improving outcomes for children and young people. As key providers of services to children and young people, voluntary and community organisations have considerable knowledge and expertise to offer in developing strategy and planning provision.

The DfES has published a strategy for working with voluntary and community organisations to improve services for children and young people. The strategy indicates the ways the DfES will strengthen its connections with voluntary and community organisations that work with children, young people and families. It describes what the government is doing to support effective working with local voluntary and community organisations through the *Every Child Matters: Change for Children* programme (see 'Further reading' at the end of this chapter).

Children's trusts

Children's trusts are the new way in which local authorities are encouraging co-operation between all agencies working with children, young people and families. Children's trusts bring together all services for children and young people in a local area so that they can focus on improving outcomes for all children and young people. Children's trusts will provide more integrated and responsive services for children and their families. People will work in effective multi-disciplinary teams and services will be co-located in children's centres or extended schools. Local authorities will also involve voluntary and community organisations at all levels of children's trusts including the planning, commissioning and delivery of children's services.

Children's centres

Children's centres are excellent examples of integrated service provision for children and their families. Primary Care Trusts, local authorities, JobCentre Plus, education and childcare providers, social services, and community and voluntary organisations work in partnership to deliver holistic services that reflect the needs of local communities.

A children's centre.

The expansion of the children's centre network means that there should be up to 2500 centres in England by 2008. Children's centres will be established to provide services in all of the most disadvantaged areas. The Ten Year Childcare Strategy recommends that more co-located and accessible children's services be established. Children's trusts will also be able to develop children's centres in response to local demand (DfES, 2004b).

Extended schools

As part of the Five Year Strategy for Children and Learners, all primary and secondary schools will be expected to provide a core offer of services to parents. Local authorities and children's trusts will bring together local partners to plan and develop extended services that meet the needs of local communities.

The Ten Year Childcare Strategy includes a childcare offer for school-aged children that provides a guarantee of childcare provision between 8 am and 6 pm all year round. This offer builds on existing childcare provision in schools, such as breakfast and after-school clubs. By 2010, all primary schools will provide this offer, either on site or in partnership with other schools and local childcare providers. Also by 2010 all secondary schools will provide a network of provision including out-of-school activities such as sports, arts and holiday activities (DfES, 2004b).

KEY TASK

1. Investigate the rights of children and young people in your local community.
2. Find out what local provision is being made to meet these rights, for example: voluntary and community organisations; children's trusts; children's centres; extended schools.

NVQ links – Level 3: PW6.1

Policies and procedures reflecting children's and young people's rights

You must know and understand the importance of having policies and procedures within the setting that reflect the rights of children and young people. You must also know and understand your organisation's strategies and policies that have an impact on children's and young people's rights, and how to evaluate these – for example, the setting's policies and procedures relating to equal opportunities, anti-discriminatory practice, diversity and inclusion (see Chapter 10). The setting's policies and procedures should reflect the rights of children and young people as set out in the UN Convention on the Rights of the Child (see above).

Ten ways to reflect the rights of children and young people

1. Demonstrate a knowledge and understanding that children under the age of 18 have rights (e.g. displaying posters/leaflets about children's rights). (*Article 1*)

2. Ensure all children and young people in the community have equal rights to participate in the play setting regardless of their race, religion, abilities or family background (e.g. through anti-discriminatory and open-access policies). (*Article 2*)

3. Work towards what is best for each child (e.g. providing appropriate play opportunities to meet each child's developmental needs). (*Article 3*)

4. Follow national legislation concerning children's rights (e.g. the outcomes in the national framework such as providing children with opportunities to achieve personal and social development, and enjoy recreational activities). (*Article 4*)

5. Listen to children's views and take their opinions into account when making decisions that affect them (e.g. consulting and involving children and young people in decision-making within the play setting). (*Article 12*)

6. Share appropriate information with children and young people (e.g. involving them in record-keeping as appropriate to their age/level of development). (*Article 13*)

7. Allow children and young people to think and believe what they like as long as they do not stop others from enjoying their rights (e.g. encouraging freedom of expression through play activities). (*Article 14*)

8. Encourage children's participation in groups and organisations (e.g. providing information about activities available to children and young people in the play setting and the wider community). (*Article 15*)

9. Encourage children with disabilities to lead full and independent lives (e.g. adapting activities to enable all children to participate fully within the play setting). (*Article 23*)

10. Provide opportunities for all children to relax, play and join in a range of activities (e.g. providing appropriate play opportunities within the play setting). (*Article 31*)

The child's right to play

Play is not only essential to the all-round development of children and young people – it is a universal right. Article 31 of the UN Convention on the Rights of the Child states that, 'The child has the right to rest and to engage in leisure, play and recreational activities and participate in cultural and artistic activities.'

Play enables children and young people to:

⭐ make connections with their world

⭐ build positive relationships with others

⭐ take calculated risks and develop survival skills

⭐ make choices and experience control

⭐ make sense of their lives in a meaningful context.

In 1926, the then British Prime Minister, Lloyd George, stated: 'Play is a child's first claim on the community. No community can infringe that right without doing deep and enduring harm to the minds and bodies of its citizens' (Play Wales and PlayEducation, 2001). His statement demonstrates the paramount importance of local communities providing play opportunities for all children. Being denied opportunities for play can cause immense damage not only to children but also to society as a whole. Play (or the lack of it) helps to shape children's and young people's feelings, perceptions and opinions about their world, and these will form the basis for their attitudes and behaviour in adult life. The provision of play opportunities for children and young people can help to create a more positive future for everyone in today's society.

Everyone working in the play setting should:

⭐ share a common understanding of the issues relating to the child's right to play

⭐ agree on a set of common principles for providing play opportunities

⭐ have an informed, planned and strategic approach to play provision

⭐ facilitate the development and improvement of play provision

⭐ encourage children and young people to be actively involved in decisions about play.

KEY TASK

1. Make a list of the existing policies and procedures that relate to the rights of children and young people in your play setting.

2. Suggest improvements to these policies and procedures to ensure that children's and young people's rights are met effectively within your setting.

NVQ links – Level 3: PW6.1, PW6.2

Promoting and advocating children's and young people's rights

You must know and understand how to promote and advocate children's and young people's rights. To do this effectively you need to remember the following important points.

1. Children and young people must respect the rights of others; having rights does not mean children and young people can act irresponsibly towards others.
2. Children and young people are important and valid individuals *now;* their worth is not dependent on their potential as future adults.
3. Children and young people are widely discriminated against in our society – you should be committed to working with them to make real improvements in their lives and status.
4. Children and young people should be involved in decision-making that affects their lives, either as individuals or as a group, within the play setting and local community.
5. Always take into account the vulnerability, individual needs and evolving capacity of children and young people.

(The Children's Rights Alliance for England, www.crae.org.uk/)

Children's needs

All children and young people have the following essential needs – the mnemonic (memory aid) 'PRICELESS' will help you to remember them.

- ✯ **P**hysical care: regular, nutritious meals; warmth; rest and sleep.
- ✯ **R**outines: a regular pattern to their day; with any changes explained.
- ✯ **I**ndependence: encouragement to do things for themselves and make choices.
- ✯ **C**ommunication: encouragement to talk and interact with others.
- ✯ **E**ncouragement and praise: for trying as well as achieving.
- ✯ **L**ove: from parents/carers that is unconditional (e.g. expecting nothing back).
- ✯ **E**ducation: appropriate to their ages and levels of development.
- ✯ **S**incerity and respect: honest and courteous treatment.
- ✯ **S**timulation: opportunities to explore their environment and tackle new challenges.

All children and young people have individual needs because they perceive the world differently and interact with others in different ways. All children (including identical twins) have different life experiences that affect their view of the world. They experience different social and environmental factors that along with their genetic differences shape their personalities, knowledge and skills. Children and young people may be individuals but they exist as part of various social groups, such as family, local community, school and wider society (Brennan, 1987). Playworkers must appreciate the uniqueness of every child and young person within the setting while ensuring that the needs of both the individual and the group are being met.

All political parties recognise that children and young people have the right to have their needs met. However, defining what these needs are can be a matter of political or professional judgement. (For example, you might disagree with my definition of children's needs listed above.)

In the past decade there has been a major shift in attitude towards children's rights. In the past they were mainly concerned with basic welfare needs. Now as well as their basic rights to life, health and education, children are viewed as having a much wider range of rights – including the right to engage in play activities, to express their views and to participate in making decisions that affect them directly.

Children's rights, as stated in the UN Convention on the Rights of the Child, are clear and universal: they apply to all children and young people. Also, while children's and young people's individual needs may differ, they all have the same rights. Children's rights are based on their needs, but emphasising rights rather than needs demonstrates a commitment to viewing and respecting children and young people as valued citizens (The Children's Rights Alliance for England, www.crae.org.uk/).

An important aspect of promoting and advocating children's rights is to ensure that their play needs are met and protected (see the section on children's play needs in Chapter 3).

Promoting and advocating children's and young people's rights encourages mutual respect and positive behaviour. A commitment to children's and young people's rights demonstrates that you respect children and young people, and value them as individuals (see Chapter 8).

 KEY TASK

Design a booklet (for parents, students or volunteers) outlining how your setting promotes children's and young people's rights with regard to:

- play and social activities
- care and safety
- emotional well-being
- inclusion
- acknowledgement of their identity
- information
- consultation and decision-making.

NVQ links – Level 3: PW6.1

Encouraging children and young people to understand and assert their rights

You should encourage children and young people to understand and assert their rights under the UN Convention on the Rights of the Child. You should also ensure that they are aware of their rights under UK law (e.g. the Children Act 1989, and sex, race and disability laws – see Chapter 10).

You can help children and young people to *understand* their rights by:

- ☆ using posters, leaflets and resource packs about children's rights (e.g. the 'Rights for Young Children' posters from Oxfam, the 'What Rights?' leaflet from UNICEF and the *A Right To Know* resource pack from Article 12)
- ☆ sharing books about children's rights (e.g. *For Every Child*; *Wise Guides: Your Rights*)
- ☆ providing appropriate creative activities (e.g. designing posters/leaflets, painting pictures or making collages about children's rights)
- ☆ playing games promoting children's rights (e.g. 'On the Right Track')
- ☆ encouraging them to look up information about children's rights on websites aimed at children and young people (e.g. www.therightssite.org.uk and www.savethechildren.org.uk/rightonline/whats.html)

For details of books and other resources see the 'Further reading' section at the end of the chapter.

You can help children and young people to *assert* their rights by:

- ☆ providing choices of play activity within the setting
- ☆ encouraging their participation in the day-to-day running of the setting
- ☆ consulting and involving them in decision-making with regard to the setting
- ☆ promoting inclusion and anti-discriminatory practice (see Chapter 10)
- ☆ helping to organise a children's panel or youth forum
- ☆ providing accessible information
- ☆ providing access to confidence/assertiveness training
- ☆ providing information about other play and leisure activities in the local community
- ☆ providing information about local and national children's rights networks.

KEY TASK

Working with children and young people, develop suggestions for meeting their rights in the play setting.

NVQ links – Level 3: PW6.1

Consulting and involving children and young people in decision-making

You must know and understand the importance of children and young people being consulted and involved in decision-making. They have the right to be consulted and involved in decision-making about matters that affect them (UN Convention on the Rights of the Child, Article 12). They should also be involved in the planning, implementation and evaluation of policies that affect them or the services they use (Children and Young People's Unit, 2001).

Involving children and young people in decision-making within the play setting will help you to provide better play provision based on their real needs rather than adult assumptions about their needs, and to promote social inclusion by encouraging them to participate as active citizens in their local community.

Four ways to involve children and young people in decision-making

1. Providing a **suggestion box** for their comments and complaints about play provision and play opportunities.
2. **Questionnaires and surveys** to find out their opinions about the setting's policies and procedures, including any gaps in play provision.
3. **Consultation exercises**, such as discussion groups, drama and role-play activities, music and games to provide opportunities for children and young people to express ideas.
4. **Direct involvement**, for example, taking part in staff development and recruitment activities, assessing new play initiatives, mentoring other children and young people, providing information via leaflets, posters and IT for other children/young people.

(Children and Young People's Unit, 2001)

Consultation and involvement checklist

- Purpose of consultation and involvement
- Approaches including existing consultation structures
- Strategies for involving all the children and/or young people
- Planning and preparation (e.g. who will carry out the consultation)
- Time scale
- Dealing with opposing views
- Consider the resources needed to implement any suggestions
- Evaluate and report on the consultation process

KEY TASK

Outline the ways in which your setting consults and involves children and/or young people in decision-making.

NVQ links – Level 3: PW6.1, PW6.2

Developing and implementing play setting policies and procedures

You must know and follow the policies and procedures of your setting – for example, its policies and procedures relating to:

☆ play provision (see Chapter 4)

☆ health and safety (see Chapter 5)

☆ child protection and bullying (see Chapter 6)

☆ assisting children and young people to make transitions (see Chapter 7)

☆ responding to behaviour (see Chapter 8)

☆ inclusion and anti-discriminatory practice (see Chapter 10).

You also need to know and understand how to develop and implement these policies and procedures as consistent with your role and responsibilities in the play setting. Remember that to develop effective policies and procedures everyone should be involved at some level, including staff, children and young people and their parents/carers.

Each policy should include:

☆ policy statement, including the main aims of the policy

☆ relevance of the policy to play provision and/or play activities

☆ parent and carer involvement

☆ staff roles and responsibilities in relation to the policy

☆ staff training and support relevant to the policy

☆ implementation of the policy (e.g. details of the play setting's procedures for putting the policy into practice)

☆ evaluation and review of the policy

☆ how the contents of the policy will be shared (e.g. policy statement in staff handbook, brochure/parent information pack and on noticeboards, which also indicates the location of the policy document – staffroom, office, etc.).

1. Find out about the your play setting's policies and procedures for:
   - play provision
   - health and safety
   - inclusion and anti-discriminatory practice
   - child protection and bullying
   - responding to behaviour
   - assisting children and young people to make transitions.
2. Explain your role and responsibilities in developing, implementing and reviewing these policies and procedures.

NVQ links – Level 3: PW6.1 PW6.2

Further reading

Alderson, P. (2000) *Young Children's Rights: Exploring Beliefs, Principles and Practice*. Jessica Kingsley Publishers.

Article 12 (2002) *A Right to Know* [a resource pack about children's rights designed and created by young people for young people aged 11–18 years; the pack contains a video, a teachers'/youth workers' handbook, a photo set, a poster, and information from UNICEF and the NSPCC on children's rights].

Brown, F. (ed.) (2002) *Playwork Theory and Practice*. Open University Press.

Children and Young People's Unit (2001) *Learning to Listen: Core Principles for the Involvement of Children and Young People*. DfES, available at www.dfee.gov.uk/cypu.

Cole-Hamilton, I. and Gill, T. (2002) *Making the Case for Play: Building Policies and Strategies for School-aged Children*. National Children's Bureau.

DfES (Department for Education and Skills) (2004b) *Every Child Matters: Change for Children* and *Every Child Matters: Change for Children – Working with Voluntary and Community Organisations to Deliver Change for Children and Young People*, both available at www.everychildmatters.co.uk.

Fajerman, L. (2001) *Children are Service Users Too: A Guide for Consulting Children and Young People*. Save the Children Publications.

Fortin, J. (2004) *Children's Rights and the Developing Law* (2nd edn). LexisNexis Butterworths.

Franklin, B. (ed.) (2001) *The New Handbook of Children's Rights: Comparative Policy and Practice*. Routledge.

Hand, P. (2003) *First Steps to Rights: Activities for Children Aged 3–7 Years*. Oxfam.

Miller, J. (1996) *Never Too Young: How Young Children Can Take Responsibility and Make Decisions*. Save the Children/National Early Years Network.

Naik, A. (1999) *Wise Guides: Your Rights*. Hodder Children's Books.

National Playing Fields Association, Children's Play Council and Playlink (2000) *Best Play: What Play Provision Should Do for Children*. National Playing Fields Association.

Shepherd, C. and Treseder, P. (2002) *Participation – Spice it up!* Save the Children.

Shier, H. (1996) *Article 31 Action Pack – Children's Rights and Children's Play*. Playtrain.

Siraj-Blatchford, I. (1994) *The Early Years: Laying the Foundations for Racial Equality*. Trentham Books.

Treseder, P. (1997) *Empowering Children and Young People*. Save the Children.

UK Committee for UNICEF (2000) *The Convention on the Rights of the Child*. UNICEF. (Includes a children's version of the Convention.)

UNICEF (2002) *For Every Child: The Rights of the Child in Words and Pictures*. Red Fox.

Wade, H. and Badham, B. (2003) *Hear by Right: Standards for the Active Involvement of Children and Young People*. National Youth Agency and Local Government Association.

Waters, P. (2003) *'On the Right Track': A Promoting Children's Rights Game*. KC The Bear Scheme (Tel: 01904 466220).

Willow, C. (2002) *Participation in Practice: Children and Young People as Partners in Change*. The Children's Society.

3 Play and child development

Key points

- ⚽ What is play?
- ⚽ The importance of play
- ⚽ Children's play needs
- ⚽ Identifying children's and young people's play needs and preferences
- ⚽ The sequence of children's development
- ⚽ Children's social development
- ⚽ Children's physical development
- ⚽ Children's intellectual development
- ⚽ Children's language development
- ⚽ Children's emotional development
- ⚽ The sequence of children's social play
- ⚽ Observing children's play and development

What is play?

There are many different definitions of play. Adults, children and young people may each have their own. The government's review into children's play defines play as 'what children and young people do when they follow their own ideas, in their own way and for their own reasons' (DCMS, 2004).

In playwork the following definition of play, based on the work of Bob Hughes and Frank King, is widely accepted: 'Play is freely chosen, personally directed, intrinsically motivated behaviour that actively engages the child' (National Playing Fields Association, Children's Play Council and Playlink, 2000).

This means that play is:

- ✭ freely chosen – children choose *what* they do, themselves
- ✭ personally directed – children choose *how* they do something
- ✭ intrinsically motivated – children choose *why* they do something: children's play is performed for no external goal or reward.

(Play Wales and PlayEducation, 2001)

Play can also be described as follows:

> Play can be fun or serious. Through play children explore social, material and imaginary worlds and their relationship with them, elaborating all the while a flexible range of responses to the challenges they encounter. By playing, children learn and develop as individuals, and as members of the community.

> (National Playing Fields Association, Children's Play Council and Playlink, 2000)

All children and young people play, unless they are living in extremely difficult conditions (forced into child labour, say, or to be child soldiers) or they are critically ill (Lindon, 2002). Some children with disabilities or long-term health problems may need additional support to enable them to participate in play activities (see Chapter 4).

The importance of play

Play is an essential part of children's development and learning. It is the central way in which the majority of children explore and develop an understanding of their world. Children and young people learn through play. The term 'play' is often used to refer to children's activities that are considered to be unimportant and frivolous by many people – notably some teachers, parents and especially politicians! It is up to playworkers to stress the importance of play to those who are sceptical about its benefits.

Play helps children's and young people's development and learning by providing opportunities for:

- ✭ self-chosen and well-motivated learning
- ✭ challenging and interesting experiences
- ✭ taking responsibility for own learning
- ✭ gaining confidence and independence
- ✭ co-operative work between children
- ✭ developing a wide range of physical skills
- ✭ developing problem-solving skills and improving concentration
- ✭ encouraging imagination and creativity.

Children's play needs

Play is not an extra – something to be done to keep children quiet and occupied while adults are busy or as a reward for when other tasks have been done. It is an essential part of children's and young people's development and learning.

Children's play needs include opportunities to:

- ✭ access safe play spaces
- ✭ engage in a wide range of play activities and use a variety of play materials
- ✭ learn about and understand the physical world
- ✭ develop individual skills and personal resources
- ✭ communicate and co-operate with others
- ✭ develop empathy for others
- ✭ make sense of the world in relation to themselves
- ✭ do their own learning, in their own time and in their own way.

Suggestions on ways to provide for children's play needs are included at the end of the section for each aspect of development outlined below.

Identifying children's and young people's play needs and preferences

You should be able to identify children's and young people's play needs and preferences. Play needs are the individual needs of children for play. Preferences are children's choices with regard to play.

You can help to identify children's play needs and preferences by researching playwork theory and practice to find out about children's play and development, observing children and young people playing, and consulting children and young people about their play needs and preferences.

Consulting with children and young people about their play needs and preferences

You should consult children and young people about their play needs and preferences and take account of their ideas. You can do this by talking with them and asking for their suggestions about play spaces and resources. (There is more about consulting children and young people in Chapter 2.)

KEY TASK

1. Collect information on the play needs and preferences of the children and/or young people in your setting using these methods:
   - research playwork theory and practice
   - observe the children and/or young people playing
   - consult the children and/or young people about their play needs and preferences.
2. Use this information to identify their play needs and preferences and make suggestions for possible play opportunities and resources.
3. You could present this information in a booklet or information pack on children's play for parent helpers, volunteers and students.

NVQ links – Level 2: PW2.1; Level 3: PW9.1

The sequence of children's development

When looking at children's development it is important to use a holistic approach. This means you should remember to look at the 'whole' child. When planning play opportunities for children and young people you should consider all aspects of their development:

- ☆ Social
- ☆ Physical
- ☆ Intellectual
- ☆ Communication (language)
- ☆ Emotional.

Please note that the idea of the 'SPICE' mnemonic was originated by Fraser Brown in 1985. In playwork, SPICE usually refers to:

- ☆ Social interaction
- ☆ Physical activity
- ☆ Intellectual stimulation
- ☆ Creative expression
- ☆ Emotional stability.

(Davy, 1998)

I prefer to include creativity as part of children's intellectual development and to have a separate listing for communication instead. Use whichever headings are most appropriate for your setting and the children and/or young people you work with.

It is actually more accurate to think of a *sequence* of children's development rather than *stages* of development. This is because the term 'stages' refers to development that occurs at *fixed ages* while the term 'sequence' indicates development that follows the same basic pattern *but not necessarily at fixed ages*.

You should really use the term 'sequence' when referring to all aspects of children's development. However, the work of people such as Mary Sheridan provides a useful guide to the milestones of *expected* development – that is, the usual pattern of children's development, or norm. As well as their chronological age, children's development is affected by many other factors (for instance, social interaction, play opportunities, early learning experiences, special needs).

The developmental charts in this chapter do *indicate specific ages, but only to provide a framework to help you understand children's development. You should always remember that all children are unique individuals and develop at their own rate.*

Children's social development

Children's social development involves developing their social skills as part of the socialisation process. This involves the development of:

- ★ acceptable behaviour patterns
- ★ self-control and discipline
- ★ independence (including self-help skills such as feeding, toileting, dressing)
- ★ awareness of self in relation to others
- ★ positive relationships with others
- ★ understanding the needs and rights of others
- ★ moral concepts (for example, understanding the difference between right and wrong; making decisions based on individual morality).

Children model their attitudes and actions on the behaviour of others. They imitate the actions and speech of those they are closest to (for instance, acting at being 'mum', 'dad', 'playworker' or 'teacher', copying the actions and mannerisms of adults around the home, school or play setting). All adults working with children and young people need to be aware of the significant impact they have on their social (and emotional) development by providing positive role models. When working with children and young people you should strike a balance between allowing for their increasing need for independence and providing adequate supervision with appropriate guidelines for socially acceptable behaviour (see Chapter 8).

Social and emotional development have been listed separately to assist your understanding of these two complex aspects of children's development, but you will notice that there are overlaps between the two aspects. Children's social development is outlined here; information on children's emotional development starts on page 66.

The sequence of social development: 4 to 16 years

Age 4–7 years

- ✭ Enjoys the company of other children; may have special friend(s).
- ✭ Uses language even more effectively to communicate, share ideas, engage in more complex play activities.
- ✭ Appears confident and competent in own abilities.
- ✭ Co-operates with others, takes turns and begins to follow rules in games.
- ✭ Seeks adult approval; may blame others for own mistakes to escape disapproval.
- ✭ Observes how others behave and will imitate them; has a particular role model.
- ✭ May copy unwanted behaviour (e.g. swearing, biting, kicking to gain adult attention).

Age 7–11 years

- ✭ Continues to enjoy the company of other children; wants to belong to a group; usually has at least one special friend.
- ✭ Uses language to communicate very effectively, but may use it in negative ways (e.g. name-calling or telling tales) as well as positively to share ideas and participate in complex play activities often based on TV characters or computer games.
- ✭ Is able to play on own; appreciates own space away from others on occasion.
- ✭ Becomes less concerned with adult approval and more concerned with peer approval.
- ✭ Is able to participate in games with rules and other co-operative activities.

Age 11–16 years

- ✭ Continues to enjoy the company of other children/young people; individual friendships are still important; belonging to group or gang becomes increasingly important but can also be a major source of anxiety or conflict.
- ✭ The desire for peer approval can overtake the need for adult approval and may cause challenges to adult authority at home, school or in the play setting, particularly in the teenage years.
- ✭ Participates in team games/sports or other group activities including clubs and hobbies; can follow complex rules and co-operate fully but may be very competitive.
- ✭ Strongly influenced by a variety of role models especially those in the media (e.g. sport and film stars and pop stars).
- ✭ Is able to communicate very effectively and uses language much more to resolve any difficulties in social interactions.
- ✭ Can be very supportive towards others (e.g. people with special needs or those experiencing difficulties at home, school, in the play setting or the wider community).

> **Ten ways to provide for children's social play needs**
> 1. **Set goals and boundaries** to encourage socially acceptable behaviour as appropriate to the children's ages and levels of development. Using appropriate praise and rewards can help. (See Chapter 8.)
> 2. **Encourage children to help tidy up.** You could help the children to design certificates with pledges such as 'I promise to help tidy up after each play activity'.
> 3. **Encourage children's self-help skills.** Be patient and provide time for them to do things independently (e.g. choosing play activities and selecting own materials).
> 4. **Provide play opportunities to encourage children's self-help skills** (e.g. dressing-up helps younger children learn to dress independently in a fun way).
> 5. **Provide opportunities for children to participate in social play** (e.g. encourage them to join in team games, sports and other co-operative activities).
> 6. **Use books and stories about everyday situations** to help children understand ideas about fairness, jealousy and growing up.
> 7. **Use puppets and play people** to act out potential conflict situations and help children work out possible solutions.
> 8. **Encourage children to take turns** during play activities and games.
> 9. **Encourage children to share** toys and other play equipment.
> 10. **Encourage children to focus on their own abilities.** Emphasise co-operation and sharing rather than competition. Any comparisons should be related to each child improving their own individual skills.

Children's physical development

Physical development involves children's increasing ability to perform more complex physical activities involving gross motor skills, fine motor skills and co-ordination.

Gross motor skills

Gross motor skills involve whole-body movements. Examples include walking, running, climbing stairs, hopping, jumping, skipping, cycling, swimming, climbing play apparatus, and playing badminton, basketball, football, hockey, netball, rugby or tennis. Children need strength, stamina and suppleness to become proficient in activities involving gross motor skills.

Fine motor skills

Fine motor skills involve whole-hand movements, wrist action or delicate procedures using the fingers – for example, the 'palmar grasp' (grabbing and holding a small brick), the 'pincer grip' (using the thumb and index finger to pick up a pea) and the 'tripod grasp' (holding a crayon, pencil or pen). Examples of fine motor skills include drawing, painting, writing, model-making, playing with wooden/plastic bricks or construction kits, cutting with scissors, and doing up/undoing buttons, shoelaces and other fastenings. Children need good concentration levels and hand–eye co-ordination (see below) to become proficient in activities involving fine motor skills.

Co-ordination

Co-ordination involves hand–eye co-ordination, whole-body co-ordination and balance. Examples of hand–eye co-ordination include drawing, painting, using scissors, writing and threading beads. Examples of whole body co-ordination include crawling, walking, cycling, swimming and playing football or netball. Examples of balance include hopping and gymnastics. Co-ordination plays an important part in developing children's gross and fine motor skills. Co-ordination and balance are needed to improve children's gross motor skills.

You should provide appropriate play opportunities for children and young people to develop their physical skills. Remember that some children may be limited in their physical abilities due to physical disability, sensory impairment or other special needs.

The sequence of physical development: 4 to 16 years
Age 4–7 years

- ✸ Can dress/undress self but may still need help with intricate fastenings and shoelaces.
- ✸ Has improved gross motor skills and co-ordination so is more proficient at running, jumping, climbing and balancing.
- ✸ Has some difficulty with hopping and skipping.
- ✸ Has improved ball skills but still learning to use a bat.
- ✸ May learn to ride a bicycle (with stabilisers).
- ✸ Enjoys swimming activities.
- ✸ Fine motor skills continue to improve: has better pencil/crayon control; is more competent at handling materials and making things.
- ✸ Enjoys action songs plus singing and dancing games.

Age 7–11 years

- ✸ Can dress/undress self, including fastenings and shoelaces.
- ✸ Grows taller and thinner; starts losing baby teeth.
- ✸ Improved gross motor skills and co-ordination lead to proficiency in climbing, running, jumping, balancing, hopping and skipping.
- ✸ Can hit a ball with a bat.
- ✸ Learns to ride a bicycle (without stabilisers).
- ✸ Learns to swim (if taught properly).

- ★ As fine motor skills improve, handwriting becomes easier and more legible.
- ★ Can do more complex construction activities.
- ★ Continues to enjoy singing and dancing games.

Age 11–16 years

- ★ Can dress/undress self, including intricate fastenings and shoelaces.
- ★ Grows taller and thinner; continues losing baby teeth.
- ★ Physical changes of puberty.
- ★ Improved gross motor skills and co-ordination lead to proficiency in climbing, running, jumping, balancing, hopping and skipping, swimming.
- ★ Enjoys team games and sports.
- ★ Rides a bicycle with competence and confidence.
- ★ Improved fine motor skills makes handwriting easier and more legible.
- ★ Can do more complex construction activities.
- ★ Continues to enjoy singing and dancing, but often prefers performing set dance routines rather than participating in dancing games.

Children engaged in physical play activity.

Ten ways to provide for children's physical play needs

1. **Select play activities**, **tools and materials** that are appropriate to the ages and levels of development of the children.

2. **Provide play opportunities that encourage children to explore and experiment** with their physical skills both indoors and outdoors, with and without play apparatus or other equipment.

3. **Maintain children's safety** by providing appropriate adult supervision and checking that any equipment used meets required safety standards and is positioned on an appropriate surface. Ensure the children know how to use any equipment correctly and safely (see Chapter 5).

4. **Provide play opportunities that allow children to repeat actions** until they are confident and competent. Provide specific tools and activities to help children practise their physical skills. Encourage children to persevere with tackling new skills that are particularly difficult by reassuring them that everyone needs practice and patience to learn new skills.

5. **Use everyday routines** to develop children's fine motor skills (e.g. getting dressed, dealing with fastenings and shoelaces, helping prepare or serve food, washing up, setting out/clearing away play activities). (Remember: *safety*.)

6. **Provide play opportunities** to help the children practise fine motor skills (e.g. bricks, jigsaws, play dough, sand, construction kits, drawing).

7. **Help children to develop body awareness** through action songs such as 'Head, Shoulders, Knees and Toes'.

▶

8. **Encourage and praise children** as they become competent in each physical skill.
9. **Allow children to be as independent** as possible when developing their physical skills. (See the section on risk during play activities in Chapter 4.)
10. **Adapt activities and/or use specialist equipment** for children with special needs to enable their participation in physical activities as appropriate (see Chapter 4).

Children's intellectual development

Intellectual (or cognitive) development involves the process of gaining, storing, recalling and using information. The interrelated components of intellectual development are: thinking, perception, language, problem-solving, concepts, memory, concentration and creativity.

To develop as healthy, considerate and intelligent human beings, children and young people require intellectual stimulation as well as physical care and emotional security. They are constantly thinking and learning, gathering new information and formulating new ideas about themselves, other people and the world around them.

The sequence of intellectual development: 4 to 16 years

Age 4–7 years

- ☆ Is very curious and asks lots of questions.
- ☆ Develops interest in reading for themselves.
- ☆ Enjoys imaginative and creative play activities.
- ☆ Enjoys construction activities; spatial awareness increases.
- ☆ Knows, matches and names colours and shapes.
- ☆ Follows three-step instructions.
- ☆ Enjoys jigsaw puzzles and games.
- ☆ Concentrates for longer (e.g. on TV programmes and longer stories) and can recall details.
- ☆ Learns to read and write.
- ☆ Shows awareness of right and wrong, and the needs of others.
- ☆ Begins to see other people's points of view.
- ☆ Stores and recalls more complex information using language.

Age 7–11 years

- ☆ Learns to read more complex texts and develops writing skills.
- ☆ Enjoys number work, but may still need real objects to help mathematical processes.

* Enjoys experimenting with materials and exploring the environment.
* Develops creative abilities as co-ordination improves (e.g. more detailed drawings).
* Begins to know the difference between real and imaginary, but still enjoys imaginative play (e.g. acting out ideas, pretending to be characters from TV or film).

Children engaged in creative play activity.

* Interested in more complex construction activities.
* Has longer attention-span; does not like to be disturbed during play activities.
* Follows increasingly more complex instructions.
* Enjoys board games and other games with rules; also computer games.
* Develops a competitive streak.
* Has increased awareness of right and wrong, and the needs of others.
* Sees other people's points of view.
* Seeks information from various sources (e.g. encyclopaedia, Internet).
* Processes expanding knowledge and information through language.

Age 11–16 years

* Reads more complex texts with improved comprehension and extends writing skills.
* Develops understanding of abstract mathematical/scientific processes (e.g. algebra, physics).
* Continues to enjoy experiments and exploration of the wider environment.
* Develops more creative abilities (e.g. very detailed drawings and stories).
* Knows the difference between real and imaginary.
* Has increased concentration levels.
* Continues to follow more complex instructions.
* Continues to enjoy board games and computer games that require strategy skills.
* Has a competitive streak and may have particular interests that allow them to show off their intellectual abilities (e.g. chess, computer clubs).
* Has well-defined understanding of right and wrong; can consider the needs of others.

☆ Sees other people's points of view.

☆ Continues to seek information from various sources (e.g. encyclopaedia, Internet).

☆ Continues to process increasing knowledge and information through language.

Ten ways to provide for children's intellectual play needs

1. **Provide play opportunities and materials to increase children's curiosity** (e.g. outings, toys, games and books).

2. **Encourage children to be observant by pointing out details in the environment** (e.g. colours, shapes, smells, textures; interesting objects such as birds, vehicles; talking about weather conditions; taking them on outings; gardening; keeping pets).

3. **Participate in children's play to extend their development and learning** by asking questions, providing answers and demonstrating possible ways to use play equipment. Demonstrate how things work or fit together when the children are not sure what to do. Make sure your help is wanted (and necessary). Use verbal prompts where possible to encourage children to solve a problem themselves.

4. **Provide repetition** by encouraging children to play with toys and games more then once; each time they play, they will discover different things about these activities.

5. **Provide gradually more challenging play activities** but do not push children too hard by providing activities that are obviously too complex; instead of extending their abilities this will only put them off due to the frustration of not being able to do the activity.

6. **Remember safety**. It is important to allow children the freedom to explore their environment and to experiment with the properties of different materials, but always ensure that materials and equipment are suitable for the children. (See the section on risk during play activities in Chapter 4.)

7. **Encourage children's auditory perception** through activities such as singing rhymes and songs; clapping games; awareness of animal noises/environmental sounds; taped songs, rhymes, music, everyday sounds and stories; sharing books and stories; 'sound lotto'.

8. **Encourage children's visual perception** through activities involving exploration of the environment including outings to a local park or farm; looking at books, pictures, displays, photographs; using magnification to highlight details (e.g. magnifying glass, binoculars, telescope); matching games, jigsaws, lotto; activities requiring letter and/or number recognition, including board games.

9. **Encourage children's tactile exploration and creativity** through activities that involve exploratory and creative play, such as doing arts and crafts; playing with sand, water, clay, dough or wood; playing with manufactured materials (e.g. plastic construction kits like LEGO®, Stickle Bricks, Mega Bloks®).

10. **Encourage children's use of their taste and smell senses** through cooking activities; finding out about different tastes – sweet, sour, bitter, salty; and different smells – sweet and savoury, flowers, fruit and vegetables. (Remember: *safety*.)

Children's language development

Language is the key factor in all children's development as it provides them with the skills they need to communicate with others, relate to others, explore their environment, understand concepts, formulate ideas and express feelings. Children (and adults) use a variety of different ways to communicate. These modes of language are essential to being able to communicate effectively with others and to being fully involved in a wide range of social interactions.

You should provide opportunities for children and young people to develop the necessary skills to become competent at communicating using these different modes of language. Opportunities for talk are especially helpful in promoting the development and use of language. When working with children and young people, you must be aware of and provide for appropriate experiences to enable the children to develop effective communication skills.

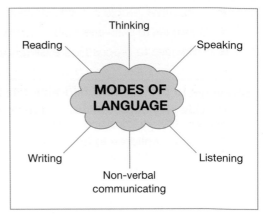

Modes of language.

The sequence of language development: 4 to 16 years

Age 4–7 years

- ★ May use a vocabulary of about 1500 to 4000 words.
- ★ Uses quite complex sentence structures.
- ★ Asks lots of questions using what, when, who, where, how and especially *why*!
- ★ Shows interest in more complex books and stories.
- ★ Develops early literacy skills.
- ★ Gives fairly detailed accounts of past events.
- ★ Vocalises ideas and feelings.
- ★ Can listen to and follow detailed instructions.
- ★ Can deliver complex verbal messages.
- ★ Enjoys songs and rhymes.
- ★ Shows interest in simple poetry.

Age 7–11 years

- ★ Has extensive vocabulary of between 4000 and 10,000 words.
- ★ Uses more complex sentence structures.
- ★ Develops more complex reading skills, including improved comprehension.
- ★ Develops more complex writing skills, including more accurate spelling, punctuation and joined-up writing.
- ★ Continues to enjoy books, stories and poetry.
- ★ Gives very detailed accounts of past events and can anticipate future events.

- ★ Vocalises ideas and feelings in more depth.
- ★ Listens to and follows more complex instructions.
- ★ Appreciates jokes due to more sophisticated language knowledge.
- ★ Uses literacy skills to communicate and to access information (e.g. story and letter writing, use of dictionaries, encyclopaedia, computers, Internet, e-mail).

Age 11–16 years

- ★ Has an extensive and varied vocabulary of between 10,000 and 20,000 words.
- ★ Uses appropriate language styles for different occasions (e.g. standard English for formal situations).
- ★ Has more complex reading skills, including detailed comprehension skills (e.g. can comment on structure and themes of a book or other piece of writing).
- ★ Has more complex writing skills, including accurate spelling and punctuation; neat and legible joined-up writing.
- ★ Can use different writing styles including word-processing on a computer.
- ★ Continues to enjoy more complex texts, including fiction, poetry and factual books.
- ★ Gives very detailed accounts of past events using varied expression and vocabulary.
- ★ Can anticipate future events *and* give detailed reasons for possible outcomes.
- ★ Vocalises ideas and feelings in greater depth, including justifying own views and opinions.
- ★ Listens to and follows complex sets of instructions.
- ★ Appreciates complex jokes and word play.
- ★ Continues to use literacy skills to communicate and to access information (e.g. taking notes, writing essays and letters; using dictionary/thesaurus, encyclopaedia; computers, Internet, e-mail).

Ten ways to provide for children's language/communication play needs

1. **Talk to children and young people about anything and everything!**
2. **Show children what you are talking about** (e.g. use real objects/situations, pictures, books, and other visual or audio aids).
3. **Use straightforward sentences** with words appropriate to the children's level of understanding and development; avoid over-simplifying language; do *not* use 'baby talk' – children need to hear adult speech to learn language.
4. **Use repetition to introduce/reinforce new vocabulary and ideas**. Do *not* make children repeat things back over and over; this is boring and frustrating.
5. **Copy children's sounds/words** including any extensions or corrections to positively reinforce and extend the children's vocabulary, sentence structures, etc. For example, the child says: 'Ball' and you could reply, 'Yes, that is Tom's red ball.' Or the child may say, 'Moo!' and you could reply, 'Yes, the cow goes "moo"!' *Never* tell children off for making language errors; it will only make them reluctant to communicate in the future. Making mistakes is part of the language learning process.
6. **Be lively!** Use your tone of voice and facial expressions to convey your interest in what is being communicated.

7. **Remember turn-taking in language exchanges.** Ask questions to stimulate the children's responses and to encourage speech.
8. **Look at the children when you are talking with them.** Remember to be at their level (e.g. sit on a low chair or even on the floor; do *not* tower over them).
9. **Let the children initiate conversations** and listen to what they have to say.
10. **Share a variety of books, stories and rhymes** with children and young people.

Children's emotional development

Emotional development can be defined as the development of personality and temperament. This includes how each child:

- ☆ develops as a unique individual
- ☆ feels about and sees themselves
- ☆ *thinks* other people see them
- ☆ expresses their individual needs, desires and feelings
- ☆ relates to others
- ☆ interacts with their environment.

You need to understand the sequence of children's emotional development in order to provide them with the appropriate assistance and support to promote their emotional well-being. (See Chapter 7 for further information on this.)

The sequence of emotional development: 4 to 16 years

Age 4–7 years

- ☆ Becomes more aware of the feelings and needs of others.
- ☆ Tries to comfort others who are upset, hurt or unwell.
- ☆ May occasionally be aggressive as still learning to deal with negative emotions.
- ☆ Uses language to express feelings and wishes.

Child engaged in imaginative play.

- ★ Uses imaginative play to express worries and fears over past/future experiences (e.g. hospital visits, family disputes/upheaval).
- ★ Has an occasional **emotional outburst** when tired, stressed or frustrated.
- ★ Argues with other children but may take some time to forgive and forget.
- ★ Confidence in self can be shaken by 'failure'.
- ★ May have an 'imaginary friend'.

Age 7–11 years

- ★ Becomes less **egocentric** as understands feelings, needs and rights of others.
- ★ Still wants things that belong solely to them (e.g. very possessive of own toys, puts own name on everything they possess).
- ★ Becomes more aware of own achievements in relation to others but this can lead to a sense of failure if they feel they don't measure up; hates to lose.
- ★ May be very competitive; rivalry may lead to aggressive behaviour.
- ★ Argues with other children but may take even longer to forgive and forget.
- ★ Has increased awareness of the wider environment (e.g. the weather, plants, animals, people in other countries).

Age 11–16 years

- ★ Sensitive to own feelings and those of others, with a growing understanding of the possible causes for why people feel and act as they do.
- ★ Emotional changes due to puberty.
- ★ Understands issues relating to fairness and justice.
- ★ Can anticipate people's reactions and consider the consequences of own actions.
- ★ Is increasingly able to see different viewpoints in order to resolve difficulties in relationships.
- ★ Has confidence in own skills and ideas; is more able to be assertive rather than aggressive or passive.
- ★ May have very strong opinions or beliefs, leading to arguments with adults and peers; may hold grudges and find it difficult to forgive or forget.
- ★ Has more understanding of complex issues concerning the wider environment (e.g. ethics, philosophy, religion, politics).

Ten ways to provide for children's emotional play needs

1. **Be positive by using praise and encouragement** to help children focus on what they are good at. Point out all the things that make each child special.
2. **Treat every child in the play setting as an individual**. Each has unique abilities and needs. Help them to maximise their individual potential.
3. **Encourage children to measure any achievements by comparing these to their *own* efforts**. Foster co-operation between children rather than competition.

►

4. **Have high but realistic expectations**. Remember *nothing succeeds like success*, so provide appropriate play activities that are sufficiently challenging while still allowing the children opportunities for enjoyment and success.

5. **Take an interest in children's efforts as well as their achievements**. Remember the *way* children participate in play activities is more important than the end results (e.g. sharing resources, helping others and contributing ideas).

6. **Give children opportunities to make decisions and choices**. Letting them participate in decision-making, even in a small way, helps them to feel positive and important; it also prepares them for making appropriate judgements and sensible decisions later on (see Chapter 2).

7. **Share books and stories about real-life situations** showing children (and adults) that the children can identify with. Promote equality of opportunity by providing positive images of children and adults through books and stories as well as songs/rhymes.

8. **Encourage children to focus on their skills and abilities in positive ways** (e.g. an 'I can …' tree with positive statements about what the children *can* do).

9. **Provide opportunities for imaginative play** that encourage children to explore different roles in positive ways (e.g. dressing-up clothes, cooking utensils, dolls and puppets).

10. **Be consistent about rules and discipline**. All children need consistency and a clearly structured framework for behaviour so that they know what is expected of them (see Chapter 8). Remember to label the behaviour not the child as this is less damaging to their emotional well-being (e.g. 'That was an unkind thing to say' rather than 'You are unkind').

The sequence of children's social play

Children go through a recognised sequence of social play. Younger children tend to engage in more solitary or parallel play activities because they are more egocentric; while older children are capable of more co-operative play activities as they can take turns, share play equipment and follow rules more easily. There will be times when quite young children can be engaged happily in play activities with some interaction with other children (associative play) such as dressing-up, home corner, doing jigsaws, simple construction or painting. There will be occasions when older children become engrossed in solitary or parallel play activities with no interaction with other children (for example, doing

Children engaged in social play.

detailed drawings and paintings, building intricate constructions that require complete concentration to the exclusion of everyone else).

A child's level of social interaction during play activities depends on the individual child and their previous experiences of play, the play activity itself and the social context (e.g. the setting and other people present).

The sequence of social play
- **Solitary play**: playing alone.
- **Parallel play**: playing alongside other children without interaction.
- **Associative play**: playing alongside other children with limited interaction.
- **Co-operative play**: playing together.
- **Complex co-operative play**: playing together including following agreed rules.

Observing children's play and development

Careful observations enable you to assess children's and young people's individual play needs and preferences, levels of development, range of skills and behaviour patterns. The methods for observing children and young people will depend on the setting's record-keeping policy and any legal requirements. (See the section on record-keeping in Chapter 10.) You may compile a portfolio of relevant information about each child. A portfolio could include:

- ✯ observations
- ✯ examples of the child's activities (e.g. paintings, drawings)
- ✯ photographs of the child during play activities
- ✯ checklists of the child's progress.

Assessment of this information can help highlight and celebrate the child's strengths as well as identify any difficulties they may have in accessing particular play activities. The information can also form the basis for the ongoing planning of appropriate play opportunities.

Observations and assessments should cover all relevant aspects of child development, including: physical skills; language and communication skills; social and emotional behaviour during different play activities. There are various methods for observing and recording children's play and development, including: free description, structured description, pre-coded categories or checklists; sampling. Your college tutor/assessor will give you guidelines for the methods most appropriate to your role as a playworker in your particular play setting. Your observations and assessments must be in line with your setting's policy for record-keeping, and relevant to the play activities of the children and/or young people you work with. You must follow the setting's policy regarding confidentiality at all times. Before doing any key tasks for NVQ assessment involving observations of children or young people you *must* negotiate with the playworker who supervises your work when it will be possible for you to carry out your observations, and have written permission to do so.

> **EXERCISE:** Find out what your setting's policies are regarding child observations, record-keeping and confidentiality. Keep this information in mind when doing your own observations of children and/or young people.

The basic principles of observation

The following are some important points to consider when observing children and young people.

1. **Confidentiality** must be kept at all times. You *must* have your supervisor's permission before making formal observations of children or young people.

2. **Be objective** – only record what you actually see and hear, not what you think or feel. For example, the statement 'The child cried' is objective, but to say 'The child is sad' is subjective, because you do not know what the child is feeling; the child could be crying for any number of reasons (e.g. to draw attention to itself or to show discomfort).

3. **Remember equal opportunities.** Consider children's cultural and social backgrounds (for example, children may be very competent at communicating in their community language, but may have more difficulty in expressing themselves in English; this does *not* mean they are behind in their language development).

4. **Be positive!** Focus on the child's strengths not just on any difficulties they may have. Look at what the child *can* do in terms of play and use this as the foundation for providing future play opportunities.

5. **Use a holistic approach.** Remember to look at the 'whole' child. You need to look at *all* areas of a child's development in relation to the particular aspect of play and development you are focusing on. For example, when observing a child's drawing skills, as well as looking at their intellectual development you will also need to consider their physical development (fine motor skills when using a pencil), their language development and communication skills (vocabulary and structure of any language used), and their social and emotional development (interaction with others and behaviour during the activity).

6. **Consider the child's feelings.** Try not to make it obvious that you are observing; keep your distance where possible, but be close enough to hear the child's language. Where observation is obvious (e.g. tape recording) explain to the child in simple terms what you are doing. Try not to interact with the child (unless it is a participant observation – see below), but if they do address you, be polite and respond positively, keeping your answers short.

7. **Practise.** The best way to develop your skills at observing children's play and development is to have a go at doing observations, and keep on doing them.

Methods of observation

⭐ **Time sampling**: observation of child's behaviour at regular intervals during a set period of time (e.g. every ten minutes during a play session). Time sampling can provide a clearer picture of behaviour changes throughout a session or day and help to identify when certain behaviour occurs and during which activities.

⭐ **Event sampling**: observations of particular events as they occur (e.g. child's emotional outbursts). A record is made of the number of times the target behaviour occurs, when it occurs and how long it lasts.

⭐ **Participant observation**: where the observer is also involved in the child's activity.

⭐ **Non-participant observation**: involves being as unobtrusive as possible while other members of staff assist the child as necessary during the activity.

⭐ **Target child**: observation that concentrates on one particular child.

⭐ **Trail or movement**: observations to monitor behaviour. On a plan of the play area, lines are drawn indicating the movements of the child, with brief notes about the length of time spent on each activity, the child's behaviour and any social interaction.

Other useful methods for observing learning and/or behaviour include checklists, coded observations and diaries. Some observations of children may be unplanned – for instance, you may take note of a child's unusual behaviour during an activity).

Your college tutor or assessor should give you guidelines on how to present your observations. Otherwise you might find the suggested format in the accompanying box useful.

Suggested format for presenting observations

Date of observation: ....

Method: ....

Start time: ....

Finish time: ....

Number of children/staff: ....

Permission for observation: ....

Type of play setting: *e.g. holiday play scheme, out-of-school club* ....

Immediate context/background information: *including the activity and its location* ....

Description of child/children: *including age in years and months* ....
....

Aims: *why you are doing this particular observation* ....
....

Observation: *the observation may be a written report, a tape recording with written transcript, a pie chart or bar graph, or tick chart* ....

▶

Assessment: *include the following:*

- *did you achieve your aims?*
- *your assessment of the child's play, development and/or behaviour, looking at all aspects of the child's development with particular emphasis on the focus area (e.g. drawing skills)*
- *references to support your comments*

Personal learning: *what you have gained from doing this observation (e.g. what you have learned about this aspect of child development and using this particular method of observing children – for instance, was this the most appropriate method of observation for this type of play activity?)*

Recommendations:

- *on how to encourage/extend the child's play and development in the focus area (e.g. make suggestions for activities and experiences to develop the child's drawing skills)*
- *for any aspect of the child's play and development that you think requires further observation and assessment*

References/bibliography: *details of all the books used to complete your assessment*

KEY TASK

1. Observe a child during a play activity.
2. In your assessment, include information on:
   - the type of play activity observed
   - the child's play needs
   - the development and skills demonstrated by the child
   - the child's behaviour during the play activity
   - the child's language and communication skills
   - the child's level of social interaction
   - suggestions for extending the child's play and development in this area.

Use relevant sections in this chapter (and any play and development or psychology books you have) to help you with your assessment.

Remember to follow your setting's guidelines for child observation.

NVQ links – Level 2: PW2.1; Level 3: PW9.1

Further reading

Bilton, H. (2004) *Playing Outside: Activities, Ideas, and Inspiration for the Early Years*. David Fulton Publishers.

Broadhead, P. (2003) *Early Years Play and Learning: Developing Social Skills and Co-operation*. Routledge Falmer.

Brown, F. (ed.) (2002) *Playwork: Theory and Practice*. Open University Press.

Bruce, T. (2001) *Learning Through Play*. Hodder & Stoughton.

Davy, A. (2001) *Playwork: Play and Care for Children 5–15* (3rd edn). Thomson Learning.

DCMS (Department for Culture, Media & Sport) (2004) *Getting Serious About Play: A Review of Children's Play*. UK Department for Culture, Media & Sport.

Einon, D. (1986) *Creative Play*. Penguin.

Gibson, R. (1998) *Usborne Playtime Activities*. Usborne Publishing Ltd.

Hughes, B. (2001) *Evolutionary Playwork and Reflective Analytic Practice*. Routledge.

Lindon, J. (2001) *Understanding Children's Play*. Nelson Thornes.

Lindon, J. (2005) *Understanding Child Development: Linking Theory and Practice*. Hodder Arnold.

Masheder, M. (1989b) *Let's Play Together*. Green Print.

Meredith, S. (1988) *Teach Your Child to Swim*. Usborne Publishing Ltd.

Morris, J. and Mort, J. (1991) *Bright Ideas for the Early Years: Learning Through Play*. Scholastic.

Moyles, J. (ed.) (1994) *The Excellence of Play*. Open University Press.

National Playing Fields Association, Children's Play Council and Playlink (2000) *Best Play: What Play Provision Should Do for Children*. NPFA.

Play Wales and PlayEducation (2001) *The First Claim: A Framework for Playwork Quality Assessment*. Play Wales.

Schaffer, H.R. (2003) *Introducing Child Psychology*. Blackwell Publishers.

Sheridan, M.D. et al. (1999) *Play in Early Childhood: From Birth to Six Years*. Routledge.

Smith, P. et al. (2003) *Understanding Children's Development*. Blackwell Publishers.

Street, C. (2002) *The Benefits of Play*. Highlight No. 195. National Children's Bureau.

Sylva, K. and Lunt, I. (2002) *Child Development* (2nd edn). Blackwell Publishers.

Woolfson, R. (1994) *Understanding Children: A Guide for Parents and Carers – A Practical Guide to Child Psychology*. Caring Books.

4 Planning and supporting play

Key points

- ⚙ The playworker's role in planning and supporting self-directed play
- ⚙ Using objectives to evaluate play provision
- ⚙ The range of different types of play spaces
- ⚙ Planning play spaces that meet children's and young people's play needs
- ⚙ Obtaining resources for play spaces
- ⚙ Providing appropriate support for play
- ⚙ Identifying when and how to respond to play cues
- ⚙ Defining a play frame
- ⚙ Behavioural modes associated with play
- ⚙ Recognising the mood descriptors associated with play
- ⚙ Providing for a range of play types
- ⚙ Encouraging and supporting acceptable risk-taking during play
- ⚙ Ending play sessions

The playworker's role in planning and supporting self-directed play

You should aim to provide minimum intervention in children's play activities while keeping them safe from harm. You should support rather than direct their play and help to create a play environment that will stimulate their self-directed play and provide maximum opportunities for them to experience a wide variety of play types.

You can enrich children's and young people's play experiences in the following ways:

- ✪ planning and creating play spaces that meet their play needs and preferences
- ✪ obtaining and/or creating resources for a range of play spaces
- ✪ fostering positive attitudes
- ✪ providing new materials and tools to stimulate their exploration and learning
- ✪ participating in their play if and when invited.

The planning cycle

You should use information on children's and young people's play needs and preferences to plan appropriate play opportunities. You can write down your plans on a planning sheet or in an activity file. Your plans may be brief or detailed, depending on the requirements of your setting. Some activities may require more detailed preparation and organisation than others (e.g. arts and crafts, cooking, outings).

A plan for an activity could include the following sections.

1. **Title:** A brief description of the activity.
2. **When?** Date and time of the activity.
3. **Where?** Where the activity will take place (e.g. indoor play area, outdoor play area, local park or playground).
4. **Why?** Outline why you have selected this particular activity (e.g. identified children's play needs and preferences through research, observation or consultation).
5. **What?** What you need to prepare in advance (e.g. selecting or making appropriate resources; buying ingredients, materials or equipment).
6. **How?** How you will organise the activity. Consider any safety requirements. Think about tidying up after the activity (e.g. encouraging the children to help tidy up).

Evaluate the activity afterwards (for instance, note the children's response to the activity, the skills and/or learning they demonstrated, the effectiveness of your preparation, organisation and implementation). Make a note of your evaluation on the planning sheet or in the activity file. These notes will prove helpful when planning future play opportunities and for providing information to other playworkers at regular meetings (see Chapter 10).

Be flexible in planning activities

While careful planning of appropriate play opportunities is important, it should be flexible enough to allow for each child's individual interests and for unplanned, spontaneous opportunities for play. For example, an unexpected snowfall can provide a wonderful opportunity to explore and talk about snow, as well as enabling the children to express delight and fascination at this type of weather.

Children playing on a snowy day.

EXERCISE:
1. Think about how you plan and support children's and young people's self-directed play in your setting.
2. Describe your experience of an unplanned play opportunity.

Using objectives to evaluate play provision

You need to know and understand the objectives that can be used to evaluate play provision. Knowledge and understanding of the play objectives (see the accompanying box) will help you to put playwork theory into practice.

   You can use these objectives to evaluate play provision in the following ways:

☆ Observing and recording the play types demonstrated by children/young people and the relationships within the setting.

☆ Listening to the children/young people's views on the play environment and the resources available in the setting.

☆ Monitoring the policies and procedures, and how these work in practice in the play setting.

☆ Evaluating and reviewing activity plans, play opportunities and resources, as well as the policies and procedures in the play setting.

(Based on National Playing Fields Association, Children's Play Council and Playlink, 2000)

The range of different types of play spaces

It is essential for you to know about the range of different types of play spaces or play environments that support and enrich the potential for children and young people's play. 'Play spaces' are areas that support and enrich the potential for children and young people to play (SkillsActive, 2004b). 'Play environments' are environments with resources to stimulate children's and young people's play (SPRITO, 2002).

Types of play spaces or play environments include:

Adventure playground.

☆ **day care settings**, run by professional early years staff and/or playworkers, providing play opportunities (e.g. private and local authority day nurseries, out-of-school clubs)

☆ **'formal' play provision**, run by professional play staff and parent helpers/volunteers (e.g. playgroups, holiday play schemes)

☆ **'open access' play facilities**, operated by professional playworkers but where children and young people come and go as they please (e.g. adventure playgrounds, some holiday play schemes, playbuses)

☆ **'informal' play facilities** that are not staffed (e.g. public parks, play areas and playgrounds, skate parks, basketball courts, football pitches and playing fields)

☆ **non-designated play spaces** used by children and young people especially when there are no other play spaces available (e.g. local streets, outside shops, abandoned buildings, open spaces).

(DCMS, 2004)

You also need to ensure that the play provision meets the play needs and preferences of the children and young people who use the setting. You should consider the following key elements of successful play opportunities (which you can remember using the mnemonic 'VITAL'). They should be:

☆ **V**alue-based
☆ **I**n the right place
☆ **T**op quality
☆ **A**ppropriate
☆ **L**ong-term.

Characteristics of VITAL play opportunities

Value-based

☆ Children's and young people's interests and rights are respected.
☆ All children and young people are welcomed, whatever their ability or background, especially those from disadvantaged groups.
☆ Children's and young people's skills and abilities are respected.

In the right place

☆ Close to children's and young people's homes and schools or on well-used travel routes.
☆ In safe locations.
☆ Located in places that children, young people and the wider community are happy with.

Top quality

☆ Safe, welcoming and providing choice and variety.
☆ Well designed in relation to surrounding area and local community.
☆ Has balanced approach to managing risk.
☆ Well managed and maintained.

Appropriate

☆ Shaped by local needs and circumstances.
☆ Complementing other local opportunities.
☆ Taking account of all sectors of the local community.
☆ Well planned.

Long-term

⭐ Sustainable beyond the lifetime of immediate funding.

⭐ Set up to be valued and respected parts of the social fabric of the neighbourhood.

(DCMS, 2004: 19)

KEY TASK

1. List the range of existing play spaces or play environments in your local area.

2. What additional play spaces or play environments and resources do you think should be made available to meet the play needs and preferences of the children and young people in your local area?

NVQ links – Level 2: PW2.1; Level 3: PW9.1

Planning play spaces that meet children's and young people's play needs

You need to be able to plan play spaces or play environments that meet children's and young people's play needs. When doing this, remember that:

⭐ the play environment should be welcoming and provide maximum opportunities for children and young people to make choices

⭐ play resources should be varied, with sufficient quantities so that children do not have to wait too long to play with materials or equipment

⭐ children should have lots of opportunities for social interaction with other children and adults.

(Lindon, 2002)

Playworkers plan how a setting will be organised, both indoors and outdoors, and what play opportunities and resources will be available. However, such planning must take account of children's and young people's play needs and be flexible enough to allow them to enjoy play in their own way, and to make their own choices and decisions about it.

EXERCISE: Think about the planning and provision of play opportunities in your setting.

When planning play spaces (or play environments) you should remember the following important points:

1. Plan play spaces based on children's and young people's play needs and preferences – find out about children's play and development, observe children's and young people's play activities.

2. Involve children and young people in the creation of play spaces – consult them about the play opportunities and play resources they would like in the play setting.

3. Create play spaces that children and young people can adapt to their own needs – for example, flexible play areas that allow children to spread out during their play.

4. Allow children and young people to choose and explore play spaces for themselves – for example, selecting their own play activities and resources.

5. Allow children and young people to develop through play in their own ways – for example, give them the freedom to explore and enjoy their chosen play activities in their own way and in their own time.

6. Allow children's and young people's play to continue uninterrupted – participate in their play as and when invited to do so; only intervene in order to maintain their physical safety or emotional security.

7. Address the possible barriers to accessing play spaces that some children and young people may experience – ensure the play setting is inclusive and encourages participation by all the children/young people including those from ethnic minority backgrounds and those with disabilities. (See the section on diversity and inclusion in Chapter 10.)

 KEY TASK

Describe how you plan and support children's and/or young people's play in your play setting. Include examples of how you:
- meet the children's and/or young people's play needs
- involve children and/or young people in the creation of play spaces
- create play spaces that children and/or young people can adapt to their own needs
- allow children and/or young people to choose and explore play spaces for themselves
- allow children and/or young people to develop through play in their own ways
- allow children's and/or young people's play to continue uninterrupted
- address the possible barriers to accessing play spaces that some children and young people may experience.

Your examples might include:
- child observations
- work plans/activity plans
- summaries of discussions with children and/or young people
- relevant policies and procedures (e.g. equal opportunities, health and safety).

NVQ links – Level 2: PW2.1 PW2.2 PW2.3; Level 3: PW9.1 PW9.2 PW9.3

Obtaining resources for play spaces

Every play setting should be equipped with appropriate play resources appropriate to the age range of the children and/or young people. You should know how to obtain and/or create the resources needed for a range of play spaces. You may need to work within the budget available for resources and, if necessary, find alternative ways to obtain or create resources. Children and young people benefit from a wide range of play resources, not just those that are commercially produced. Depending on the play setting, you should be able to provide a wide selection of play resources. For example:

- ✯ **recycled materials** to provide opportunities for children/young people to construct models, etc.
- ✯ **the outdoor environment** to provide opportunities for exploring the natural world (e.g. gardening, visiting local parks and playgrounds)
- ✯ **natural materials** to provide opportunities for exploring different materials and their properties (e.g. sand, water, cooking ingredients)
- ✯ **homemade materials** for creative activities (e.g. homemade play dough – encouraging children to make the play dough themselves enriches their play and learning experience)
- ✯ **clean**, **unwanted clothing** for dressing-up activities (recycling again!) not just commercially produced outfits
- ✯ **commercially produced resources** that are well made, durable and safe for children's use, as well as being good value for money (e.g. construction kits and tools, climbing equipment, child-size domestic play equipment); remember that quality is more important than quantity
- ✯ **space** for children's imaginary games that require little or no props.

Remember to make use of any community resource facilities such as book loans from local libraries (usually free to non-profit organisations) and borrowing play equipment from toy libraries. Contact the local authority or disability charities for information on schemes they may operate for hiring or purchasing specialist play equipment for children with disabilities.

Resources for the play setting include the following.

- ✯ **Consumables** (resources that get used up) such as paint, glue, paper; ingredients for cooking activities; food and drinks for meals/snacks; cleaning materials. Keep track of these resources to ensure that they do not run out, by doing regular stock takes and reporting to the person responsible for reordering.
- ✯ **Equipment** (resources that do not get used up) such as furniture, books, computers and play equipment (e.g. climbing frames, construction kits, board games). Check these resources for wear and tear to ensure they are safe for continued use, and report any problems or damage to the person responsible for resources. (See the section in Chapter 5 on safety checks.)

★ **Finance** for the play setting (e.g. the money needed to buy consumables and new equipment, pay staff wages, pay for the rent and/or maintenance of the building). (See the section in Chapter 11 on managing a budget.)

★ **Adults** (the people who run and organise the play setting): they may be paid staff, parent helpers or volunteers.

Adult resources

Adults are one of the most important resources in a play setting. Ensure that the setting is making the best use of its adult resources (e.g. playworkers, assistant playworkers, parent helpers and volunteers) in order to:

★ respond to children's and young people's play needs

★ stimulate children's and young people's play and development

★ encourage children's and young people's ideas, opinions and active participation

★ provide appropriate support for children's and young people's self-directed play

★ safeguard children's and young people's health and well-being.

(For more detailed information see the section in Chapter 11 on effective planning and fair allocation of work.)

Managing resources

It is essential that all resources within the setting be used efficiently and appropriately without undue waste, especially if the setting has a limited budget. Remember the following important points.

★ Discuss the efficient use of resources at team meetings.

★ Pay attention to other play provision in the local area.

★ Consult children and young people about the play resources *they* would like.

★ Plan ahead (e.g. long-term plans for the play setting including funding).

★ Monitor the quality and value for money of the resources in the play setting.

★ Be aware of the environmental impact of the resources used by the play setting (e.g. use recycled materials such as paper; recycle clean household junk for use in creative activities; use and promote Fair Trade products).

★ Allocate responsibility for different areas of resources to spread the workload.

A designated member of staff should have specific responsibility for replenishing supplies of consumables (e.g. pencils, paper and card, paint, cooking ingredients) as necessary. Stock levels should be monitored on a regular basis. Staff and children/young people should know how to use all play resources correctly and safely, with care and respect; and with regard for health and safety and waste. Care should be taken to ensure that resources reflect the cultural and linguistic diversity of the local community, and that all children/young people have equality of access. Visual aids should also be available – for example, videos, maps, posters, pictures, interesting objects or

artefacts related to topics or themes, and computer software. Display materials for use in play areas and around the setting should also be available.

As part of your role you may need to make regular checks to ensure that essential materials or equipment are not running out. You may need to keep a weekly check on consumables such as art and craft materials, cooking ingredients, and so on. Clearing away equipment and materials provides you with a regular opportunity to check whether any supplies are running low. Items such as soap and paper towels may need to be checked every day. There will be an inventory, or stock list, that is checked on a regular basis. Larger items, such as furniture, may be included on an inventory that is checked annually. There should be a setting procedure for doing this.

KEY TASK

1. List the main play resources available in your setting under these headings:
   - Consumables
   - Equipment
   - Finance
   - Adults.
2. What are your responsibilities for obtaining and/or creating the necessary resources for your play setting?

NVQ links – Level 2: PW2.2; Level 3: PW9.2

Providing appropriate support for play

You should know how to provide appropriate support for play. You can provide appropriate types of support for children's and young people's self-directed play in the following ways.

★ Provide flexible planning and minimal adult supervision.
★ Enable them to choose from a broad range of play opportunities and resources.
★ Enable them to choose whether or not they wish to be involved in play activities.
★ Give them freedom to choose how to use the available materials.
★ Provide them with access to a wide range of materials and allow them to determine their play in their own way.
★ Provide plenty of space for their play activities, especially for physical games and imaginative play.

- ☆ Encourage them to sort out fair ways to take turns on play equipment.
- ☆ Keep the numbers of children/young people in group activities to a reasonable size to enable everyone to enjoy play.
- ☆ Create a stimulating and enjoyable play environment that also maintains their physical safety and emotional well-being.
- ☆ Provide challenging play opportunities to avoid boredom; risk-taking is part of the enjoyment of play.

(Lindon, 2002)

KEY TASK

List the ways in which you provide appropriate support for children's and/or young people's self-directed play.

NVQ links – Level 2: PW2.2, PW2.3; Level 3: PW9.3

Identifying when and how to respond to play cues

You should know and understand the main stages of the play cycle. This means the course of play from start to finish – that is, from the first play cue to completion of play.

You should be able to identify when and how to respond to play cues as part of the play cycle. Play cues are 'facial expressions, language or body language that communicate the child or young person's wish to play or invite others to play' (SkillsActive, 2004b). You should observe children's and/or young people's play and respond appropriately to their play cues. Here is a brief example:

Child's Play Cue	Playworker's Response
First play cue: child smiles and uses eye contact (facial expression) to indicate wish to play.	Asks the child which particular play activity they want to do. Child chooses an activity and selects own resources.
Second play cue: child makes specific verbal request (language) for adult to join in with the play activity.	Joins in as per the child's request, e.g. having a 'cup of tea' in the playhouse.
Final play cue: child points (body language) to another play activity indicating wish to play something else.	Checks there is space for the child to do the desired play activity. Child selects resources for this activity and new play cycle begins.

Example of responding to play cues.

KEY TASK

Describe how you have observed and responded to a child/young person's play cues.

NVQ links – Level 2: PW2.3; Level 3: PW9.3

Defining a play frame

A play frame is 'a material or non-material boundary that keeps the play intact' (SkillsActive, 2004b). For example, a material boundary could be an actual physical boundary such as a specific play area (e.g. a play shop); a non-material boundary may be something imaginary such as a 'magic circle'. You must be able to support children's and young people's play frames as necessary (for example, maintaining a play frame by adopting an appropriate role during children's play such as a customer during shop play).

KEY TASK

Give two examples of how you have supported children's and/or young people's play frames.

NVQ links – Level 3: PW9.3

Behavioural modes associated with play

You need to know and understand the behavioural modes associated with play. For example:

- ✭ **personally directed** (e.g. child initiated)
- ✭ **intrinsically motivated** (e.g. play for play itself)
- ✭ **in secure context** (e.g. freedom to explore feelings or imagination in safe environment)
- ✭ **spontaneous** (e.g. unplanned play opportunities)
- ✭ **goalless** (e.g. play as a process not an end product)
- ✭ **controlled by children and young people** (e.g. choosing own activities, open-ended play opportunities).

Recognising the mood descriptors associated with play

You should also be able to recognise the following mood descriptors associated with play.

- ✪ **Active:** enthusiastic, full participation in play.
- ✪ **Altruistic:** playing with consideration for others.
- ✪ **At ease:** relaxed and comfortable during play.
- ✪ **Balanced:** in harmony with others and/or the play activity.
- ✪ **Confident:** positive and bold approach to play.
- ✪ **Happy:** displaying enjoyment and delight during play.
- ✪ **Immersed:** involved deeply, totally absorbed in play.
- ✪ **Independent:** playing without influence of others.
- ✪ **Trusting:** confidence in others involved in play.

Providing for a range of play types

You should know and understand how to provide opportunities for a wide range of play types, including the following:

- ✪ **Communication play** – play using words, nuances or gestures (e.g. telling jokes, play acting, singing, storytelling).
- ✪ **Creative play** – play allowing new responses, transformation of information, awareness of connections, with an element of surprise (e.g. enjoying creative activities, arts and crafts, using a variety of materials and tools).
- ✪ **Deep play** – play allowing the child to encounter risky experiences, to develop survival skills and conquer fears (e.g. balancing on a high beam, performing skateboarding stunts).
- ✪ **Dramatic play** – play dramatising events in which the child is not a direct participator (e.g. presenting a TV show, religious or festive celebrations).
- ✪ **Exploratory play** – play involving manipulating objects or materials to discover their properties and possibilities (e.g. playing with bricks, sand, water, clay, play dough).
- ✪ **Fantasy play** – play rearranging the world in the child's way, in a manner unlikely to occur in real life (e.g. playing at being an astronaut or king/queen).
- ✪ **Imaginative play** – play where conventional rules of the real world are not applicable (e.g. pretending to be a dog or a superhero).
- ✪ **Locomotor play** – play involving movement in all directions for its own sake (e.g. playing chase, tag, hide and seek).
- ✪ **Mastery play** – play involving control of physical aspects of the environment (e.g. digging holes, building dens).

- ✴ **Object play** – play involving hand–eye co-ordination to manipulate objects in an infinite variety of ways (e.g. examining novel uses for a paintbrush, brick).
- ✴ **Role play** – play exploring human activities on basic level (e.g. doing simple domestic chores such as sweeping with a broom, making telephone calls, driving a car, with or without play equipment).
- ✴ **Rough and tumble play** – play involving discovering physical flexibility and demonstrating physical skills (e.g. play fighting, chasing).
- ✴ **Social play** – play involving social interaction that requires following certain rules or protocols (e.g. games with rules, conversations).
- ✴ **Socio-dramatic play** – play involving enacting real-life experiences of an intense personal or interpersonal nature (e.g. playing house, shops, hospital, dentist).
- ✴ **Symbolic play** – play allowing controlled, gradual exploration and increased understanding, without risk (e.g. using piece of wood to symbolise a person).

(National Playing Fields Association,
Children's Play Council and Playlink, 2000: 33–4)

KEY TASK

List examples of each play type based on your experiences of providing play opportunities for children and/or young people.

NVQ links – Level 2: PW2.1, PW2.2; Level 3: PW9.1

These play types can be grouped into three main areas of play, as follows.

1. **Physical play:** play activities that provide opportunities for children and young people to develop their physical skills. For example, locomotor play, mastery play, rough and tumble play.
2. **Exploratory play:** play activities that provide opportunities for children and young people to understand the world around them by exploring their environment and experimenting with materials. For example, exploratory play, creative play, object play.
3. **Imaginative play:** play activities that provide opportunities for children and young people to express feelings and to develop social skills. For example, communication play, deep play, dramatic play, fantasy play, imaginative play, role play, social play (see the section in Chapter 3 on the sequence of children's social play), symbolic play.

Physical play

Children and young people should have plenty of opportunities for physical play (such as play apparatus, outdoor play, ball games and swimming). By using their whole bodies children learn to control and manage them. The more practice children get to develop gross motor skills, the more agile, co-ordinated and safe they will be, as they get older. Using lots of energy in physical play is fun and relaxing too. Children also need opportunities to develop their fine motor skills and hand–eye co-ordination (for example, playing with stacking toys and jigsaws).

Physical play enables children and young people to:

✯ develop body awareness and awareness of spatial relationships

✯ understand positional relationships (e.g. in and out, over and under)

✯ develop gross motor skills

✯ develop fine motor skills

✯ improve hand–eye co-ordination and visual perception.

Activities to encourage children's physical play

1. **Outdoor play opportunities** should be provided for children every day, such as playing in the outdoor play area, going for walks, going to the park or visiting an adventure playground. As well as the benefits of fresh air, outdoor play offers children more space to develop gross motor skills such as running, hopping, jumping, skipping, throwing and catching a ball, playing football, and doing somersaults and cartwheels.

2. **Play apparatus** can be used indoors or outdoors depending on the size of the equipment and the space available. Larger play equipment that cannot be easily (or safely) accommodated inside the setting can be used in outdoor play (e.g. climbing apparatus). When using play equipment, whether in the play setting or at a playground, you must ensure that it is safe for use as well as appropriate for the children's ages and sizes. Always check play apparatus *before* use (see Chapter 5).

3. **Jigsaw puzzles** help children with shape recognition as well as developing fine motor skills and hand–eye co-ordination. Children can tackle standard jigsaws with a few large pieces, increasing the number of pieces as they grow and improve their physical skills.

4. **Ball games** provide children with opportunities to develop ball skills such as throwing, kicking and catching. Younger children need large, lightweight balls to practise their throwing and catching skills. As they get older, smaller balls, beanbags and quoits can be used to develop their skills of throwing with more accuracy. Older children and young people can be encouraged to participate in team sports such as five-a-side football or basketball.

5. **Swimming** is an excellent all-round physical activity. Children are usually ready to learn to swim by the age of 4 or 5. If the setting does not have its own swimming pool, it may be possible to arrange regular outings to a local pool. If not, try to encourage the children and young people in your setting to use their local pool with their families or friends, depending on their ages/swimming abilities.

Children using outdoor play equipment.

Exploratory play

Exploratory play encourages and extends children's and young people's discovery skills. Play is an important way to motivate children and to assist thinking and learning in a wide variety of settings. Children learn from play situations that give them 'hands on' experience. Exploratory play encourages them to use their senses to discover the properties of different materials in pleasurable and meaningful ways. For example, playing with sand encourages them to consider the textures and functions of sand – getting the right consistency of sand to build sand castles – for instance, too wet or too dry and the sand will not stick together.

Activities to encourage children's exploratory play

1. **Painting** with brushes, sponges, string; finger painting, bubble painting, 'butterfly' or 'blob' painting, marble painting, wax resist painting; printing (e.g. with leaves, potatoes, cotton reels) and pattern-making (e.g. with rollers, stamps).

2. **Drawing** using pencils, crayons, felt tips or chalks on a variety of materials including different kinds paper, card, fabric and wood. Include colouring activities linked to the children's interests by drawing your own colouring sheets, buying ready-made colouring books or using free printable colouring pages from the Internet.

3. **Model making** using commercial construction kits (e.g. LEGO Explore®, Mega Bloks®, Stickle Bricks), wooden blocks or clean and safe 'junk' materials to enable children to create their own designs.

4. **Collage** using glue and interesting materials to create pictures with different textures, colours and shapes. Provides an enjoyable sensory experience too.

5. **Clay, play dough and plasticine** can be used creatively; they are tactile too.

6. **Cooking** provides a similar experience to working with play dough or clay except that the end product is (usually) edible. Remember to include 'no cook' activities such as icing biscuits, or making sandwiches or peppermint creams.

7. **Making music** can provide opportunities for children to explore different sounds and to experiment freely with musical instruments. Provide a portable box/trolley with a range of percussion instruments, including drum, tambourine, castanets, wood blocks, shakers, bell stick, Indian bells, triangle, xylophone and chime bars.

8. **Water play** with plain, bubbly, coloured, warm or cold water helps children learn about the properties of water (e.g. it pours, splashes, runs, soaks). Provide small containers to fill and empty, as well as a sieve and funnel.

9. **Sand play** provides opportunities for exploring the properties of sand (e.g. wet sand sticks together and can be moulded, while dry sand does not stick and can be poured). Use 'washed' or 'silver' sand (not builder's sand, which might contain cement). Provide small containers and buckets to fill and empty, as well as sieves and funnels.

Exploratory play enables children to:

* ✭ understand concepts such as shape and colour
* ✭ explore the properties of materials (e.g. textures)
* ✭ understand volume/capacity and physical forces through sand and water play
* ✭ develop problem-solving skills
* ✭ devise and use own creative ideas.

EXERCISE: Give examples of exploratory play activities from your own experiences of working with children and/or young people.

Imaginative play

Imaginative play provides opportunities for children and young people to release emotional tension and frustration or express feelings such as anger or jealousy in positive ways. Imaginative play also encourages children to look at and feel things from another person's viewpoint as well as developing communication skills to interact more effectively with others. Imaginative play activities such as role play and dressing-up enable children to overcome fears and worries about new experiences or people, to feel more important and powerful, and to feel more secure by being able to temporarily regress to earlier levels of development.

Activities to encourage children's imaginative play

1. **Role play** includes *domestic play* (e.g. playing/imitating 'mum' or 'dad', or pretending to be a baby while other children act as parents, later play imitates other role models such as carers, playworkers, teachers, characters from TV, books); *shop play* (e.g. post office, hairdressers, café, where other roles can be explored). Pretending to visit the dentist, clinic, optician or hospital, or setting up a home corner, a health centre or hospital can also provide for this type of play. Also include *drama* activities.

2. **Dressing-up activities**: pretending to be parents, carers, playworkers, teachers, film/TV superheroes, characters from computer games or consoles, kings and queens, allows children to experiment with being powerful and in control. Pretending to be someone else can also help children to understand what it is like to be that person, and encourages empathy and consideration for others.

3. **Dolls and puppets** can help children deal with their feelings (e.g. jealousy over a new baby can be expressed by shouting at a teddy or doll). Puppets are also a useful way of providing children with a 'voice' and may encourage shy or withdrawn children to express themselves.

4. **Miniature worlds** include small-scale toys such as dolls' houses, toy farms and toy zoos, as well as vehicle play where children can act out previous experiences or situations while sharing ideas and equipment with other children; this can also help them establish friendships.

Imaginative play enables children to:

- ☆ develop language and communication skills
- ☆ practise and rehearse real-life situations
- ☆ improve self-help skills such as getting dressed
- ☆ express feelings in positive ways
- ☆ share ideas and co-operate with other children.

> **EXERCISE:** List examples of imaginative play activities from your own experiences of working with children and/or young people.

 KEY TASK

1. Observe children and/or young people involved in a play activity.
2. Then comment on the following:
   - the play activity
   - the age/level of development of the children/young people
   - their play needs and preferences
   - the play type
   - the behavioural modes demonstrated by the children/young people
   - the mood descriptors associated with the children/young people's play.
3. Think about how you could provide future play opportunities to extend the children/young people's development within this type of play.

NVQ links – Level 2: PW2.1, PW2.2; Level 3: PW9.1

Encouraging and supporting acceptable risk-taking during play

You should encourage and support acceptable risk-taking during play activities as appropriate to children's and young people's ages/levels of development. Always follow the relevant setting policies and procedures (for example, health and safety policy, risk assessment and risk management procedures) (see Chapter 5).

Children and young people need opportunities to explore and experiment through play and to try out new, exciting play activities. Many play activities have risks – especially physical activities such as climbing, exploring and swimming: 'Risky activity, and risk taking itself, is recognised as an essential part of growing up' (Child Accident Prevention Trust, 2002a).

As children and young people play, they will make mistakes and accidents will happen. By exploring their environment and experimenting with their physical skills and intellectual abilities, children and young people develop confidence and competence in their own abilities. Play spaces and play opportunities should be sufficiently challenging and have different levels of difficulty to enable children and young people to fully explore these challenges. Without these challenges and opportunities to assess risks, children and young people will not develop the survival skills they will need later in life (Institute of Leisure and Amenity Management, 1999).

Seven ways to encourage and support acceptable risk-taking during play activities

1. Assess and manage the levels of risk in play areas, either through supervision or design.
2. Help individual children and young people to make a realistic assessment of their abilities to avoid them being under- or over-confident.
3. Take precautions to reduce the severity of injuries if children and young people make inaccurate judgements (e.g. provide appropriate safety surfaces in outdoor play areas to reduce the impact of falls).
4. Inform children and young people of the potential dangers of play activities so that they can make their own decisions.
5. Provide opportunities for children and young people to take calculated risks (e.g. challenging climbing frames, adventure playgrounds).
6. Provide appropriate safety information.
7. Consult and involve the children and young people in developing play activities that are challenging and interesting to them.

 KEY TASK

1. Outline your setting's policies and procedures that are relevant to risk-taking during play activities (e.g. health and safety policy, risk assessment and risk management procedures).
2. List examples of how you encourage and support acceptable risk-taking during play activities according to these policies and procedures *and* the ages/levels of development of the children and/or young people you work with.

NVQ links – Level 2: PW3.1, PW3.2; Level 3: PW7.1, PW7.2, PW9.4

Ending play sessions

You must be able to end each play session in a way that is appropriate to the ages/levels of development of the children and young people with whom you work, and the requirements of the play setting. For example, warn the children in advance that the play session is coming to an end so that they can finish off what they are doing. Young children especially dislike having their play activities stopped suddenly, so giving them a five- or ten-minute warning can help to avoid emotional outbursts.

Ensure that the play area is clean and tidy at the end of the play session. Encourage the children to tidy up and put away play resources as appropriate to their ages and levels of development. Remember to follow the setting's procedures for tidying up and putting away resources. Let children have a chance to review their play activities as individuals or in groups ('circle time' is an excellent way to finish a play session). Make a note of the children's views as these may form the basis for planning future play sessions.

Follow the setting's procedures for ensuring the safety of the children and young people when leaving the play setting (for instance, young children must be collected by a known adult) (see Chapter 5). When the children have gone complete any required records (see the section in Chapter 10 on record-keeping).

KEY TASK

Describe how you have ended a play session.

NVQ links – Level 2: PW2.4

Further reading

Ball, D. (2002) *Playgrounds: Risks, Benefits and Choices*. Health & Safety Executive.

Bilton, H. (2004) *Playing Outside: Activities, Ideas, and Inspiration for the Early Years*. David Fulton Publishers.

Brown, F. (ed.) (2002) *Playwork: Theory and Practice*. Open University Press.

Bruce, T. (2001) *Learning Through Play*. Hodder & Stoughton.

Children's Play Council (2002) *More than Swings and Roundabouts – Planning for Outdoor Play*. Children's Play Council.

Davy, A. (2001) *Playwork: Play and Care for Children 5–15* (3rd edn). Thomson Learning.

DCMS (Department for Culture, Media & Sport) (2004) *Getting Serious About Play: A Review of Children's Play*. UK Department for Culture, Media & Sport.

Einon, D. (1986) *Creative Play*. Penguin.

Gibson, R. (1998) *Usborne Playtime Activities*. Usborne Publishing Ltd.

Hughes, B. (2001) *Evolutionary Playwork and Reflective Analytic Practice*. Routledge.

Kidsactive (2000) *Side by Side: Guidelines for Inclusive Play*. Kidsactive.

Lindon, J. (1999) *Too Safe for their Own Good? Helping Children Learn About Risk and Lifeskills*. National Early Years Network.

Masheder, M. (1989b) *Let's Play Together*. Green Print.

Morris, J. and Mort, J. (1991) *Bright Ideas for the Early Years: Learning Through Play*. Scholastic.

Moyles, J. (ed.) (1994) *The Excellence of Play*. Open University Press.

National Playing Fields Association (1996) *Children's Play Areas: Design Guide*. HMSO.

National Playing Fields Association (1997) *Play Safety: Guidelines for Outdoor Play Provision*. NPFA.

National Playing Fields Association, Children's Play Council and Playlink (2000) *Best Play: What Play Provision Should Do for Children*. NPFA.

Play Safety Forum (2002) *Managing Risk in Play Provision: A Position Statement*. National Children's Bureau.

Play Wales and PlayEducation (2001) *The First Claim: A Framework for Playwork Quality Assessment*. Play Wales.

Titman, W. (1994) *Special Places, Special People: The Hidden Curriculum of School Grounds*. WWF UK/Learning Through Landscapes

5 Health and safety in the play setting

Key points

- ✪ Statutory and regulatory health and safety requirements
- ✪ Safety checks of the indoor and outdoor environment
- ✪ Recognising the signs and symptoms of common childhood illnesses
- ✪ Regulations and procedures for storing and administering medicines
- ✪ Responding to accidents and injuries (including first aid)
- ✪ Emergency procedures in the play setting
- ✪ Risk assessment applicable to the play setting
- ✪ Maintaining children's safety during play
- ✪ Supervising children on outings
- ✪ Escorting children to and from the play setting

Statutory and regulatory health and safety requirements

As a playworker you need to be aware of the statutory and regulatory health and safety requirements for children, workers, families and visitors in the play setting. Health and safety legislation places overall responsibility for health and safety with the employer. However, as an employee working within a play setting you also have responsibilities with regard to maintaining health and safety:

Employees have responsibilities too. The Health and Safety at Work Act 1974 and the Management of Health and Safety at Work Regulations 1999 apply to them as well.

Employees must:

- ☆ take reasonable care of their own and others' health and safety
- ☆ co-operate with their employers
- ☆ carry out activities in accordance with training and instructions
- ☆ inform the employer of any serious risks.

(DfES, 2002)

The **Workplace (Health, Safety and Welfare) Regulations 1992** clarify and consolidate existing legislation. They also establish a consistent set of standards for the majority of workplaces. The regulations expand on the responsibilities placed on employers (and others in control of premises) by the **Health and Safety at Work Act 1974**. They cover, among other things:

★ health and safety in the workplace
★ welfare facilities for people at work
★ maintenance of the workplace.

The workplace and equipment need to be maintained in an efficient state, in working order and in good repair. Buildings, including mobile or temporary rooms, should be in a good state of repair and services should be in efficient working order. The regulations also cover the minimum standards for maintaining an appropriate physical working environment – for example, ventilation, temperature, humidity, lighting, cleaning, room dimensions and space. Windows, skylights and ventilators provided for the purpose of ventilation should be capable of opening, closing or adjustment without risk to health and safety. In general, indoor workplaces should be reasonably comfortable, reasonably clean, properly illuminated and adequately spacious.

The environmental requirements of the regulations apply to the workplace, but existing education standards for pupils' working space, temperature and ventilation, and so on, in schools may be more appropriate for some play settings (for example, breakfast and after-school clubs).

The **Education (School Premises) Regulations 1999** provide the statutory requirements for the minimum standards of both new and existing schools. They include a general requirement that all parts of the school's premises must be reasonably maintained to ensure the health, safety and welfare of all users. These regulations also include the specific requirements for: acoustics, ancillary facilities, drainage, heating, lighting, medical accommodation, playing fields, washrooms, staff accommodation, structural matters, ventilation, water supply and weather protection.

The **Day Care and Childminding (National Standards) (England) Regulations 2003** may apply to your setting. Standards 4, 5, 6 and 7 refer to health and safety (see the information on the Daycare Standards in Chapter 10).

All play settings must have a health and safety policy with clear procedures to implement it. As a playworker you will need to follow the legal and organisational requirements of the play setting for maintaining the health, safety and security of yourself and others at all times. You must know and understand the setting's health and safety policy, including who is responsible for health and safety as well as the procedures for reporting any concerns or problems to the appropriate person.

The **Management of Health and Safety at Work Regulations 1999** require a risk assessment of facilities, a safety policy regarding these risks, and appropriate health and safety training. You should be able to recognise any risks within the play environment and take the appropriate action to minimise them (for instance, reporting potential health and safety hazards to the relevant person). (See the section on risk assessment below.)

You will also need to use safe working practices in all that you do, which includes ensuring that someone in authority (e.g. a senior playworker and/or your line manager) knows where you are at all times in case of an emergency.

You should also know the local and national requirements regarding health, hygiene, safety and supervision in the play setting, including: access to premises; storerooms and storage areas; the health and safety requirements for the materials and equipment being used. You must follow the setting's procedures for gaining access to the premises (entry systems, visitors' book, identity tags for visitors in the play setting, and so on).

 KEY TASK

1. Find out about the statutory and regulatory requirements that apply to your play setting.
2. Find out about your setting's policy and procedures relating to health and safety.
3. Outline your role and responsibilities with regard to maintaining health and safety in the play setting.

NVQ links – Level 2: PW3.1; Level 3: PW7.1

Safety checks of the indoor and outdoor environment

You need to know the location of safety equipment in different play environments. You must be clear about the safety arrangements for the areas and children/young people you work with, including: the position of fire exits, extinguishers and blankets; first aid boxes; your role during fire drill; what to do in case of fire or other emergency, especially the procedures for children/young people with physical or sensory disabilities; escape routes and alternatives if blocked by fire, and so on.

Facilities and equipment

Storage areas should be kept tidy, with sufficient space for the materials or equipment being stored there. They should be easily accessible and lockable; any potentially hazardous materials must be stored away from children and locked away. Storage space should be organised so that heavy equipment is stored at a low level. Lightweight equipment may be stored above head level if space is limited.

One of your responsibilities may be to ensure that all equipment and surfaces are safe, hygienic and usable. If working with children who have been using messy materials such as glue or paint, you will need to wipe tables or easels clean after they have finished and clean any brushes so that they are ready for use next time. Any major cleaning tasks that are not part of your duties should be referred to the senior playworker or setting manager for attention.

All equipment in the setting should be safe and approved for safety (e.g. BSI Kitemark, European standards markings, BEAB mark of safety). You should know the operating procedures and safety requirements of the setting *before* using any equipment, and should follow any instructions carefully. Allow yourself plenty of time to do this thoroughly. Operating instructions should be available and, in many cases, an experienced/knowledgeable playworker may show you how to use the equipment beforehand. If not, it is essential to ask, especially when dealing with electrical equipment – for safety reasons and the possibility of damaging expensive equipment. You do not want to cause hundreds or even thousands of pounds' worth of damage to a computer or photocopier!

You should check equipment that you use regularly to ensure that it is safe and in proper working order. For example, check the television, video or computer is in working order before you or the children need it so that you can sort out any problems in advance. If there is a fault and the equipment is not functioning properly or not at all you need to know the appropriate procedures for dealing with faults – for example, which can be dealt with yourself and which require reporting to the appropriate person. It is also important to check equipment and materials regularly for damage and to report any to the appropriate person (such as the senior playworker or setting manager). Serious damage will have to be repaired by a professional (e.g. a technician or the setting caretaker) or the item replaced.

Toy safety

Every year in the UK over 35,000 children under the age of 15 are treated in hospital following an accident involving a toy (Child Accident Prevention Trust, 2002a). It is essential to provide children with toys that are appropriate for their age and level of development. Most toys will have a suggested age range. It is a legal requirement for all toys sold in the European Union to carry a CE mark but this does not necessarily guarantee safety or quality. When selecting toys for children always look for one of these safety marks:

* ☆ European Standard BS EN 71, to show that the toy has been tested to the agreed safety standards
* ☆ the Lion Mark, to show that the toy has been made to the highest standards of safety and quality.

Outdoor play areas and playgrounds

There is a duty under Sections 3 and 4 of the Health and Safety at Work Act 1974 to ensure the health and safety of users of playground equipment as far as is reasonably practicable (RoSPA, 2004a). Evidence of good practice in ensuring the health and safety of users includes compliance with the relevant safety standards – for example, EN 1176 for children's playground equipment and EN 1177 for playground surfaces. Safety checks for the outdoor play area and/or playground include:

- ☆ inspecting the play area and playground equipment on a regular basis
- ☆ reporting any faults to the appropriate person promptly
- ☆ ensuring that children do not use the faulty equipment until mended or replaced
- ☆ getting the necessary repairs done as quickly as possible
- ☆ having an annual inspection by an independent specialist.

EXERCISE:
1. List the main play equipment used in your setting.
2. How did/could you find out how to use each piece of play equipment?
3. What are the setting's safety arrangements regarding the use of indoor and outdoor play equipment?
4. What are the setting's procedures for reporting faulty or broken play equipment?

Toilet and wash areas

It is important that toilet and wash facilities are maintained in a clean and orderly condition, with adequate lighting and ventilation. In play settings, there will usually be separate provision for children and staff. There should be an adequate supply of drinking water that is easily accessible.

Play settings should ensure that toilet facilities are maintained to high standards of hygiene. There should be adequate supplies of toilet paper, soap, warm water and disposable paper towels and/or access to hot-air driers. The cleaning routines for toilets and washbasins should be regular and thorough to maintain high standards of hygiene. To minimise the spread of infection, the setting should advise parents whose children have diarrhoea that the children should stay away from the setting until they no longer have symptoms.

Your role might involve checking children's toilet areas to see that they are used correctly and that children wash their hands after using the toilet or before handling food. You may be required to assist very young children (or children with physical disabilities) with their toileting needs. You should know the setting's procedures for dealing with children who wet or soil themselves, including the location of appropriate spare clothing.

You may need to provide reassurance and support for a girl who starts menstruation but does not have any sanitary protection (girls as young as 8 or 9 could start their first period while at the setting). You should know the setting's procedures for dealing with this situation, including accessing emergency supplies of sanitary protection and its disposal. If you are a male playworker then you must know who to go to for help if this situation occurs.

If you experience any concerns or problems with children/young people when carrying out hygiene routines, you should report these to the senior playworker or your line manager. This includes reporting any hazard or unsafe situation you discover when using the setting's toilet or wash facilities.

KEY TASK

1. Find out about the legal and organisational requirements for the toilet and wash areas in your play setting.
2. What is your role and what are your responsibilities for checking these areas?

NVQ links – Level 2: PW4.2

The movement and activity of children

Play settings cater for the access, egress and movement of children, families, workers and visitors, either as pedestrians or in vehicles, including delivery vans and taxis for children with special needs. Traffic routes should be properly organised so that both pedestrians and vehicles can move safely in and around the setting. Particular care should be taken of everyone using or having access to the premises, especially young children and people with disabilities.

The setting may have to cope with the large-scale movement of children and workers during busy periods – for example, at the start and end of sessions. Care should be taken to avoid accidents such as slips, trips or falls, particularly in main corridors and staircases. Floor surfaces should be appropriate for their use and free from hazards or obstructions that might cause people to trip or fall. Particular attention should be paid to:

- ☆ holes, bumps and uneven surfaces
- ☆ wear and tear on carpeted areas
- ☆ procedures for dealing with spillages
- ☆ snow and ice on external pathways
- ☆ precautionary measures prior to repairs (e.g. barriers, alternative routes).

Recognising the signs and symptoms of common childhood illnesses

You need to be aware of the range of common illnesses that may affect children and young people. These include allergies, asthma, bronchitis, chicken pox, colds, diabetes, diarrhoea, earache, flu, glandular fever, headache, measles, meningitis, mumps, sore throat and worms.

Responding to signs of illness

You should know what to do if children come to the play setting when they are unwell – for example, when they have a cold. Children do not need to be kept away from the setting because of a cold unless their symptoms are very bad. Make sure that a box of tissues is available for children to use and that used tissues are disposed of properly to avoid the spread of germs. You also need to know what to do if a child or young person becomes ill while at the play setting.

Give verbal reassurance to children who are feeling unwell or just miserable. Younger children may seek physical comfort such as a cuddle or sitting on your lap. This is fine in a busy room but may be misinterpreted in a quiet corner (see Chapter 6).

You need to be able to recognise the differences between children who are pretending to be ill, feeling 'under the weather', and experiencing a health problem. By knowing the usual behaviour and appearance of the children you work with, you will be able to recognise any significant changes that might indicate possible illness.

The signs of possible illness in children and young people include:

- ☆ changes in facial colour (e.g. becoming pale or very red)
- ☆ changes in temperature (e.g. becoming very hot or cold, becoming clammy or shivering – a fever usually indicates that the child has an infection)
- ☆ changes in behaviour (e.g. not wanting to play when would usually be very keen)
- ☆ being upset or generally distressed
- ☆ having reduced concentration levels or even falling asleep
- ☆ scratching excessively (check the setting's policy regarding head lice)
- ☆ complaining of persistent pain (e.g. headache or stomach ache)
- ☆ coughing or sneezing excessively
- ☆ diarrhoea and/or vomiting
- ☆ displaying a rash – this could indicate an infection or allergic reaction; make sure you are aware of any children who may have severe allergic reactions (see the section on children and young people with special medical needs).

(Watkinson, 2003)

Ensure that you know what to do when children are sick – for example, where or to whom to send them. You may need to stay with a sick child while someone else summons assistance. You need to know who to report signs of illness to (see below).

When responding to the signs of illness you should:

- ☆ summon assistance for any health emergency as appropriate to your role and responsibilities (see below)
- ☆ report any concerns about health problems to the senior playworker
- ☆ follow the setting's policies and procedures relating to illness
- ☆ give advice as appropriate to the child's age, level of development and the illness
- ☆ inform the child's parent/carer if this is part of your role.

If you have any concerns regarding the health of the children you should always inform the senior playworker. You need to be able to recognise any changes in a child's behaviour or appearance that may indicate a possible health problem and report these appropriately.

Whatever the illness, you should know where and when to seek assistance. You should also know what types of written record are required and to whom you should report any concerns regarding a child's health. Check whether you are allowed to contact parents/carers directly regarding a sick child or whether this is the responsibility of someone else (e.g. the senior playworker).

KEY TASK

1. Find out about your setting's policy and procedures for responding to children's illnesses or allergies.
2. Outline your role and responsibilities for responding to children's illnesses or allergies.

NVQ links – Level 2: C35.1; Level 3: PW7.3

Regulations and procedures for storing and administering medicines

Play settings should ensure that their health and safety procedures cover the needs of *all* children and young people who use them. The setting may have some children with medical needs. Some of these will be short term (for example, a child finishing a course of antibiotics or recovering from an accident/surgery). Some children may have long-term medical needs due to a particular condition. The medical conditions in children that usually cause concern in play settings are asthma, diabetes, epilepsy and severe allergic reaction (anaphylaxis). The setting will need additional procedures to maintain the health and safety of children with medical needs; this may include an individual healthcare plan (see below). The setting has a responsibility to ensure that all relevant workers are aware of children with medical needs and are trained to provide additional support if necessary.

The manager of the play setting and other playworkers must treat medical information in a sensitive and *confidential* manner. The manager should agree with the child (if appropriate) and their parent/carer, which workers should have access to records and other information about the child's medical needs in order to provide a good support system. However, where medical information is not given to workers they should not usually be held responsible if they provide incorrect medical assistance in an emergency but otherwise acted in good faith.

Parents are responsible for their own children's medication. Children under the age of 16 should not be given medication without parental written consent. The play setting's manager usually decides whether the setting can assist a child who needs medication during a session. The setting will have a form for the parent to sign if their child requires medication while at the setting.

Most children with long-term medical conditions will not require medication while at the setting. If they do, children can usually administer it themselves depending on their age/ability, medical condition and type of medication. The setting's policy should encourage self-administration where appropriate and provide suitable facilities for children to do so in safety and privacy.

Playworkers have no legal duty to administer medication or to supervise a child taking it. This is a voluntary role similar to that of being a first aider. The setting's manager, parents/carers and relevant health professionals should support playworkers who volunteer to administer medication by providing information, training and reassurance about their legal liability. Arrangements should be made for when the playworker responsible for providing assistance is absent or unavailable.

Playworkers providing support for children with medical needs must know and understand:

- ★ the nature of the child's medical condition
- ★ when and where the child may need additional support
- ★ the likelihood of an emergency arising (especially if it is potentially life threatening)
- ★ what action to take if an emergency occurs.

The health and safety of children and workers must be considered at all times. Safety procedures must be in place regarding the safe storage, handling and disposal of medicines. Some medication (e.g. reliever inhaler for asthma or adrenalin device for severe anaphylaxis) must be quickly available in an emergency and should not be locked away. Relevant workers and the children concerned must know where this medication is stored.

Children and young people with special medical needs

Some children and young people with long-term medical needs may require a healthcare plan to provide the setting's staff with the necessary information to support them and to ensure their safety. A written healthcare plan should be drawn up in consultation with the child or young person (if appropriate), their parents and the relevant health professionals.

The healthcare plan should include:

- ★ details of the child's or young person's medical condition
- ★ any special requirements (e.g. dietary needs, such as avoiding nuts)
- ★ medication and its possible side-effects
- ★ what to do and who to contact in an emergency
- ★ how staff can support the child/young person in the play setting.

Responding to accidents and injuries (including first aid)

When responding to accidents or injuries that occur within the play setting, you should remain calm and follow the relevant procedures. You must immediately call for qualified assistance (e.g. the designated first aider or the emergency services) and take appropriate action in line with your role and responsibilities within the play setting. If you are a designated first aider then you can administer first aid; if not, you can comfort the injured person by your physical presence and talking to them until the arrival of a designated first aider, doctor, paramedic or ambulance staff. You will then help to establish and maintain the privacy and safety of the area where the accident or injury occurred, and provide support for any other people involved. When qualified assistance arrives you should give clear and accurate information about what happened. Afterwards, you will need to follow the setting's procedures for recording accidents and injuries. This will normally involve recording the incident in a special book. Serious accidents are usually recorded on an official form. Accuracy in recording accidents and injuries is essential because the information may be needed for further action by senior staff or other professionals. Certain types of accident must be reported to an official authority under the **Reporting of Injuries**, **Diseases and Dangerous Occurrences Regulations 1985** – for example, commercial and voluntary sector play settings must report to the local Environmental Health Office; local authority and school settings must report to the Health & Safety Executive.

First aid arrangements

You must know and understand the first aid arrangements that apply in your setting, including the location of first aid equipment/facilities and the designated first aider(s).

First aid notices should be displayed clearly in all rooms; make sure you read them. First aid information is usually included in induction programmes to ensure that new staff and children know about a setting's first aid arrangements. Detailed information on a setting's first aid policy and procedures will also be in the staff handbook.

All playworkers must do their best to maintain the safety and welfare of children and young people using the play setting's facilities; their actions should be as those of a responsible parent, especially in emergencies. Playworkers have no legal obligation to give first aid, but any member of staff can volunteer to take on first aid responsibilities. If so, the employer must arrange appropriate training and guidance for them. A designated first aider must complete a training course approved by the Health & Safety Executive.

Accident/Incident Report Form

Date: Time:

Location of accident/incident:

Address:

Person reporting the accident/incident:

Address:

Details of the accident/incident: (Continue on reverse and additional sheets if necessary)

Action taken: (Continue on reverse and additional sheets if necessary)

Witnesses or others informed of accident/incident: (Continue on reverse and additional sheets if necessary)

1. Name:

Address:

2. Name:

Address:

Any further action required: (Continue on reverse and additional sheets if necessary)

Signed: Date of report:

Number of additional sheets:

Accident/incident report form.

The aims of first aid

1. To preserve life by:
   * providing emergency resuscitation
   * controlling bleeding
   * treating burns
   * treating shock.
2. To prevent the worsening of any injuries by:
   * covering wounds
   * immobilising fractures
   * placing the casualty in the correct and comfortable position.
3. To promote recovery by:
   * providing reassurance
   * giving any other treatment needed
   * relieving pain
   * handling gently
   * moving as little as possible
   * protecting from the cold.

The priorities of first aid

* **A** is for Airway: establish an open airway by tilting back the forehead so that the child can breathe easily.
* **B** is for Breathing: check that the child is breathing by listening, looking and feeling for breath.
* **C** is for Circulation: apply simple visual checks that the child's blood is circulating adequately, by watching for improved colour, coughing or eye movement.

First aid equipment

First aid equipment must be clearly labelled and easily accessible. All first aid containers must be marked with a white cross on a green background. There should be at least one fully stocked first aid container for each building within the setting, with extra first aid containers available on split-sites/levels, distant playing fields/playgrounds, any high-risk areas (e.g. kitchens), and for outings. Here are some suggestions for the contents of a first aid kit:

* a first aid manual or leaflet
* assorted bandages, including a wrapped triangular bandage, a one-inch and a two-inch strip for holding dressings and compresses in place
* medium and large individually wrapped sterile unmedicated wound dressings
* two sterile eye pads
* safety pins
* adhesive tape

- ⭐ sterile gauze
- ⭐ a pair of sharp scissors
- ⭐ tweezers
- ⭐ child thermometer
- ⭐ disposable gloves.

All playworkers must follow basic hygiene procedures and take the usual precautions for avoiding infection. Staff should use protective disposable gloves and be careful when dealing with spillages of blood or other body fluids, including the disposal of dressings, and so on.

◎ KEY TASK

1. Find out about your setting's policy and procedures for dealing with accidents and injuries, including the provision of first aid.
2. Describe your role and responsibilities in the event of an accident or injury in the setting.

NVQ links – Level 2: PW3.2, C35.1; Level 3: PW7.3

Emergency procedures in the play setting

You need to know about the fire alarms and emergency procedures for your setting. The fire alarm signals the need to evacuate the building. You should give calm, clear and correct instructions to the people involved in the emergency as appropriate to your role in implementing emergency procedures within the setting. You will need to make sure that any children/young people for whom you are responsible leave the building in the appropriate manner (e.g. walking, no running or talking). This will help to maintain calm and minimise panic as the children focus on following the appropriate evacuation procedures. All rooms must have evacuation instructions, including exit routes, prominently displayed. You also need to know what to do if there is a bomb scare or an intruder in the setting. Evacuation procedures would usually be the same as for a fire. You should report any problems with emergency procedures to the relevant colleague (e.g. senior playworker or setting manager).

If you work with children with special needs, you must know how to assist them in the event of an emergency – for example, a child with physical disabilities may need to leave the building via a special route or require access to a lift. You should check with the senior playworker or setting manager about the exact procedures to follow.

Visitors to the setting should normally be asked to sign in (and out) so that the people responsible for health and safety know who is in the building (and where) in case of emergencies.

You should know where the fire alarm points and fire exits are, the location of fire extinguishers and fire blankets and their use. There may be different types of extinguisher for use with different hazardous substances (for instance, in kitchens water must not be used to put out oil or electrical fires as this can make the situation worse). Carbon dioxide extinguishers will be located in the necessary places.

Missing children

A register of children attending the setting should be taken at the start of each session. It should also be taken for children participating in outings away from the setting and a duplicate left with the setting's manager. Children should be made aware (or reminded), at each session, of the boundaries of the setting. Children should be supervised at all times. However, despite these safeguards they may still go missing from the setting.

You need to be aware of the setting's procedures for dealing with missing children. These procedures may include:

☆ contacting the senior playworker or setting manager immediately

☆ calling the register to check which child is missing

☆ searching rooms, play areas and grounds to ensure the child has not hidden or been locked in anywhere within the setting

☆ the setting manager contacting the police and the parents/carers.

If a child is found to be missing while on an outing the playworker should:

☆ contact the setting manager immediately

☆ check the register again

☆ keep the rest of the group together while searching the area

☆ contact the setting manager again (who will contact the police and the child's parents/carers).

If a child or young person insists on leaving the setting and cannot be persuaded by playworkers to stay, then their parents/carers must be contacted immediately. If the setting manager decides the child is unsafe then the police may also be called.

KEY TASK

1. Find out about your setting's fire and evacuation procedures.
2. Briefly outline the setting's procedures in the event of a fire or other emergency evacuation, including your specific role.
3. Briefly outline your setting's procedures for dealing with missing children.

NVQ links – Level 2: C35.2; Level 3: PW7.3

Risk assessment applicable to the play setting

You must know and understand the importance of children and young people being given opportunities to play within an environment that will not harm their health and safety. However, they still need to be provided with play activities that have levels of challenge and risk that will help them to develop confidence and independence. (See the section in Chapter 4 on encouraging and supporting acceptable risk-taking.)

1. The purpose of risk assessment is to:
   ★ undertake a systematic review of the potential for harm
   ★ evaluate the likelihood of harm occurring
   ★ decide whether the existing control measures are adequate
   ★ decide whether more needs to be done.

2. The sequence for risk assessment is:
   ★ classify the activity
   ★ identify potential hazard(s)
   ★ evaluate possible risks
   ★ evaluate control measures
   ★ specify any further action.

3. Once the risk assessment has been carried out the hierarchy for control measures is:
   ★ eliminate hazard
   ★ reduce hazard
   ★ isolate hazard
   ★ control hazard.

4. Once the risk assessment and control measures have been completed no further action need be taken unless there is a significant change in the play area.

(RoSPA, 2004c)

You should know and understand how to assess and minimise the risks associated with possible hazards in the play setting. For example:

★ unsafe buildings, fixtures and fittings
★ unsafe equipment, including play resources
★ hazardous substances (e.g. cleaning materials)
★ hygiene hazards in toilet or kitchen areas
★ security hazards (e.g. inadequate boundaries, unauthorised visitors).

You should also know the procedures for risk assessment and dealing with hazards in your setting. For example:

⭐ the responsibilities for carrying out risk assessments in the setting

⭐ which hazards you can deal with yourself

⭐ which hazards must be reported to someone else

⭐ what to do if you are not sure about a hazard (e.g. assessing the risks, who to approach for help)

⭐ appropriate levels of supervision required during play to minimise potential hazards

⭐ assessing and dealing with unacceptable risks.

KEY TASK

1. Outline the procedures for risk assessment and dealing with hazards in your play setting.

2. List your responsibilities for dealing with the following types of possible hazard that can occur in the play setting:
   - unsafe buildings, fixtures and fittings
   - unsafe equipment, including play resources
   - hazardous substances (e.g. cleaning materials)
   - hygiene hazards in toilet or kitchen areas
   - security hazards (e.g. inadequate boundaries, unauthorised visitors).

NVQ links – Level 2: PW3.1; Level 3: PW7.1

Maintaining children's safety during play

You are responsible for maintaining children's and young people's safety while they are in the play setting. You must know and follow the setting's policies and procedures for maintaining safety during play. It is important to provide challenging and exciting play opportunities that encourage children and young people to develop and explore, while maintaining their physical safety and emotional welfare. (See the section in Chapter 4 on encouraging and supporting acceptable risk-taking.)

Accidents are common in children and young people because they are developing and learning rapidly and it can be difficult for adults to keep up with their changing developmental abilities. Accidents also occur because children and young people are naturally curious and want to explore their environment and, in doing so, may expose themselves to danger. The setting should provide play opportunities that encourage children's and young people's curiosity and exploration, while protecting them from unnecessary harm. They need to learn how to deal with risk so that they can keep themselves safe as they grow up. Bumps, bruises, minor cuts and scrapes are all part of play and learning but there is no need for children or young people to suffer serious injury. To avoid accidents the setting should provide adult care and supervision as well as ensuring safe play equipment design and appropriate modifications to the play environment (Child Accident Prevention Trust, 2004a).

The design, location and maintenance of play areas is important for maintaining children's safety during play. For example:

★ the layout must ensure that activities in one area do not interfere with other areas

★ play areas for younger children should be separated from those for older children

★ paths must be situated safely, away from equipment areas (especially swings)

★ clear sight lines in the play area make it easier to supervise children

★ secure fencing is required if there are roads, rivers or ponds close to the play area

★ safe access for children with disabilities should be considered

★ lighting must be adequate for safety and supervision

Twelve ways to maintain children's safety during play

You should maintain children's and young people's safety during play by:

1. knowing and following the relevant policies and procedures of the play setting
2. assessing the health, safety and security of the play setting before, during and after play opportunities and activities
3. identifying and assessing play and other behaviour that may cause harm to the health, safety and welfare of the children and young people involved
4. ensuring that the children and young people involved in play opportunities have the relevant information about health, safety and welfare
5. ensuring children, young people and adults in the play setting are following health, safety and security procedures
6. supporting and supervising children and young people as appropriate to their ages/levels of development and the level of risk involved in the play opportunity
7. maintaining an acceptable level of challenge and risk for the children and young people involved in accordance with the policies and procedures of the play setting
8. encouraging children and young people to help manage risk for themselves
9. encouraging children's and young people's awareness of their own and others' safety
10. encouraging the children and young people to take responsibility for their health, safety and welfare and that of others
11. ensuring your own play with children and young people does not endanger their health, safety and welfare
12. knowing and following the play setting's procedures for dealing with and reporting accidents or incidents that occur during play opportunities.

(SkillsActive, 2004b; SPRITO, 2002)

★ repair and replace old or worn play equipment

★ ensure all play equipment is suitable for the age of the children using it

★ use impact-absorbing surfaces such as rubber, bark chips and other such materials.

(Child Accident Prevention Trust, 2004b)

Making sure that children and young people are aware of safe behaviour when using play equipment can also help to maintain their safety and protect them from unnecessary accidents. Examples of safe behaviour include:

★ not walking in front of swings or other moving equipment

★ not pushing or shoving

★ being aware of younger children and those with disabilities

★ removing scarves or other items that could get caught in equipment

★ taking extra care when using high play equipment such as climbing frames.

(Child Accident Prevention Trust, 2004b)

KEY TASK

1. Find out about your setting's policy and procedures relating to health and safety, and maintaining children's safety during play.

2. Outline your role and responsibilities with regard to maintaining children's safety during play.

NVQ links – Level 2: PW3.1, PW3.2; Level 3: PW7.1, PW7.2, PW9.4

Supervising children on outings

Outings provide excellent opportunities for you to encourage and extend all aspects of children's and young people's development and learning. There are many different places where you can take children and young people on outings. Some outings are short, simple, cheap and easy to organise. Others take more organisation, involve a whole day and can be more exciting, but also more expensive. Outings can be divided into indoor and outdoor activities.

Examples of indoor activities include visits to:

★ art gallery

★ aquarium

★ butterfly centre

★ cinema

★ indoor adventure play

- ☆ library
- ☆ museum
- ☆ swimming pool
- ☆ theatre
- ☆ toy library.

Examples of outdoor activities include:

- ☆ adventure playgrounds
- ☆ bird sanctuary
- ☆ botanical gardens
- ☆ bug hunt
- ☆ castle
- ☆ farm
- ☆ nature walk
- ☆ parks and playgrounds
- ☆ safari park or zoo
- ☆ seaside
- ☆ wildlife park.

The types of outing you organise and supervise will depend on the type of play setting, the children's interests, ages and levels of development, as well as what is available to do in your area. You can find out about activities and places of interest for children and young people at your local library or information centre.

> **EXERCISE:** Find out about activities and places of interest suitable for outings at your local library or information centre.

Young people on an outing.

Ten golden rules for outings

All outings with children and young people should be both safe and enjoyable. To make this possible follow these ten golden rules:

1. Check the outing is suitable for the ages and levels of development of the children and/or young people.
2. Obtain written permission from the children's parents/carers.
3. Ensure the destination, leaving time and expected return times are written down.
4. Know how to get there (e.g. location, route and mode of transport).
5. Check the seasonal conditions, weather and time available.
6. Assess any potential dangers or risks (e.g. activities near water, suitability and safety of playground equipment).
7. Ensure the children's safety and well-being at all times (see below).
8. Carry essential information/equipment such as identification, emergency contact numbers, mobile phone, first aid, spare clothing, food, money and any essential medication.
9. Make sure you and the children are suitably dressed for the occasion (e.g. sensible shoes or boots for walks; waterproof clothing for wet weather; sunhat and sun screen in hot weather; clean, tidy clothes for cinema, theatre and museum visits).
10. Talk to the children about their surroundings during the outing and take things slowly by proceeding at the children's pace to maximise their enjoyment and learning.

Maintaining children's safety on outings

The health and safety of children and young people on outings is part of the setting's overall health and safety policy. The most senior playworker on the outing will usually have overall responsibility and act as group leader. Any other playworkers present will also have responsibility for children and young people on outings at all times. You should be clear about your exact role and responsibilities for organising and supervising outings.

When organising and supervising outings, remember these important points:

- ☆ know and follow the relevant organisational and legal requirements for outings
- ☆ plan travel arrangements that are appropriate to the requirements of the outing
- ☆ ensure your information about travel arrangements is up to date and correct
- ☆ ensure that all consent forms are complete
- ☆ ensure the children and staff are prepared for the outing
- ☆ ensure the timely departure and arrival of adults and children involved in the outing
- ☆ keep equipment, belongings and travel documents safe and secure during the outing
- ☆ maintain the safety and well-being of the children and young people during the outing
- ☆ encourage acceptable behaviour from the children and young people during the outing

- ⭐ ensure that first aid equipment is complete and meets organisational and legal requirements
- ⭐ ensure the correct number of children and young people are accountable throughout the outing
- ⭐ keep any required records accurate and up to date.

(SkillsActive, 2004b; SPRITO, 2002)

You should be aware of children and young people who might require closer supervision during outings (for example, children with disabilities or behavioural difficulties). Additional safety procedures to those used in the play setting may be necessary to support children with medical needs during outings (for instance, arrangements for taking medication). Sometimes it might be appropriate to ask the parent/carer to accompany the child to provide extra help and support during the outing.

Organising emergency procedures is a fundamental part of planning an outing. All participants – including staff, children and parents – should know who will take charge in an emergency during the outing and what their individual responsibilities are in the event of an emergency. (See the section above on dealing with a medical or health emergency.)

KEY TASK

Give a reflective account of your involvement in an outing or trip.

NVQ links – Level 2: PW5.2; Level 3: B228.1 B228.2

Escorting children to and from the play setting

Some playworkers may be involved in escorting children and young people to and from the setting – for example, collecting children from school and taking them to an out-of-school club at another location. To ensure children's and young people's safety and security, you must follow the play setting's procedures for:

- ⭐ collecting the relevant information for the children and young people to be escorted
- ⭐ ensuring the staff/child ratio meets organisational and legal requirements
- ⭐ ensuring that everyone involved is aware of the travel arrangements
- ⭐ ensuring that staff are at the meeting point at the agreed time

★ escorting the children and young people in a safe manner using the agreed route and mode of transport

★ ensuring the children and young people enter the play setting in a safe manner

★ carrying out the agreed procedures for children and young people who are not at the meeting point.

(SkillsActive, 2004b; SPRITO, 2002)

EXERCISE: If applicable, describe the procedures for escorting children and young people to and from your play setting.

Further reading

Balmforth, N. (1992) *Outdoor Play Areas for Children*. ILAM.

Balmforth, N. (1995) *Safety in Indoor Adventure Play Areas*. ILAM, NPFA and RoSPA.

Balmforth, N. *et al.* (1993) *The Complete Playground Book*. SUP.

Cook, B. and Heseltine, P.J. (1998) *Assessing Risk on Children's Playgrounds*. RoSPA.

Dare, A. and O'Donovan, M. (2000) *Good Practice in Child Safety*. Nelson Thornes.

DfES (2003) *The National Standards for Under 8s Day Care and Childminding: Out of School Care*. DfES.

Heseltine, P.J. (1997) *The Children's Playground*. RoSPA.

Paterson, G. (2002) Foreword, in *First Aid For Children Fast*. Dorling Kindersley in association with the British Red Cross.

Yearley, J. (2000) *Safety Recommendations for Recreational Facilities for Young People*. RoSPA.

6 Child protection

Key points

- ✪ The law regarding child protection
- ✪ What is child abuse?
- ✪ Child protection and the requirements of the play setting
- ✪ The playworker's responsibilities for child protection
- ✪ Identifying signs and indicators of possible abuse
- ✪ Factors that may make children more vulnerable to abuse
- ✪ Responding to suspicions of abuse
- ✪ Responding to a child's disclosure of abuse
- ✪ The confidentiality of information relating to abuse
- ✪ Helping children to protect themselves
- ✪ Dealing with bullying

The law regarding child protection

Information on child protection issues can be found in the guidance document *Working Together to Safeguard Children*, prepared and issued jointly by the Department of Health, the Home Office and the Department for Education in 1999. This replaces *Working Together Under the Children Act 1989*, published in 1991. This new guidance is still informed by the requirements of the Children Act 1989, which provides a comprehensive framework for the care and protection of children. The guidance also echoes the principles covered by the United Nations Convention on the Rights of the Child, endorsed by the UK Government in 1991, and takes on board the European Convention of Human Rights, especially Articles 6 and 8. In addition, Section 11 of the Children Act 2004 places a statutory duty on specified agencies (e.g. local authorities) to make arrangements to ensure that they safeguard and promote children's welfare.

Working Together to Safeguard Children sets out how agencies and professionals should work together to promote the welfare of children and protect children from abuse and neglect. The document applies to those working in education, health and social services, as well as the police and the probation service. It is relevant to those working with children and their families in the statutory, independent and voluntary sectors. The document sets out:

- ★ a summary of the nature and impact of child abuse and neglect
- ★ how to operate best practice in child protection procedures
- ★ the roles and responsibilities of different agencies and practitioners
- ★ the role of area child protection committees
- ★ the procedures to be followed when there are concerns about a child
- ★ the actions to be taken to safeguard and promote the welfare of children experiencing, or at risk of, significant harm
- ★ the important principles to be followed when working with children and families
- ★ training requirements for effective child protection.

As a further safeguard to children's welfare, the **Protection of Children Act 1999** requires childcare organisations (including any organisation concerned with the supervision of children) not to offer employment involving regular contact with children, either paid or unpaid, to any person listed as unsuitable to work with children on the Department of Health List and the Department for Education and Employment's List 99. The Criminal Records Bureau acts as a central access point for criminal records checks for all those applying to work with children and young people. (See the information on enhanced disclosures in Chapter 1.)

What is child abuse?

The Children Act 1989 defines child abuse as a person's actions that cause a child to suffer 'significant harm' to their health, development or well-being. Significant harm can be caused by:

- ★ punishing a child too much
- ★ hitting or shaking a child
- ★ constantly criticising, threatening or rejecting a child
- ★ sexually interfering with or assaulting a child
- ★ neglecting a child (for example, not giving them enough to eat or not ensuring their safety).

The Department of Health defines child abuse as the abuse or neglect of a child by inflicting harm or by failing to prevent harm. Children and young people may be abused by someone known to them (e.g. parent, sibling, babysitter, carer or other familiar adult). It is very rare for a child or young person to be abused by a stranger.

Types of child abuse

- **Physical abuse** involves causing deliberate physical harm to a child and may include: burning, drowning, hitting, poisoning, scalding, shaking, suffocating or throwing. Physical abuse also includes deliberately causing, or fabricating the symptoms of, ill-health in a child (e.g. Munchausen's syndrome by proxy).
- **Emotional abuse** involves the persistent psychological mistreatment of a child and may include: making the child feel inadequate, unloved or worthless; imposing inappropriate developmental expectations on the child; threatening, taunting or humiliating the child; exploiting or corrupting the child.
- **Sexual abuse** involves coercing or encouraging a child to engage in sexual activities to which the child does not or cannot consent because of their age or level of understanding. These sexual activities may involve physical contact such as penetrative and/or oral sex, or encouraging the child to watch the adult masturbate or to look at pornographic material.
- **Neglect** involves the persistent failure to meet a child's essential basic needs for food, clothing, shelter, loving care or medical attention. Neglect may also include when a child is put at risk by being left alone without proper adult supervision.

(DOH, 2003)

Child protection and the requirements of the play setting

All play settings should establish and maintain a safe environment for children/young people and deal with circumstances where there are child welfare concerns. Through their child protection policies and procedures for safeguarding children, play settings have an important role in the detection and prevention of child abuse and neglect.

As playworkers have close contact with children and young people, they should be aware of the signs of possible abuse or neglect and know what to do if they have concerns about a child's welfare (see below). The setting should have clear procedures, in line with the local Area Child Protection Committee (ACPC) procedures, on the situations in which playworkers should consult senior colleagues and external agencies (e.g. social services and the police) when they have concerns about the welfare of a child or young person. Local voluntary play organisations can seek guidance from their national bodies (or from the ACPC) on the requirements for staff training and how they can safeguard the children and young people for whom they provide play services.

The play setting's child protection procedures

The play setting's child protection policy should include information on the roles and responsibilities of staff members and the procedures for dealing with child protection issues. For example:

- ☆ all playworkers should attend child protection training
- ☆ the play setting must comply with local ACPC procedures
- ☆ if any member of staff is concerned about a child s/he must inform a senior colleague; the member of staff must record information regarding such concerns on the same day; this record must give a clear, precise and factual account of their observation
- ☆ confidentiality is of crucial importance and incidents should be discussed only with the relevant persons (e.g. senior colleague or external agency)
- ☆ the senior playworker decides whether the concerns should be referred to external agencies (e.g. social services and/or the police)
- ☆ the setting should work co-operatively with parents unless this is inconsistent with the need to ensure the child's safety
- ☆ if a referral is made to social services, the senior playworker must ensure that a report of the concerns is sent to the social worker dealing with the case within 48 hours
- ☆ particular attention must be paid to the attendance and development of any child identified as 'at risk' or who has been placed on the child protection register.

> EXERCISE: Find out about your setting's child protection policy and procedures.

The playworker's responsibilities for child protection

All adults who work with children have a duty to safeguard and promote their welfare. You need to be aware of:

- ☆ the signs of possible abuse, neglect and bullying
- ☆ to whom you should report any concerns or suspicions
- ☆ the setting's child protection policy and procedures
- ☆ the setting's policy against bullying
- ☆ the setting's procedures for actively preventing all forms of bullying among children
- ☆ the setting's procedure to be followed if a staff member is accused of abuse.

You may be involved in child protection in the following ways.

- ☆ You may have concerns about a child and refer these concerns to a senior colleague in the play setting (who will then refer matters to social services and/or the police as appropriate).

☆ You may be the senior playworker who is responsible for referring concerns about a child's welfare to social services or the police.

☆ You may be approached by social services and asked to provide information about a child or to be involved in an assessment or to attend a child protection conference. This may happen regardless of who made the referral to social services.

☆ You may be asked to carry out a specific type of assessment, or provide help or a specific service to the child as part of an agreed plan, and to contribute to the reviewing of the child's progress (including attending child protection conferences).

(DOH, 2003)

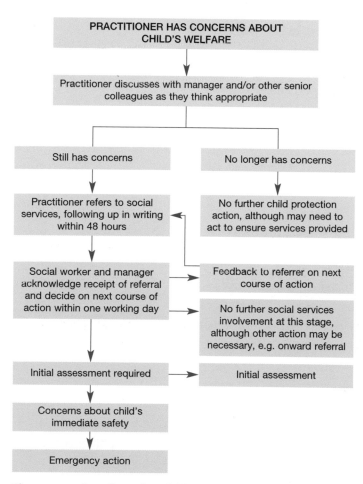

The processes for safeguarding children.
(From 'Working Together to Safeguard Children', DOH, 1999)

Identifying signs and indicators of possible abuse

You need to be aware of the signs and indicators of possible child abuse and neglect, and to whom you should report any concerns or suspicions. You may have contact with children or young people on a daily basis and so have an essential role to play in detecting signs and indicators of possible abuse or neglect: outward signs of physical abuse, uncharacteristic behaviour patterns, failure to develop in the expected ways.

Indicators of *physical abuse* include:

- ★ recurrent unexplained injuries or burns
- ★ refusal to discuss injuries
- ★ improbable explanations for injuries
- ★ watchful, cautious attitude towards adults
- ★ reluctance to play and be spontaneous
- ★ shrinking from physical contact
- ★ avoidance of activities involving removal of clothes (e.g. swimming)
- ★ aggressive or bullying behaviour
- ★ being bullied
- ★ lack of concentration
- ★ difficulty in trusting people and making friends.

Indicators of *emotional abuse* include:

- ★ delayed speech development
- ★ very passive and lacking in spontaneity
- ★ social isolation (e.g. finding it hard to play with other children)
- ★ unable to engage in imaginative play
- ★ low self-esteem
- ★ easily distracted
- ★ fear of new situations
- ★ self-damaging behaviour (e.g. head-banging, pulling out hair)
- ★ self-absorbing behaviour (e.g. obsessive rocking, thumb-sucking)
- ★ eating problems (e.g. overeating or lack of appetite)
- ★ withdrawn behaviour and depression.

Indicators of *sexual abuse* include:

- ★ sudden behaviour changes when abuse begins
- ★ low self-esteem
- ★ using sexual words in play activities uncharacteristic for age/level of development
- ★ withdrawn or secretive behaviour

- ☆ starting to wet or soil themselves
- ☆ demonstrating inappropriate seductive or flirtatious behaviour
- ☆ frequent public masturbation
- ☆ fear of physical contact
- ☆ depression resulting in self-harm (or an overdose)
- ☆ bruises, scratches, burns or bite marks on the body.

Indicators of *neglect* include:

- ☆ slow physical development
- ☆ constant hunger and/or tiredness
- ☆ poor personal hygiene and appearance
- ☆ frequent lateness or absenteeism
- ☆ undiagnosed/untreated medical conditions
- ☆ social isolation (e.g. poor social skills)
- ☆ compulsive stealing or begging.

(Indicators of possible bullying are dealt with towards the end of this chapter.)

KEY TASK

What are your setting's procedures for reporting the signs of possible abuse?

NVQ links – Level 2: C36.1; Level 3: PW6.4, PW12.3

Factors that may make children more vulnerable to abuse

As we have seen, there are various types of child abuse: physical, emotional, sexual or neglect. In all types, there are certain factors that may make children more vulnerable to abuse: child-related factors, parent-related factors or social factors.

Child-related factors

- ☆ Being disabled or suffering from ill-health
- ☆ Being born prematurely or of low birth weight
- ☆ Being the result of a difficult or unwanted pregnancy
- ☆ Being fostered, adopted or a step-child
- ☆ Being the 'wrong' sex

Parent-related factors

- ★ Being abused as a child
- ★ Experiencing domestic violence
- ★ Having a mental health problem
- ★ Misusing alcohol or drugs
- ★ Being a teenage parent or emotionally immature
- ★ Being a single parent
- ★ Having poor coping or parenting skills
- ★ Having several young children

Social factors

- ★ Lack of social support
- ★ High crime rate
- ★ High unemployment rate
- ★ High poverty rate
- ★ Overcrowded or inadequate housing
- ★ Racial harassment
- ★ Little or no access to leisure/play opportunities

Responding to suspicions of abuse

Playworkers working closely with children and young people in play settings are well placed to identify the early signs of abuse, neglect or bullying. In addition, many children and young people may view the play setting as 'neutral territory' where they feel more able to talk with an adult they trust about what is happening to them. If you have concerns that a child or young person at your setting may be experiencing possible abuse or neglect then you *must* report these concerns *promptly* to the relevant person (e.g. a senior colleague or external agency).

 KEY TASK

1. What are your responsibilities for reporting information on possible abuse to a senior colleague or external agency?
2. Give a reflective account of how you have handled concerns about possible physical, emotional or sexual abuse or neglect. Remember confidentiality.

NVQ links – Level 2: C36.1; Level 3: PW6.4, PW12.1, PW12.3

Allegations of abuse against staff or volunteers

If a child or parent makes a complaint of abuse against a member of staff or volunteer, the person receiving the complaint must take it seriously and follow the relevant procedures in line with local ACPC procedures. Professionals who are independent of the setting should investigate all allegations of abuse made against staff or volunteers.

If you have reason to suspect that a child or young person may have been abused by another member of staff, either in the setting or elsewhere, you must inform a senior colleague immediately. You should make a record of the concerns, including a note of anyone else who witnessed the incident or allegation. The senior playworker will not investigate the allegation itself, or take written or detailed statements, but will assess whether it is necessary to refer the matter to social services.

If the senior playworker decides that the allegation warrants further action through child protection procedures, a referral will be made direct to social services. If the allegation constitutes a serious criminal offence it will be necessary to contact social services and the police before informing the member of staff. If it is decided that it is not necessary to refer the matter to social services then the senior playworker will consider whether there needs to be an internal investigation. If the complaint is about the senior playworker, then the ACPC should be contacted for information on the necessary procedures to be followed.

> EXERCISE: Find out about your setting's procedures for dealing with allegations of abuse made against staff or volunteers.

Responding to a child's disclosure of abuse

A child or young person may make a personal disclosure to a member of staff relating to an experience in which the child may have been significantly harmed. A child may make a disclosure to you at an inappropriate place or time. If this happens, you should talk again individually to the child before the end of the day. You may be able to discuss the issue with a senior colleague without giving the name of the child. If not, you should follow the setting's confidentiality policy and child protection procedures.

If a child makes a personal disclosure that s/he has been abused in some way, you should:

- ★ listen to what the child has to say
- ★ accept what the child is saying
- ★ allow the child to talk openly

- ⭐ listen to the child rather than ask direct questions
- ⭐ not criticise the alleged perpetrator of the abuse
- ⭐ reassure the child that what has happened is not his or her fault
- ⭐ stress to the child that telling someone was the right thing to do
- ⭐ reassure the child, but not make promises that you might not be able to keep
- ⭐ not promise the child to keep the disclosed information confidential (as it might be necessary for the matter to be to referred to social services)
- ⭐ explain simply to the child what has to be done next and who has to be told.

After a child has made a disclosure to you:

- ⭐ make brief notes as soon as possible after the conversation
- ⭐ do not destroy the original notes, as the courts may need these
- ⭐ record the date, time, place and any noticeable non-verbal behaviour as well as the words used by the child
- ⭐ draw a diagram to indicate the position of any bruising or other injury
- ⭐ record only statements and observations rather than interpretations or assumptions.

Dealing with a disclosure from a child or being involved in a child protection case can be a very distressing and stressful experience. You may require support too and should discuss with a senior colleague how to access support when dealing with a case of child abuse or neglect.

KEY TASK

1. Give a reflective account of how you have handled a child's personal disclosure of physical, emotional or sexual abuse, or neglect. Remember confidentiality.
2. How and to whom should you pass on information from a child's personal disclosure of abuse? (For example, your role and responsibilities for providing information on the disclosure to a senior colleague or external agency.)

NVQ links – Level 2: C36.2; Level 3: PW6.4, PW12.2

The confidentiality of information relating to abuse

Child protection raises issues of confidentiality that must be clearly understood by everyone within the play setting. You must be absolutely clear about the boundaries of your legal and professional role and responsibilities with regard to the confidentiality of information relating to abuse. A clear and explicit confidentiality policy that staff, children and parents can all understand should ensure good practice throughout the setting. (See the section on confidentiality in Chapter 10.)

Playworkers have a legal duty of confidentiality with regard to the personal information they hold about children and their families. Any information you receive about children (and their families) in the course of your work should be shared only within appropriate professional contexts. All information, including child protection records, should be kept securely, in a safe, private place within the setting.

The law allows the disclosure of confidential personal information in order to safeguard a child or children. Usually personal information should only be disclosed to a third party (e.g. social services) after obtaining the consent of the person to whom the information relates. In some child protection matters it may not be possible or desirable to obtain such consent. The Data Protection Act 1998 allows disclosure without consent in some circumstances (e.g. to detect or prevent a crime, to apprehend or prosecute an offender).

The safety and well-being of children and young people must always be the playworker's first consideration. Playworkers cannot offer or guarantee absolute confidentiality, especially if there are concerns that a child is experiencing, or at risk of, significant harm. They have a responsibility to share relevant information about the protection of children with other professionals, particularly the investigative agencies (e.g. social services and the police). If a child confides in you and requests that the information is kept secret, it is important that you explain to them in a sensitive manner that you have a responsibility to refer cases of alleged abuse to the appropriate agencies for their sake. Within that context, the child should, however, be assured that the matter will be disclosed only to people who need to know about it.

As a playworker you should:

* ☆ be absolutely clear about your setting's child protection policy
* ☆ know and understand your exact role and responsibilities with regard to confidentiality and child protection issues
* ☆ ensure that, if a child asks to speak to you in confidence, s/he is told beforehand that unconditional confidentiality may not always be possible if someone is in danger of abuse
* ☆ if confidentiality is to be breached, the child needs to know who will be told and why, what the outcome is likely to be, and how s/he will be supported
* ☆ know who to contact if further advice, support or counselling is needed, and when to contact them
* ☆ ensure all children and their parents/carers are aware of the setting's confidentiality policy and how it works in practice
* ☆ make sure children are informed of sources of confidential help (e.g. local advice services, Childline).

Find out about your setting's policy and procedures with regard to the confidentiality of information in child protection matters.

NVQ links – Level 2: C36.1, C36.2; Level 3: PW6.4, PW12.1, PW12.2, PW12.3

Helping children to protect themselves

An effective child protection policy will promote a caring and supportive environment in the play setting and create an atmosphere in which children and young people feel that they are secure, valued, listened to and taken seriously. The setting's child protection policy should support children's development in ways that foster their security, confidence and independence. The policy should be regarded as central to the welfare and well-being of all children and young people and should incorporate the following aims:

- ✬ encourage children to have positive self-esteem and self-image
- ✬ help children view themselves as part of the setting and local community
- ✬ nurture children's abilities to establish and sustain relationships with families, peers, adults and the outside world
- ✬ provide time, space and opportunities for children to explore, discuss and develop key ideas relating to child protection openly with peers and adults, in a safe and secure environment
- ✬ equip children with the necessary skills to make reasoned, informed choices, judgements and decisions
- ✬ work with parents and carers to build an understanding of the setting's responsibility to ensure the welfare and well-being of all children
- ✬ establish and maintain child protection procedures so that all staff know how to act if they have concerns or need support regarding a particular child
- ✬ ensure that staff are aware of local child protection procedures so that information is passed on effectively to the relevant professional or agency
- ✬ keep members of the setting well informed about child protection issues, and develop effective and supportive liaison with outside agencies
- ✬ provide a model for open and effective communication between children, parents, playworkers and other adults working with children.

Child protection not only involves the detection of abuse and neglect but also the *prevention* of abuse by helping children and young people protect themselves. As part of this preventive role you should help children and young people to understand what is and is not acceptable behaviour towards them, stay safe from harm, speak up if they have worries or concerns, develop awareness and resilience, and prepare for their future responsibilities as adults, citizens and parents.

Being actively involved in prevention helps children and young people to keep safe both now and in the future. They need to know how to take responsibility for themselves and to understand the consequences of their actions. They must know and understand:

- ★ that they all deserve care and respect
- ★ their rights and how to assert them
- ★ how to do things safely and how to minimise risk
- ★ how to deal with abusive or potentially abusive situations
- ★ when and how to ask for help and support.

To do this, children and young people need opportunities to develop the following skills: positive self-esteem; negotiation and assertiveness techniques; critical thinking and good judgement; coping strategies; ability to access support.

Positive self-esteem

Helping children and young people develop positive self-esteem can be a major preventive strategy (Moon, 1992). All children begin with the potential for high self-esteem, but their interactions with others contribute to whether positive self-esteem is encouraged or diminished. Experiences in early childhood can have a very significant effect on children's self-esteem, although sometimes it is not until adolescence or adulthood that any serious psychological and social problems become apparent. Nevertheless, children and young people are very resilient and can rebuild their self-esteem, even if their early experiences were difficult or damaging. (See Chapter 7 for more detailed information on developing positive self-esteem.)

Negotiation and assertiveness techniques

You should help children and young people to know and understand their rights and how to assert them (see Chapter 2). Ensure that they understand that no one should take away their right to be safe.

Encouraging children and young people to develop negotiation skills is often an essential part of helping them to keep themselves safe. You can introduce or reinforce negotiation skills by encouraging children to think about how they negotiate in everyday situations (for example, at bedtime, sharing play equipment, staying out late, using the computer/games console, visiting friends, watching TV). Encourage them to explore the idea of compromise and use role play to help them practise how to negotiate in difficult situations, such as being bullied (see below). You can also help children to develop assertiveness techniques by using role play and puppets to explore the differences between being aggressive, passive and assertive (see Chapter 8).

Critical thinking and good judgement

Critical thinking and decision-making are also essential for helping children and young people keep themselves safe. You can help them to develop these skills by encouraging them to participate in decision-making within the setting (see Chapter 2) and providing opportunities for co-operation (see Chapter 8).

You should also encourage children and young people to trust their own feelings and good judgement in difficult situations. By learning to trust their inner feelings, they can avoid many potentially risky situations. Use role play to help them think about what they should do if their friends want them to do something they dislike or feel uncomfortable about (for example, going to a party or nightclub, going to a pub, getting drunk, having sex, shoplifting, taking drugs). Peer pressure can be very strong; encourage them to decide and set limits about what they will and will not do so that they know how to cope before the situation arises.

Make sure that children and young people understand the dangers of situations that may put their personal safety at risk, such as:

* being left at home alone
* playing in deserted or dark places
* being out on their own
* getting lost (e.g. on outings)
* walking home alone, especially in the dark
* talking to strangers
* accepting lifts from strangers, including hitchhiking.

As children and young people get older they need opportunities to explore their environment and to develop their independence. To do this safely they will need to know and understand about acceptable risk-taking. Risk-taking can be explored through stories (e.g. 'Jack and the Beanstalk') and TV programmes. Children and young people can think about and discuss the risks taken by their favourite characters. Encourage them to identify some of the risks they take in their own lives and look at ways they can minimise risk. Puppets and role play can be used to help them deal with potentially risky situations. (There is more information on risk-taking in play activities in Chapter 4.)

Coping strategies

Children and young people should be aware of a range of coping strategies for dealing with potentially risky situations, like those listed below.

1. Never talk to strangers. If a stranger approaches, ignore them, pretend not to hear them and walk or run away.
2. Never go up to a car when someone stops to ask for directions – it could be a trick to get them into the car. Pretend not to hear, keep at a distance and walk away.

3. Always try to stay with others, as there is safety in numbers.

4. If being followed or threatened by someone, get to a place with people (e.g. a shop or play area in a park). Go to the door of a house and pretend to ring the bell, or ring the bell if the person continues to follow or threaten.

5. Avoid anyone who is being offensive, drinking heavily, taking drugs or acting in an inappropriate way. If someone acts in an over-familiar way or gets too close, say 'No!' forcefully and get help.

6. If being bullied say 'No' without fighting, get friends to help and tell an adult. (See below for information on dealing with bullying.)

7. Do not fight to protect or retain possessions (e.g. if someone tries to steal a bag or mobile phone). Possessions can be replaced but people cannot. Keeping safe is more important. (It is also a good idea to keep mobiles and wallets safely out of sight in public places.)

8. Always tell a parent or carer their destination and contact details. Memorise their own telephone number and address from as young as possible. Know how to contact parents, carers or neighbours in an emergency.

9. Communicate their limits to friends. Learn to say and mean 'No' to situations they dislike or feel uncomfortable about. If necessary they can use their parents as an excuse (e.g. 'I can't do that because my dad won't let me').

10. Know and understand 'The Keepsafe Code' (see below).

(www.kidscape.org.uk)

Accessing support

Children and young people need to know where to go for help and support in difficult situations. They should be encouraged to identify people in the play setting and the local community who help them to keep safe. For example, worries about bullying or problems at home or school can be discussed with a playworker; if they get lost they can ask a police officer for assistance.

Encourage children and young people to think of a trusted adult (such as parents, another relative, teacher, playworker) they could talk to about a difficult situation, such as abuse, bullying or negative peer pressure. Ensure that they understand that if they go to an adult for help, especially within the play setting, they will be believed and supported. Provide them with information about other sources of help and support (e.g. Childline, the Samaritans).

EXERCISE: Think about the ways your setting helps children to protect themselves.

The Keepsafe Code

1. Hugs
2. Body
3. No
4. Run or get away
5. Yell
6. Tell
7. Secrets
8. Bribes
9. Code

(See below for more details about these.)

1. **Hugs**. Hugs and kisses are nice, especially from people we like. Even hugs and kisses that feel good and that you like should never be kept secret.

2. **Body**. Your body belongs to you and not to anyone else. This means all of your body. If anyone harms you or tries to touch your body in a way which confuses or frightens you, say 'No', if possible, and *tell*.

3. **No**. If anyone older than you, even someone you know, tries to touch you in a way you don't like or that confuses you, or that they say is supposed to be a secret, say 'No' in a very loud voice.

4. **Run or get away**. Don't talk to anyone you don't know when you are alone or just with other children. You don't have to be rude, just pretend you didn't hear and keep going. If a stranger, or a bully, or even someone you know tries to harm you, get away and get help. Make sure you always go towards other people or to a shop, if you can.

5. **Yell**. Wherever you are, it is all right to yell if someone is trying to hurt you. Practise yelling as loud as you can in a big, deep voice by taking a deep breath and letting the yell come from your stomach, not from your throat.

6. **Tell**. Tell a grown-up you trust if you are worried or frightened. If the first grown-up you tell doesn't believe or help you, keep telling until someone does. It might not be easy, but even if something has already happened that you have never told before, try to tell now. Who could you tell?

7. **Secrets**. Secrets such as surprise birthday parties are fun. But some secrets are not good and should never be kept. No bully should ever make you keep the bullying a secret and no one should ask you to keep a kiss, hug or touch secret. If anyone does, even if you know that person, tell a grown-up you trust.

8. **Bribes**. Don't accept money or sweets or a gift from anyone without first checking with your parents. Most of the time it will be fine, like when you get a present for your birthday from your grandma. But some people try to trick children into doing something by giving them sweets or money. This is called a bribe – *don't ever take one!* Remember, it is possible that you might have to do what a bully or older person tells you, so that you can keep yourself safe. Don't feel bad if that happens because the most important thing is for you to be safe.

9. **Code**. Have a code word or sign with your parents or guardians that only you and they know. If they need to send someone to collect you, they can give that person the code. Don't tell the code to anyone else.

(Kidscape, 2001)

Dealing with bullying

Research suggests that 85 per cent of 5- to 11-year-olds have experienced bullying in some form (e.g. name-calling, being hit or kicked). In 2000, a survey of 11- to 16-year-olds found that '36 per cent of children said they had been bullied in the last 12 months; 26 per cent had been threatened with violence and 13 per cent had been physically attacked' (MORI; Association of Teachers and Lecturers, 2000). As bullying occurs both inside and outside of schools, play settings should have an anti-bullying policy that clearly sets out the ways in which they try to prevent or reduce bullying and deal with bullying behaviour when it happens.

What is bullying?

Bullying can be defined as behaviour that is:

★ deliberately hurtful or aggressive
★ repeated over a period of time
★ difficult for victims to defend themselves against.

There are three main types of bullying.

1. Physical: hitting, kicking, taking belongings.
2. Verbal: name-calling, insulting, making offensive remarks.
3. Indirect: spreading nasty stories about someone, exclusion from social groups, being made the subject of malicious rumours, sending malicious e-mails or text messages.

Name-calling is the most common type of bullying. Children and young people can be called nasty names because of their individual characteristics, ethnic origin, nationality, skin colour, sexual orientation or disability. Verbal bullying is common among boys and girls. Boys experience more physical violence and threats when being bullied than girls. However, physical attacks on girls by other girls are becoming more common. Girls tend to use more indirect types of bullying, which can be more difficult to detect and deal with (DfES, 2000).

Supporting children experiencing bullying

Any child or young person can experience bullying but certain factors may make bullying more likely. While there is *never* an acceptable excuse for bullying behaviour, children and young people are more likely to experience bullying if they:

- ★ are shy or have an overprotective family environment
- ★ are from a different racial or ethnic group to the majority of children/young people
- ★ appear different in some obvious respect (e.g. stammering)
- ★ have special needs (e.g. a disability or learning difficulties)
- ★ behave inappropriately (e.g. are a 'nuisance' or intrude on others' play activities)
- ★ possess expensive accessories (e.g. mobile phones or computer games).

Recognising when a child is being bullied

Children and young people who are experiencing bullying may be reluctant to attend the play setting and are often absent. They may be more anxious and insecure than others, have fewer friends and often feel unhappy and lonely. They can suffer from low self-esteem and negative self-image; they may see themselves as failures; they may feel stupid, ashamed and unattractive.

Possible signs that a child or young person is experiencing bullying include:

- ★ suddenly not want to go to the setting when they usually enjoy it
- ★ unexplained cuts and bruises
- ★ possessions have unexplained damage or are persistently 'lost'
- ★ becoming withdrawn or depressed but will not say what is the matter.

While the above signs may indicate that a child is being bullied, they may also be symptomatic of other problems, such as child abuse (see above).

Helping children who are being bullied

The behaviour of some children can lead to them experiencing bullying, although this does not justify the behaviour of the bullies. For example, some children may:

- ★ find it difficult to play with other children
- ★ be hyperactive
- ★ behave in ways that irritate others
- ★ bully weaker children
- ★ be easily roused to anger
- ★ fight back when attacked or even slightly provoked
- ★ be actively disliked by the majority of children using the setting.

Playworkers and the child's parents/carers should work together to identify any such behaviour. The child needs help to improve their personal and social skills, including assertiveness techniques and conflict resolution (see Chapter 8).

You may be able to provide support for a child who is being bullied by:

- ★ encouraging the child to talk
- ★ listening to the child's problems
- ★ believing the child if they say they are being bullied
- ★ providing reassurance that it is not their fault; no one deserves to be bullied
- ★ discussing the matter with a senior colleague
- ★ taking appropriate action, following the setting's policy on anti-bullying.

Dealing with persistent and violent bullying

Where a child does not respond to strategies to combat bullying, the setting should take tough action to deal with persistent and violent bullying. It should have a range of sanctions to deal with this type of bullying. Everyone within the setting should know what sanctions will be applied. These sanctions should be fair and used consistently.

You can help deal with bullying behaviour by:

- ★ knowing the setting's policy and strategies for dealing with it
- ★ using appropriate sanctions for such behaviour (e.g. exclusion from certain activities)
- ★ providing help for the bully so they can recognise that this behaviour is unacceptable (e.g. discussion, mediation, peer counselling)
- ★ working with playworkers and parents to establish community awareness of bullying
- ★ making sure all children and young people know that bullying will not be tolerated
- ★ understanding that the play setting can permanently exclude children or young people who demonstrate persistent bullying behaviour, especially physical violence.

STOP the bullies now!
LOOK out for your friends.
LISTEN to your friends who are sad or upset.
TALK to your playworkers or parents.

Example of child's anti-bullying poster.

KEY TASK

1. Outline your setting's anti-bullying policy and main strategies for dealing with bullying behaviour.
2. Give a reflective account of how you have handled concerns about bullying. Remember confidentiality.
3. Devise an activity to encourage children and/or young people to speak up about bullying (e.g. story, discussion, role play, drama or poster making).

NVQ links – Level 3: PW6.4, PW12.1, PW12.2

Further reading

Department of Health (1989) *An Introduction to the Children Act 1989*. HMSO.

Department of Health (2003) *What to do if You're Worried a Child is Being Abused*. DOH (free copies of this booklet are available via the DOH website at www.dh.gov.uk).

Department of Health, Home Office and DfEE (1999) *Working Together to Safeguard Children*. HMSO.

Donnellan, C. (ed.) (2003) *Dealing with Bullies*. Independence Educational Publishers.

Elliott, M. (1998) *Bullying Wise Guide*. Hodder Children's Books.

Elliott, M. (2002) *Teenscape: A Personal Safety Programme for Teenagers*. Kidscape.

Elliott, M. and Kilpatrick, J. (2002) *How to Stop Bullying: A Kidscape Training Guide*. Kidscape.

Hobart, C. and Frankel, J. (1998) *Good Practice in Child Protection*. Nelson Thornes.

Houghton, D. and McColgan, M. (1995) *Working with Children*. Collins Educational.

Kay, J. (2003) *Protecting Children*. Continuum International Publishing.

Lindon, J. (2003) *Child Protection* (2nd edn). Hodder & Stoughton.

NSPCC (1997) *Turning Points: A Resource Pack for Communicating With Children*. NSPCC.

Russell, G. (2003) *Words Hurt Too: Young People and Bullying*. UK Youth.

Sullivan, K. (2000) *The Anti-bullying Handbook*. Oxford University Press.

7 Children's health and well-being

Key points

- ⚽ The importance of promoting children's health and well-being
- ⚽ The role of the playworker in promoting children's health and well-being
- ⚽ Promoting healthy eating and food safety
- ⚽ Promoting children's emotional well-being
- ⚽ Developing positive self-esteem
- ⚽ Coping with transitions
- ⚽ Helping children adjust to the play setting

The importance of promoting children's health and well-being

Childhood and adolescence are critical periods for establishing lifestyle habits that will affect children and young people's health and development both now and in their adult lives. Promoting children's health and well-being within a supportive environment encourages them to:

- ✩ access appropriate advice and support for health-related issues
- ✩ attain good physical and mental health
- ✩ make healthy lifestyle choices
- ✩ understand and manage risk
- ✩ develop responsible behaviour patterns
- ✩ participate in physical activity and sport in school and the local community.

(DOH, 2004)

Promoting health and well-being can be particularly helpful for children and young people who are experiencing negative social or environmental factors. For example, actively promoting children's emotional well-being may help to reduce the numbers of young people involved in teenage pregnancies, alcohol/drug misuse, truancy and crime (Goleman, 1996).

Promoting health and well-being is important because it helps children and young people to deal with risk and meet new challenges, work for and achieve educational success, identify and keep personal values, understand and respect equal opportunities, and develop and maintain better health and emotional well-being.

The play setting will have policies and procedures relating to children's health and well-being. These may cover aspects such as those listed below.

★ **Health and safety**: health and safety in the play setting; first aid; risk taking.

★ **Emotional health and well-being**: self-esteem; teasing; bullying.

★ **Physical activity**: sport and fitness; leisure activities; swimming.

★ **Healthy eating**: eating a healthy breakfast; eating a balanced diet; weight problems.

★ **Personal hygiene**: taking care of personal hygiene; dental care.

★ **Sex education**: human life cycle; puberty; emotional aspects of sexual relationships.

★ **Drug education**: drug facts; alcohol; tobacco; illegal substances; peer pressure.

See Chapter 5 for detailed information on health and safety.

> EXERCISE: Find out about your setting's policies and procedures relating to children's health and well-being.

The role of the playworker in promoting children's health and well-being

You can promote health and well-being by helping children and young people to:

★ develop and maintain positive self-esteem

★ take responsibility for their own actions

★ have confidence in themselves and their own abilities

★ make and keep meaningful and rewarding relationships (see Chapter 8)

★ be aware of their own feelings and those of others

★ consider and respect the differences of other people (see Chapter 2)

★ be active participants as citizens of a democratic society (see Chapter 2)

★ develop and sustain healthy lifestyles

★ keep safe and maintain the safety of others (see Chapter 6).

Accessing information on healthy lifestyles

The Internet (for example: www.support4learning.org.uk and www.wiredforhealth.gov.uk) can provide access to a wide range of information on health issues relevant to the age and development of children and young people, including:

- ✯ healthy eating, nutrition, food safety, weight problems and eating disorders
- ✯ dentists and oral hygiene
- ✯ first aid and medicines
- ✯ personal safety and bullying
- ✯ common illnesses and medical conditions (e.g. asthma, epilepsy, diabetes)
- ✯ drugs, alcohol, smoking
- ✯ sports, fitness and health
- ✯ emotional well-being, mental health and counselling
- ✯ stress at home and at school, including exam stress
- ✯ sexual health, HIV and AIDS.

There is a series of Department of Health and Department for Education and Employment interactive websites for children and young people exploring a wide range of health issues:

1. **Welltown** for 5 to 7 year olds – www.welltown.gov.uk
2. **Galaxy-H** for 7 to 11 year olds – www.galaxy-h.gov.uk
3. **LifeBytes** for 11 to 14 year olds – www.lifebytes.gov.uk
4. **Mind, Body and Soul** for 14 to 16 year olds – www.mindbodysoul.gov.uk.

Information on healthy lifestyles is also available from national and local organisations, including the voluntary sector, community and neighbourhood resources. (For further information see Appendix A.)

KEY TASK

1. Find out what information on healthy lifestyles for children and young people is available in your local area. Check out:
   - community centres
   - health centres
   - Internet resources
   - local libraries
   - youth projects.
2. Describe how you have encouraged and supported children and/or young people to improve and maintain their own healthy lifestyle.
3. Plan and provide a play opportunity that encourages physical activity.

NVQ links – Level 3: PW13.1

Providing an effective role model for a healthy lifestyle

Working with children and young people is a rewarding but often challenging or even stressful occupation. You need to take responsibility for your own health and emotional well-being, and take the necessary action to tackle or reduce stress in your life. To get the most out of your personal and professional life, you need to:

- ✮ develop and maintain confidence in your own abilities
- ✮ take care of your emotional well-being
- ✮ take regular exercise
- ✮ have a healthy diet
- ✮ make the most of your free time
- ✮ make new friends and develop new skills
- ✮ take time to relax and enjoy yourself.

As a playworker you can provide a positive role model for children and young people by:

- ✮ remembering and using people's names
- ✮ talking to colleagues and children/young people in an appropriate manner
- ✮ listening attentively to others
- ✮ following up problems (e.g. getting help or giving advice as appropriate to your role)
- ✮ assisting colleagues under pressure (e.g. helping to prepare resources)
- ✮ following the setting's health and safety procedures
- ✮ using hygienic and safe practices at all times.

Remember, a healthy play environment should be clean, hygienic and safe. The setting should also be a welcoming and secure environment where there are positive working relationships between all who are employed there. (See Chapter 10, 'Professional practice'.)

Promoting healthy eating and food safety

Ensuring healthy eating and food safety within the setting enables children and young people to maintain their health and well-being by:

- ✮ developing and growing properly
- ✮ maintaining a healthy weight
- ✮ protecting their skeleton and nervous system
- ✮ improving their immune system to fight off illness and infection
- ✮ preventing dental decay

⭐ keeping fit and healthy through a balanced diet and exercise

⭐ avoiding unnecessary illness (e.g. food poisoning due to poor hygiene).

The setting should remind children and young people (especially younger children) about the importance of personal hygiene and the need for proper hand washing after using the toilet or before handling food.

KEY TASK

Working with a group of children and/or young people, design a poster that illustrates the importance of personal hygiene – for example, hand washing after using the toilet or before handling food.

NVQ links – Level 2: PW4.2; Level 3: PW13.1

Basic knowledge of food hygiene

The Chartered Institute of Environmental Health Foundation Certificate in Food Hygiene (formerly the Basic Food Hygiene Certificate) is an essential qualification for all food and beverage handlers (including playworkers) and covers the basic principles of safe food handling. Many colleges include this certificate as part of their playwork courses. If you do not have this certificate already then the course is available at most local colleges and covers:

⭐ food poisoning trends and reasons

⭐ bacteria and micro-organisms

⭐ personal hygiene

⭐ food safety legislation

⭐ pest control

⭐ cleaning and disinfecting.

The play setting's procedures for preparing and storing food

You should follow your setting's procedures for preparing and storing food. If you are responsible for the preparation and handling of food you should be aware of, and comply with, regulations relating to food safety and hygiene (DfES, 2003). For example, if the setting provides meals for children then the kitchen facility must comply with the Food Safety Act 1990 and the Food Safety Regulations 2002. Children should not have access to the kitchen unless it is being used solely for a supervised children's activity (DfES, 2003).

You should know the relevant areas for eating and drinking in the setting, for both yourself and the children/young people you work with – for example, the canteen or school hall; designated classroom in a school or room in a community centre; playworkers may eat with the children or eat packed lunches in the staffroom.

Providing a satisfying, varied and balanced diet

Depending on the type of play setting, you may need to provide regular drinks and food for the children. Children attending the play setting for a full day should be offered a midday meal or packed lunch that can be provided by parents. Fresh drinking water should be available to children at all times. Any food and drink provided by the setting should be properly prepared, nutritious and comply with any special dietary requirements (DfES, 2003).

Healthy eating involves getting the right nutrients from a satisfying, varied and balanced diet. Children, young people and adults need the following nutrients to enable their bodies to work efficiently: carbohydrates, proteins, fats, vitamins and minerals. We also need fibre and water to remove waste products and avoid dehydration.

A balanced diet includes a wide variety of food so that sufficient quantities of the different nutrients are consumed. Ensure that children and young people understand that healthy eating does not have to be boring – a balanced diet can include foods they enjoy eating. For example, eating

A balanced diet.

biscuits, cakes or crisps is OK in small amounts as long as they also eat plenty of the foods with the nutrients they need the most of. These include bread, cereals and potatoes; meat, fish and vegetarian alternatives; milk and dairy products; fruit and vegetables.

Remember the following guidelines for a healthy, balanced diet.

* Enjoy eating food.
* Eat a variety of different foods.
* Eat the right amount to be a healthy weight.
* Eat plenty of foods rich in starch and fibre.
* Eat plenty of fruit and vegetables.
* Do not eat too many foods that contain lots of fat.
* Do not have sugary foods or drinks too often.
* Drink plenty of water.

(British Nutrition Foundation, 2003)

Cultural and specific dietary requirements

If your play setting provides meals and/or snacks and drinks for children then their parents/carers should provide information on any special dietary requirements, preferences or food allergies the child may have. A record should be made of this information during the registration process and the relevant staff should be aware of, and follow, these requirements.

Remember that children and young people from some families may follow strict rules about religious dietary requirements. For example, Jews do not eat pork or shellfish and many eat only kosher foods; Muslims do not eat pork and many will eat only halal foods; Hindus and Sikhs do not eat beef or are vegetarians/vegans; some Buddhists are also vegetarians. Find out if children are required to follow a certain diet during specific religious festivals (e.g. Muslims who have reached puberty, or 15 years of age, are required to fast from sunrise to sunset during Ramadan). If you are celebrating the cultural diversity of the setting by preparing and sharing foods from different cultures, check first whether the children are allowed to do this.

Children and young people from some families are vegetarian or vegan, not for religious reasons but as part of their lifestyle choices. You must also be aware of the special dietary requirements of children and young people with food allergies, especially those that can be potentially life threatening such as a peanut allergy. You should also be aware of the children's individual food preferences and any foods their parents do not wish them to eat.

Consulting children on the selection and preparation of food and drinks

Consulting children and young people on the selection and preparation of food encourages their independence and decision-making skills. Involving them in helping to serve meals/snacks and clear away afterwards also encourages their independence as well as helping them take responsibility for looking after their play environment. Always follow any health and safety regulations as well as your setting's procedures for these activities.

Encourage children to try a variety of different foods, but be careful not to force them to eat. Remember, some children eat

Healthy eating in a play setting.

more than others and the same child may eat differing amounts at different times. For example, they may eat less if tired, ill or upset, or they may eat more after energetic play or during a growth spurt. Many younger children prefer plain and familiar food they can eat with their fingers, but they also need opportunities to develop the skills of using a spoon, fork and then knife. You should encourage children to use safe, child-sized versions of these as appropriate to their age, level of development and culture.

If possible, eat with the children and use the time to share the events of the day so far. Mealtimes should be pleasant and social occasions. Eating with adults provides children with a positive role model – they can benefit from seeing you enjoying food and trying new foods, and observing your table manners.

 KEY TASK

1. What are your setting's procedures for the preparation and storage of food?

2. Plan and prepare a meal or snack for a group of children and/or young people in your setting. Remember the following:
   - healthy and balanced diet
   - specific dietary requirements, including food allergies
   - individual preferences.

3. Include the children/young people in the planning and preparation of the meal or snack as appropriate to their age and level of development and the procedures of the setting.

NVQ links – Level 2: PW4.1, PW4.2; Level 3: PW13.2

Promoting children's emotional well-being

The pressures of modern living in the twenty-first century can affect the emotional well-being of children, young people and adults. For example:

★ parents in the UK work longer hours than in any other country in Europe; consequently working parents have less time to spend with their children

★ National Curriculum demands have led to a return to more formal methods of teaching, with increased emphasis on academic achievement for all children (e.g. baseline assessment, literacy and numeracy hours, end of key stage tests)

★ technological advances and concerns about personal safety mean many children and young people spend more time in front of televisions, computers and games consoles than playing outdoors with friends.

Academic intelligence or achievement has very little to do with emotional well-being. According to research, IQ contributes 20 per cent to the factors that lead to success in life, while other factors contribute to the other 80 per cent. These other factors include environmental and social factors, luck (being in the right place at the right time or the wrong place at the wrong time, say), and emotional intelligence or competence (Goleman, 1996).

In Britain we tend to place great importance on people's qualifications and job status. We perhaps need to focus more on their emotional intelligence or well-being as this would lead to people having better life skills (for instance, making better use of leisure time, maintaining positive relationships, being able to pass exams, getting satisfying and challenging jobs, and being better parents).

You can promote children's emotional well-being by providing opportunities for them to:

★ learn about their feelings
★ understand the feelings of others
★ develop their creative abilities (e.g. art and craft, drama, musical activities)
★ participate in physical activities, games and sport
★ interact with other children and make friends (e.g. play together)
★ develop emotional intelligence.

Emotional intelligence

Emotional intelligence, or emotional well-being, involves developing: positive self-esteem and self-image; the emotional strength to deal with life's highs and lows; the confidence to face the world with optimism; an awareness of own feelings and those of other people.

We all need to feel valued – to feel that who we are and where we come from is respected, and that our ideas and abilities are important. On this solid emotional platform the building blocks for a stimulating and fulfilling life can be successfully constructed. Even if these building blocks are damaged by life experiences, personal difficulties, tragedy or trauma they can be rebuilt in childhood, adolescence and even adulthood.

Five ways to develop children's emotional intelligence

You can help children and young people to develop emotional intelligence by:

1. **developing their self-awareness** including helping them to establish a positive self-image and to recognise their own feelings
2. **helping them to handle and express feelings** in appropriate ways (e.g. through creative, imaginative and physical play)
3. **encouraging their self-motivation** by helping them to establish personal goals (e.g. developing self-control and self-reliance)
4. **developing their empathy for other people** by encouraging them to recognise the feelings, needs and rights of others
5. **encouraging positive social interaction** by helping them to develop effective interpersonal skills through play and other co-operative group activities in the play setting and in the local community.

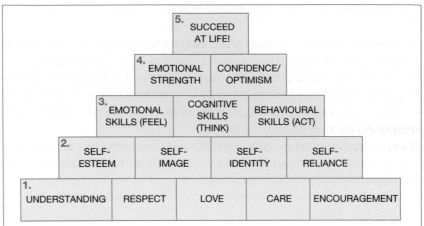

Key:
1. These **foundation stones** are established by parents, grandparents and carers in childhood; as adults we can regain them through partners/spouses, close friends, etc.
2. These **self-building blocks** are influenced by others including family, carers, teachers, playworkers, friends, peers, colleagues, etc. throughout life.
3. These **skills** can be developed as a child and/or as an adult.
4. These **qualities** can be demonstrated as a child and/or as an adult.
5. **Individual achievements** in different areas of life as a child and as an adult.

Emotional building blocks.

EXERCISE:
1. Design your own 'personal flag'. Use words and pictures to describe the following: my happiest memory; my best qualities; my significant achievements; my current goal.
2. Try this activity with a small group of children or young people.

Example of child's personal flag.

The expression of feelings

Another essential aspect of supporting children's emotional well-being is helping them to recognise and deal with their own feelings and those of others. Feelings can be defined as: an *awareness* of pleasure or pain; physical and/or psychological *impressions*; the *experience of emotions* such as anger, joy, fear or sorrow. There is an enormous range of emotions that are experienced by humans as feelings.

We all experience a variety of personal emotions that are related to our individual perceptions of self and our responses to life experiences. Personal emotions include:

* ★ happiness, joy, pleasure and satisfaction
* ★ despair, grief, pain and sadness
* ★ courage, enthusiasm, excitement and impulsiveness
* ★ anxiety, caution, fear and reluctance.

We also experience *interpersonal emotions* that affect the way we relate to other people and how they respond to us. Interpersonal emotions include:

* ★ acceptance, affection, love and kindness
* ★ anger, contempt, hate and malice
* ★ compassion, patience, respect and trust
* ★ distrust, impatience, insensitivity and jealousy.

In British society we are often encouraged to keep our feelings to ourselves. Males are discouraged from showing sensitive emotions; females are discouraged from demonstrating aggressive emotions. Babies and very young children naturally demonstrate clearly how they feel by crying, shouting and rejecting objects. They will openly show affection and other emotions such as jealousy or anger. Young children do not understand that others can be physically or emotionally hurt by what they say or do. Gradually, children and young people become conditioned to accept that the feelings and needs of others do matter.

We need to ensure that children and young people do not forget their own feelings and emotional needs by becoming too concerned with the feelings of others or trying to please others. Children and young people need to know that it is natural to feel a wide range of emotions and that it is acceptable to express strong feelings such as love and anger openly, as long as they do so in positive and appropriate ways.

You can help by encouraging children and young people to:

* ★ identify and name their own feelings
* ★ express these feelings in positive ways
* ★ recognise feelings in other people

☆ deal with emotional responses from others in appropriate ways

☆ deal with conflict situations (see Chapter 8).

As a playworker you can help children and young people to express their feelings through the following means:

☆ **Books, stories and poems** about feelings and common events experienced by other children/young people to help them recognise and deal with these in their own lives.

☆ **Creative activities** to provide positive outlets for feelings (e.g. pummelling clay to express anger); painting/drawing pictures or writing stories and poems that reflect their feelings about particular events/experiences.

Children engaged in role play activity.

☆ **Physical play or sports** involving vigorous physical activity that allows a positive outlet for anger or frustration.

☆ **Drama or role-play activities** to act out feelings (e.g. jealousy concerning siblings, worries over past experiences, fears about future events such as a visit to dentist).

KEY TASK

Describe how you have encouraged and supported children's and/or young people's emotional well-being.

NVQ links – Level 3: PW13.1

Developing positive self-esteem

A person's self-esteem is changeable; sometimes we feel more positive about ourselves than at other times. Even if we have had past experiences that resulted in negative or poor self-esteem, we can overcome this and learn to feel more positive about ourselves.

Self-esteem involves:

- ☆ feelings and thoughts about oneself (positive or negative)
- ☆ respect or regard for self (or lack of it)
- ☆ consideration of self
- ☆ self-image (perception of self).
- ☆ self-worth (value of self).

How we feel about ourselves depends on a number of factors:

- ☆ *who* we are with at the time
- ☆ the social context (e.g. *where* we are)
- ☆ current and past *relationships*
- ☆ past *experiences* (especially in early childhood).

We cannot *see* self-esteem, but we can assess children's and young people's (and adults') levels of self-esteem by their emotional responses, attitudes and actions.

People with positive or high self-esteem are usually:

- ☆ calm and relaxed
- ☆ energetic, enthusiastic and well motivated
- ☆ open and expressive
- ☆ positive and optimistic
- ☆ self-reliant and self-confident
- ☆ assertive
- ☆ reflective (e.g. aware of own strengths and weaknesses)
- ☆ sociable, co-operative, friendly and trusting.

People with negative or low self-esteem tend to be:

- ☆ anxious and tense
- ☆ lacking in enthusiasm, poorly motivated and easily frustrated
- ☆ secretive and/or pretentious
- ☆ negative and pessimistic
- ☆ over-dependent, lacking in confidence and constantly seeking the approval of others; *or* over-confident, arrogant and attention-seeking
- ☆ aggressive *or* passive
- ☆ self-destructive *or* abusive towards others
- ☆ resentful and distrustful of others.

Reasons for low self-esteem

Babies and very young children feel naturally positive about themselves and what they do or do not want. As their self-reliance develops, children and young people become more aware of their own capabilities in comparison with others and this can affect the way they feel about themselves.

Possible reasons for low self-esteem include being:

★ anxious and tense

★ deprived of basic needs or having these needs inadequately met

★ denied the expression of feelings or having these feelings ignored

★ put down, ridiculed or humiliated

★ coerced into participating in inappropriate activities

★ made to feel that their ideas and opinions are unimportant

★ denied appropriate information or explanations

★ over-protected (we all learn more by making our own mistakes)

★ excessively disciplined (especially if labelled as being 'bad' or 'naughty')

★ under-disciplined; lack of rules and discipline can lead to inappropriate behaviour

★ physically abused or threatened with violence

★ sexually abused.

(Lindenfield, 1995)

Ten ways to encourage positive self-esteem

1. Treat every child as an individual with unique abilities and needs.
2. Be positive by using praise and encouragement to help children and young people to focus on what they are good at.
3. Help children and young people maximise their individual potential.
4. Encourage children to measure their achievements by comparing them to *own* efforts.
5. Have high but realistic expectations of *all* children and young people.
6. Take an interest in each child's efforts as well as achievements.
7. Encourage positive participation during play activities (e.g. sharing resources, helping others, contributing ideas).
8. Give children and young people opportunities to make decisions and choices.
9. Promote equality of opportunity by providing positive images of children, young people and adults through books, stories and songs.
10. Remember to label the behaviour not the child as this is less damaging to their self-esteem (e.g. say 'That was an unkind thing to say' rather than 'You are unkind').

EXERCISE:
1. Think of as many *positive* words to describe yourself using the same initial as your first name e.g. *caring, creative*, Carlton; *magnificent, marvellous*, Miriam; *sensitive, sharing*, Shazia; *terrific, tremendous* Tom.
2. Try this activity with friends, colleagues or a group of children and/or young people.

Coping with transitions

The process of adjusting to a new situation is known as a transition. Transitions involve the experiences of change, separation and loss. A transition may involve the transfer from one setting to another. For example:

* home to nursery, playgroup or school
* primary school to secondary school
* secondary school to college or work
* mainstream to or from special school
* school to play setting.

A transition may involve children dealing with changes within the same setting. For example:

* moving from one year group to another (e.g. Year 1 to Year 2)
* moving from one key stage to another (e.g. Key Stage 1 to Key Stage 2)
* staff changes due to illness, maternity leave, promotion, retirement, etc.

A transition may also involve other significant changes in the child's life, such as:

* death or serious illness of a family member or close friend
* parental separation or divorce
* moving to a different area, county or country
* moving house
* going into hospital
* death of a favourite pet
* arrival of a new baby or step-brothers and sisters
* going on holiday (especially visiting another country).

To cope with transitions, children and young people need:

* help to prepare for such transitions
* help to accept transitions and settle into new settings or with new adults
* reassurance from adults to maintain their feelings of stability, security and trust
* adult assistance to adjust to different social rules and social expectations
* help in adapting to different group situations.

Helping children adjust to the play setting

Children's responses to transitions often depend on the way they are prepared for new settings. The need for preparation was not recognised in the past – for example, children started school or went into hospital with little or no preparation beforehand and parental involvement was positively discouraged.

> EXERCISE: What was your first day at school like? Describe how you were prepared for this new situation.

Factors affecting adjustment to the play setting

Factors that may affect children's adjustment to a new setting include:

- ★ the child's age and level of maturity
- ★ previous experiences in a play setting, which may have been positive or negative
- ★ special needs (e.g. physical disability, sensory impairment, communication difficulties, behavioural and/or emotional difficulties)
- ★ having moved to a new area, county or even country
- ★ special family circumstances (e.g. parental separation or divorce, bereavement, serious illness)
- ★ returning to the setting after a prolonged illness or accident.

Possible problems in adjusting to the play setting

Many children and young people may experience some anxiety and stress when they first attend a new setting due to:

- ★ encountering an unfamiliar group of children who may have established friendships
- ★ adapting to the length of time in the setting (e.g. staying for breakfast and after-school club can make a long day for some, especially younger children)
- ★ experiencing a culture and/or language different from home or previous play setting
- ★ coping with unfamiliar routines and rules within the play setting
- ★ worrying about doing the wrong thing
- ★ participating in unfamiliar activities (e.g. self-directed play, sports, drama)
- ★ being overwhelmed or scared by an unfamiliar physical environment.

Strategies for reassuring children new to the play setting

To alleviate some of the anxiety and stress experienced by children and young people during transitions, appropriate preparation is now seen as an essential part of successful transitions in most settings, including nurseries, schools and play settings. Most have established procedures for preparing children and young people for transitions.

The first days (or even weeks) that children and young people spend in a new play setting require a sensitive approach from playworkers to enable them to cope with separation from their parents and/or their adjustment to new routines and staff.

Ten ways to reassure children new to the play setting

1. Follow a clear, daily routine to provide stability and security for the children.
2. Provide opportunities for children to express their feelings and concerns over separating from parents or starting in a new setting.
3. Work with other playworkers to identify children's and young people's individual needs during the transition period.
4. Provide activities and experiences appropriate to these needs.
5. Show an active interest in the children's play activities.
6. Give particular praise and encouragement for participation not just achievement.
7. Work with children and young people to establish clear boundaries and rules.
8. Reassure younger children about their parents' eventual return.
9. Prepare parents for possible *temporary* effects of the transition (for example, children may demonstrate their feelings of anxiety by being clingy, hostile, aggressive or by regressing to a previous developmental level).
10. Settling in can often be more stressful for the parents/carers than their children; encouraging them to be relaxed, calm and confident will help their children, who can sense the adults' anxiety.

 KEY TASK

1. What are the procedures in your play setting for welcoming and settling in children and/or young people new to the setting?
2. Describe how you have developed and improved the procedures for preparing children and/or young people for transitions.

NVQ links – Level 3: PW8.1, PW6.2

Further reading

Bartholomew, L. and Bruce, T. (1993) *Getting to Know You: A Guide to Record-Keeping in Early Childhood Education and Care*. Hodder & Stoughton.

Clarke, J. (2004) *Body Foods for Busy People*. Quadrille Publishing Ltd.

Dare, A. and O'Donovan, M. (2002) *A Practical Guide to Child Nutrition* (2nd edn). Nelson Thornes.

Goleman, D. (1996) *Emotional Intelligence*. Bloomsbury.

Houghton, D. and McColgan, M. (1995) *Working with Children*. Collins Educational.

Kamen, T. (2000) *Psychology for Childhood Studies*. Hodder & Stoughton.

Lindenfield, G. (2000) *Self Esteem: Simple Steps to Developing Self-Reliance and Perseverance*. HarperCollins.

Masheder, M. (1989b) *Let's Play Together*. Green Print.

Matthews, A. (1990) *Making Friends: A Guide to Getting Along with People*. Media Masters.

Mort, L. and Morris, J. (1989) *Bright Ideas for Early Years: Getting Started*. Scholastic.

Murphy, S. (2004) *My Fitness Journal*. Ryland, Peters & Small.

Petrie, P. (1989) *Communicating with Children and Adults: Interpersonal Skills for Those Working with Babies and Children*. Hodder Arnold.

Roet, B. (1998) *The Confidence to be Yourself*. Piatkus.

Whiting, M. (2001) *Managing Nursery Food*. Orchard Books.

Woolfson, R. (1989) *Understanding your Child: A Parents' Guide to Child Psychology*. Faber & Faber.

Yeo, A. and Lovell, T. (1998) *Sociology for Childhood Studies*. Hodder & Stoughton.

8 Promoting positive relationships and behaviour

Key points

- ✪ The importance of good working relationships with children and young people in the play setting
- ✪ Understanding 'appropriate' and 'inappropriate' behaviour when interacting with children and young people
- ✪ Valuing children's individuality, ideas and feelings
- ✪ Effective communication with children and young people
- ✪ Being sensitive to children's communication difficulties
- ✪ Involving children in decision-making and encouraging them to make choices
- ✪ Negotiating and setting goals and boundaries for behaviour
- ✪ Helping children to understand the importance of positive relationships
- ✪ Promoting positive behaviour
- ✪ Dealing with negative behaviour
- ✪ Helping children to deal with conflict themselves

The importance of good working relationships with children and young people in the play setting

Your job involves working closely with individuals and groups of children and young people. Your relationships with children and young people must be professional without being too distant. To develop good working relationships with them you need to know and understand:

- ☆ the setting's behaviour policy
- ☆ strategies for promoting positive behaviour
- ☆ strategies for dealing with negative behaviour
- ☆ the setting's special needs and/or inclusion policy (see Chapter 10)
- ☆ the setting's child protection policy and the procedures to follow if a child tells you something that you feel concerned about (see Chapter 6)
- ☆ the setting's confidentiality policy (see Chapter 10)
- ☆ the nature of your relationship with children's parents/carers (see Chapter 9).

It is important to establish and maintain good working relationships with children and young people in the setting because this helps to promote positive behaviour and thus prevent or reduce disruptive behaviour. This creates a positive play environment for children and young people as well as a positive work environment for you and your colleagues.

You can help to create good working relationships with children and young people by:

- ☆ learning and using children's and young people's preferred names
- ☆ using effective communication skills and encouraging these in the children
- ☆ identifying their needs and interests to provide appropriate play opportunities
- ☆ helping to organise a stimulating environment to encourage play opportunities
- ☆ having well-prepared play activities and materials
- ☆ encouraging children to take appropriate responsibilities (e.g. tidying up)
- ☆ helping to encourage parental involvement where appropriate.

Your relationship with the children and young people is the central part of your role. This relationship involves:

- ☆ creating and maintaining a safe and healthy play environment
- ☆ being sensitive to children's individual needs
- ☆ providing for the physical, emotional, intellectual, language and social needs of the children by using developmentally appropriate play activities, materials and equipment
- ☆ providing praise and encouragement for children's development and learning
- ☆ having a warm, friendly and caring attitude
- ☆ showing an active interest in the children's play activities.

Playworker taking active interest in children's play activity.

One of the most essential aspects of developing a positive relationship with children and young people involves your role and responsibilities for providing play activities that will help to meet *all* their developmental needs: social, physical, intellectual, communication, emotional (SPICE) (see Chapter 3).

Understanding 'appropriate' and 'inappropriate' behaviour when interacting with children and young people

You should have a knowledge and understanding of 'appropriate' and 'inappropriate' behaviour when interacting with children and young people, including the relevant legal requirements.

'Appropriate' behaviour

When working as a playworker it is impossible to be emotionally detached – if you were, you would not be a good playworker. To work well as a playworker involves genuinely caring about children and young people. In addition to meeting children's physical and intellectual needs you also need to provide emotional security by showing a genuine interest in everything they say and do as well as providing comfort when they are upset or unwell. Children can sense when they are with someone who really cares about them.

You should be able to share in the different aspects of children's lives (such as birthdays and other special occasions) without compromising your professionalism. Though you may share the highs and lows of the children's lives, you must maintain some detachment to be an effective playworker. Personal friendships with children, young people or their parents are best avoided as they can complicate your professional relationships within the setting. However, if you are working in your local community this may not always be possible. If you *are* friends with children and/or their families outside the play setting try to keep your personal and professional life separate. For example, do not give the child preferential treatment within the play setting or gossip with parents about what occurs in the play setting. (See the section in Chapter 10 on confidentiality.)

'Inappropriate' behaviour

The UN Convention on the Rights of the Child states that 'children have the right to be protected from all forms of physical and mental violence and deliberate humiliation' (Article 19). Where parental expectations concerning punishment conflict with those of the setting, staff should point out to parents/carers the setting's legal requirements under the Children Act 1989 – that is, no physical punishment. Physical or corporal punishment is not allowed in maintained schools, day nurseries and play settings:

> Corporal punishment (smacking, slapping or shaking) is illegal in maintained schools and should not be used by any other parties within the scope of this guidance. It is permissible to take necessary physical action to prevent personal injury either to the child, other children or an adult, or serious damage to property.
>
> (DOH, 1991; Children Act 1989, Volume 2, Section 6.22)

In addition, using physical punishment is never acceptable because it teaches children and young people that violence is an acceptable means for getting your own way. Shouting and verbal abuse are also totally unacceptable. Smacking and shouting do not work; adults end up having to smack harder and shout louder to get the desired behaviour. Children and young people do not learn how to behave better by being smacked or shouted at; they are just hurt and humiliated, which can do lasting damage to their self-esteem.

Working with children and young people in a play setting can place you in a vulnerable position. You may be open to allegations of abuse made by even quite young children. Children are more aware of child abuse as child protection issues are portrayed in the media and may be discussed in angry, emotional or suspicious terms at home. Some children and young people may view making false allegations of abuse as a way of gaining adult attention or getting back at a member of staff they dislike.

To prevent possible false allegations of abuse, you should:

★ avoid being in a situation where it is just your word against that of a child

★ deal with a child's toileting accident with a colleague

★ not work late in the day alone in the setting with only one or two children

★ not place a child on your lap (especially if you are male) unless it is essential to their well-being and other staff are present

★ discuss child protection issues with your line manager/mentor soon after starting work in a play setting

★ always follow the relevant guidelines given to you by the play setting.

There may be some occasions when a child or young person who is sexually active or is contemplating sexual activity directly approaches a member of staff or volunteer. This must be viewed as a child protection issue. If this happens you should approach a senior colleague with your concerns. The senior playworker will make sensitive arrangements, in discussion with the child or young person, to ensure that parents or carers are informed, and will address child protection issues and ensure that help is provided for the child/young person and family. (See Chapter 6 for further information on child protection.)

Code of conduct for interactions with children and young people

You should have a strong commitment to children, young people, parents/carers, colleagues and the local community. You should behave at all times in a manner that shows personal courtesy and integrity. You should actively seek to develop your personal skills and professional expertise (see Chapter 10).

With regard to working with children and/or young people you should:

- ✿ remember that their social, intellectual and physical welfare and emotional well-being is the prime purpose and first concern of the setting
- ✿ act with compassion and impartiality
- ✿ express any criticism of children/young people in a sensitive manner, and avoid hurtful comments of a personal nature
- ✿ never abuse, exploit or undermine the adult/child relationship
- ✿ respect the confidentiality of information relating to children/young people unless the disclosure of such information is either required by law or is in the best interests of that particular child/young person
- ✿ ensure that any necessary records on the children/young people are based on factual, objective and up-to-date information.

(For codes of conduct for interactions with parents and colleagues see Chapters 9 and 10.)

Valuing children's individuality, ideas and feelings

Valuing children's individuality, ideas and feelings is an important aspect of respecting them and promoting their emotional well-being. This involves being sensitive to their needs. There are universal needs that are necessary to *all* children; these needs are physical or biological needs, such as food, drink and shelter, that are essential to survival. Then there are psychological needs such as love, affection, secure and stable relationships, friendships, environmental stimulation, independence, education; these needs are essential to maintaining the individual's quality of life.

Remember that children's and young people's individual needs vary. Some will have developmental needs that are in line with the expected norm for their chronological age, while others will have needs that are characteristic of much younger or older children. In recognising and attempting to meet children's needs, you should consider each child's age, physical maturity, intellectual abilities, emotional development, social skills, and past experiences and relationships. (For more detailed information see the section in Chapter 2 on children's needs.)

It is important to show sensitivity to the needs of all the children and young people in the setting. They all need to feel valued and accepted by others, especially if they might feel different from others in the setting due to a disability or because of their race/culture. You must have a positive attitude and be able to show that you value each child or young person's individuality, ideas and feelings.

Ten ways to value children's individuality, ideas and feelings

1. Introduce yourself to the children and young people when you first meet them.
2. Use the preferred names of the children and young people in your setting.
3. Give equal time to all the children and young people in your setting.
4. Be a friendly and approachable person that children and young people know will listen to them and take their views into account.
5. Listen to the views and opinions of the children and young people you work with.
6. Do not interrupt children and young people or talk over them.
7. Never make judgements about a particular child/young person based on ability, gender, race or religious beliefs.
8. Never criticise a child/young person or jump to conclusions about their behaviour without first asking them for an explanation.
9. Show children and young people that they are worthwhile, valuable and important through your positive attitude towards them, including using encouragement and praise.
10. Be alert and respond to the cues children and young people give with regard to their feelings.

Playworker listening to views of a young person.

(Houghton and McColgan, 1995)

 KEY TASK

List four ways in which you have shown you value children's individuality, ideas and feelings. Include practical examples of working with children and young people:

- with additional or special needs
- with differing social or cultural backgrounds
- male and female.

NVQ links – Level 2: PW1.1; Level 3: PW8.1

Effective communication with children and young people

The first step towards effective communication with children (and adults, too, of course) is being able to listen attentively to what they have to say. Nearly all breakdowns in communication are due to people not listening to each other. Effective communication requires good interpersonal skills, such as:

- ☆ **being available** – make time to listen to children and young people
- ☆ **listening attentively** – concentrate on what children are saying
- ☆ **using appropriate non-verbal skills** (e.g. facing the child, leaning slightly towards them, smiling, nodding, open-handed gestures, not clenched fists)
- ☆ **following the rules of turn-taking** in language exchanges; every person needs to have their say while others listen
- ☆ **being polite and courteous** – no shouting, no talking over other people, avoiding sarcasm (especially with younger children, who do not understand it and can be frightened by your strange tone of voice)
- ☆ **being relaxed, confident and articulate**
- ☆ **using vocabulary appropriate to your listener(s)**
- ☆ **encouraging others to talk** by asking 'open' questions (see below)
- ☆ **responding positively** to what is said
- ☆ **being receptive** to new ideas
- ☆ **being sympathetic** to other viewpoints (even if you totally disagree with them!)
- ☆ **providing opportunities** for meaningful communication to take place.

Active listening

Communication is a two-way process that depends on the sender (talker) and on the receiver (listener). Research has shown that adults tend to be poor listeners. You can be an active listener by listening carefully to children's talk, considering the mood of the children during play activities, and knowing how, if, and when to intervene to encourage children's use of language

Asking and answering questions

You can initiate and sustain children's talk by providing questions, prompts and cues that encourage their language and communication skills. Some questions require only limited responses or answers from children. These 'closed' questions usually receive one-word answers such as 'yes' or 'no' or the name of a person/object. These types of question do not help children to develop their own language and communication skills. 'Open' questions, on the other hand, are a positive way to encourage a variety of responses, allowing more detailed answers, descriptions and accounts of children's personal experiences, feelings and ideas. For example, the question 'Did you ride your bike?' can only be answered by 'yes' or 'no'; instead it is better to ask 'Where did you go on your bike?' and then use questions like 'What happened next?' to prompt further responses.

As well as asking questions, you need to be able to answer children's and young people's questions. Encouraging them to ask questions helps them to explore their environment more fully, to look for reasons/possible answers, and to reach their own conclusions as to why and how things happen. Always treat their questions seriously. Try to answer them truthfully and accurately. If you honestly do not know the answer, then say so and suggest an alternative way for the child to obtain an answer. For example, 'I don't know where that animal comes from, take a look in the encyclopaedia or on the Internet to find out.' You should encourage children to find their own answers as appropriate to their age and level of development.

KEY TASK

1. Listen to adults talking with children and/or young people in a variety of situations, both within and outside your play setting (e.g. on buses, in shops, in the street, in the playground). Pay particular attention to the questions asked by the adults *and* the children, and *how* they are answered.

2. Consider the following points.

   - How effective was the communication?
   - Was the adult an active listener?
   - What did the children/young people learn about language, the activity and/or the environment?

NVQ links – Level 2: PW1.1; Level 3: PW8.2

Being sensitive to children's communication difficulties

All children and young people have individual language needs, but some may have additional or special needs that affect their ability to communicate effectively with others. For example:

- ⭐ autistic spectrum disorders
- ⭐ behavioural and/or emotional difficulties
- ⭐ cognitive difficulties affecting the ability to process language
- ⭐ hearing impairment
- ⭐ physical disabilities affecting articulation of sounds.

The following are some things for you to consider when working with children or young people with communication and interaction difficulties.

★ Keep information short and to the point; avoid complex instructions.
★ Speak clearly and not too quickly.
★ Be a good speech role model.
★ Build up the child's confidence gradually (e.g. speaking one to one, then in a small group).
★ Encourage reluctant children to speak, but don't insist that they talk.
★ Use stories, cassettes and taped radio programmes to improve listening skills.

Involving children in decision-making and encouraging them to make choices

Involving children in decision-making and encouraging them to make choices is an important part of helping them to develop their independence. Encouraging independence involves helping them to develop:

★ **dependence** on their own capabilities and personal resources
★ **autonomy** (the ability to think and act for oneself)
★ **competence** in looking after self
★ **trust** in own judgement and actions
★ **confidence** in own abilities and actions.

Eight ways to encourage children to be more independent

You can encourage children and young people to become more independent by:

1. providing *freedom* for children and young people to become more independent
2. being *patient* and providing *time* for children and young people to do things for themselves (e.g. let younger children dress themselves, although it takes longer, as it is an essential self-help skill); children and young people with physical disabilities may need sensitive support in this area
3. *praising* and *encouraging* their efforts at becoming more independent
4. being aware of children's *individual needs* for independence; every child is different and will require encouragement relevant to their particular level of development; do not insist children be more independent in a particular area until they are ready
5. being sensitive to children's *changing needs* for independence; remember a child who is tired, distressed or unwell may require more adult assistance than usual
6. offering *choices* to enable children and young people to feel more in control; as they develop and mature, increase the scope of choices
7. providing *play opportunities* that encourage independence (e.g. dressing-up is a fun way to help younger children learn to dress independently)
8. using *technology* to encourage independence (e.g. specialist play equipment; voice-activated word processing; motorised wheelchairs).

Children and young people gain independence by developing self-help skills, making choices and decisions, and taking responsibility for their own actions. They need the freedom to develop their independence in ways appropriate to their overall development. Some may need more encouragement than others to become increasingly more independent and less reliant on other people. The playworker has an important role to play in encouraging children and young people to develop their independence.

(For more detailed information on involving children in decision-making see Chapter 2.)

KEY TASK

Describe how you have involved children and/or young people in decision-making and encouraged them to make choices within the setting.

NVQ links – Level 2: PW1.1; Level 3: PW8.1

Negotiating and setting goals and boundaries for behaviour

As part of your role you will be promoting the setting's policies regarding children's behaviour by consistently and effectively implementing agreed ground rules. You will help children and young people establish and follow ground rules and also to play within certain boundaries as appropriate to the setting. This includes negotiating and setting appropriate goals and boundaries for behaviour. Goals are the *expectations* for behaviour; usually starting with 'Do …'. Boundaries are the *limitations* to behaviour, often starting with 'Don't …'.

You should negotiate and set goals and boundaries that take into account:

★ the age/level of development of children and young people
★ the children's and young people's individual needs and abilities
★ the social context (e.g. the type of play setting, the play activity, the group size).

Negotiating and setting goals and boundaries involves teaching children and young people to respect other people and the possessions of others, and develop self-control.

Negotiating and setting goals and boundaries involves adults seeing things from a child's point of view, respecting children's needs and ideas, realising that children will test boundaries from time to time, having realistic expectations for children's behaviour, and recognising the limitations of some children's level of understanding and memory skills.

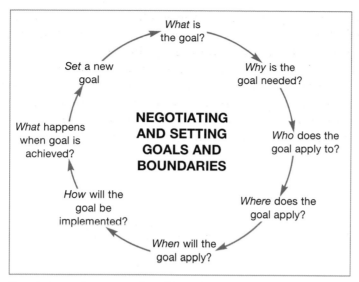

Negotiating and setting goals and boundaries.

Children and young people are more likely to keep to goals and boundaries if they have some say about them. They need to be active participants, not only in following ground rules but also in establishing them. Having a feeling of ownership makes rules more real and gives children and young people a sense of control.

Examples of ground rules
1. Treat each other with kindness and respect.
2. Show respect for the belongings and activities of others.
3. Listen to and follow instructions and directions, especially safety rules.
4. Find and return resources within the play setting.
5. Handle equipment and materials carefully.
6. Keep the setting tidy.
7. Move around the setting sensibly.

Some children may not recognise or accept ground rules, or share the same views as to what is acceptable behaviour. Remember some children from different social or cultural backgrounds may have different expectations regarding behaviour. Where children are given clear guidelines for behaviour at home, they are much more likely to understand and keep to rules, goals and boundaries in the play setting. Adults within the setting also need to be good role models for behaviour. Your use of interpersonal skills with children, young people and colleagues should provide a positive role model for behaviour and effective working relationships.

KEY TASK

1. Think about the goals and boundaries that might be appropriate to the children and/or young people you work with.
2. If possible, encourage them to draw up their own list of ground rules that promote positive behaviour in the setting.

NVQ links – Level 2: PW1.2; Level 3: PW8.3

Helping children to understand the importance of positive relationships

Observing the behaviour of parents and other significant adults (carers, playworkers, teachers and so on) affects:

- ✮ children's and young people's behaviour
- ✮ how children and young people deal with their own feelings
- ✮ how children and young people relate to others.

This is why it is so important for adults to provide positive role models for children's and young people's behaviour. Positive interactions with adults (and other children) in various settings leads to children being able to demonstrate positive ways of relating to others and using appropriate social skills. Adults who provide inconsistent or inappropriate care may unwittingly encourage difficult behaviour in children, which can lead to adults spending less time interacting with the child, resulting in the child having poor communication skills and difficulties in forming positive relationships. There is a spiralling interaction between child and adult.

Every child needs:

- ✮ **S**ecurity
- ✮ **P**raise
- ✮ **E**ncouragement
- ✮ **C**ommunication
- ✮ **I**nteraction
- ✮ **A**cceptance
- ✮ **L**ove.

The mnemonic SPECIAL will help you to remember this.

A child who has not had these needs adequately fulfilled in the first five to six years of life may remain deprived throughout childhood and adolescence (and even adulthood) because they may find it difficult to relate to other people. However, children are amazingly resilient and subsequent, sustained relationships with caring adults in a supportive environment can help them overcome early parental separation, rejection or neglect. However, it is not just parents who influence children's behaviour and self-esteem: all adults who work with children (including playworkers) influence their behaviour and self-esteem through their attitudes, words and actions.

You can encourage children and young people to have a positive view of themselves and their abilities by:

⭐ praising and encouraging their efforts as well as achievements

⭐ listening to their ideas/views to show them that they are valued and important

⭐ taking an active interest in their activities.

Being a positive role model

Being a positive adult role model helps the socialisation of children. Socialisation involves the development of:

⭐ behaviour patterns

⭐ self-control

⭐ independence

⭐ awareness of self in relation to others

⭐ effective relationships

⭐ understanding the needs and rights of others

⭐ moral concepts (e.g. understanding the difference between right and wrong; making decisions based on personal values).

Socialisation determines how children relate socially and emotionally to others. Children need to learn how to deal appropriately with a whole range of emotions, including anger and frustration, within a supportive environment. (There is detailed information about feelings in Chapter 7.) Socialisation occurs through observing, identifying the behaviour of other people, imitating and assimilating.

EXERCISE:
1. Who were your role models when you were younger?
2. What social interactions can you remember (for example, at playgroup, nursery, school, clubs; hobbies, on holiday, early friendships)?
3. How do you think these early role models and social interactions influenced your behaviour? (For example, did they have a positive or negative influence?)

Encouraging positive interactions

Babies and very young children are naturally egocentric; their belief that the world revolves around them and their wishes often makes them selfish and possessive. As children develop they begin to think and care about others as well as themselves.

We have all experienced jealousy in our relationships with others (for example, with siblings, friends, neighbours, colleagues or employers). Unchecked jealousy can be a very destructive and hurtful emotion that prevents children (and adults) from developing respect and care for others.

You can help children to cope with any feelings of jealousy they may have towards others in the following ways.

1. **Avoiding comparisons between children (especially siblings).**
   - ★ For example, do not make comments like 'You're not as quiet as your brother' or 'Why can't you behave more like that group of children?'

2. **Encouraging children to focus on their own abilities.**
   - ★ Emphasise co-operation and sharing rather than competition.
   - ★ Comparisons should be related to improving their own individual skills.

3. **Understanding the reasons for a child's jealousy.**
   - ★ Children feel better when adults acknowledge their feelings.
   - ★ Do not make children feel guilty about being jealous.

4. **Treating all children with respect and fairness.**
   - ★ Take children's individual needs into account.
   - ★ They may require different amounts of adult attention at different times.
   - ★ Equality of opportunity does not mean treating everyone exactly the same, as this would mean ignoring individual needs; it means treating individuals fairly and providing the same *chances*.

5. **Reassuring children they are accepted for *who* they are regardless of what they *do*.**
   - ★ Try to spend a few minutes with each child in your group.
   - ★ Give regular individual attention to help reduce jealousy and increase children's emotional security.

Taking turns is an essential element of learning to interact positively with other children. From about the age of 3 young children begin to co-operate with other children in play activities. By about age 5 they should be quite adept at playing co-operatively with other children. Gradually, children should be able to participate in more complex co-operative play, including games with rules, as their understanding of abstract ideas increases.

We live in a highly competitive society; we all want to be the best, fastest, strongest or cleverest. The media (television, magazines, newspapers) focus our attention on being the best. Most sports and games have only one winner, which means all the other participants are losers. To win is the aim of all contestants. Winning makes us feel good, confident and successful; losing makes us feel bad, inadequate and unsuccessful. Competitive games can prepare children and young people for the competitiveness of real life. However, competition can also contribute to a child's poor self-image and low self-esteem, aggressive behaviour, lack of compassion for others, overwhelming desire to win at any cost.

Young people playing co-operatively.

Competitive sports and games have their place and can be beneficial to children and young people as long as they emphasise: co-operation, teamwork, mutual respect, agreeing on rules and following them, that participation and the pleasure of taking part are more important than winning, and the importance of doing our *personal* best.

As well as being competitive, people can also be sociable and co-operative; we like to be part of a group or groups. Co-operative activities encourage children and young people to:

☆ be self-confident
☆ have high self-esteem
☆ relate positively to others
☆ work together and help others
☆ make joint decisions
☆ participate fully (no one is left out or eliminated)
☆ have a sense of belonging.

KEY TASK

Devise and implement an activity that could encourage children and/or young people to play together in a positive way.

NVQ links – Level 2: PW1.2; Level 3: PW8.3

Promoting positive behaviour

Behaviour can be defined as:

★ a person's actions and reactions

★ a person's treatment of others.

Behaviour involves children and young people *learning to conform* to:

★ their parents' expectations for behaviour

★ the setting's expectations for behaviour

★ wider society's expectations for behaviour.

Children and young people who are not prepared (or are unable) to conform have to accept the consequences (e.g. sanctions for inappropriate behaviour). Learning about behaviour always takes place within a social context. Certain behaviour may be appropriate in one context but inappropriate in another (for instance, parents may make allowances for their child's behaviour, but different rules apply in the play setting because adults must consider the needs of *all* children and have rules to reflect this). What is appropriate in one situation may be inappropriate in another; even within the same setting, for example, loud and boisterous behaviour is appropriate in outdoor play areas but may not be appropriate indoors, depending on the type of play setting and the nature of the play activities.

Learning to conform brings limitations to children and young people's behaviour (e.g. following ground rules).

Parental expectations for behaviour

Parents/carers have expectations for their children's behaviour based on:

- ★ the media (see below)
- ★ cultural or religious beliefs
- ★ individual variations in child-rearing practices
- ★ adherence to traditional child-rearing practices
- ★ comparisons with other children (of relatives, friends, neighbours)
- ★ perceptions of their own childhood and *their* parents' attitudes to behaviour.

Many parents may have idealistic or unrealistic expectations concerning their children's behaviour because some child care/education books and the media promote unrealistic age-related expectations so that many children do not seem to 'measure up' to what the experts say.

The trend towards smaller families (often with few or no relatives nearby) means many parents lack first-hand experience of caring for children *before* they have their own children and may feel less confident about their parenting skills. Parents of children with special needs may be unsure of what to expect from their children in terms of behaviour; they may overcompensate for their child's special needs by being overprotective or by letting the child get away with behaviour that would not be appropriate in a child of similar age/level of development.

In the past children did not dare challenge parental authority for fear of physical punishment. Today some parents still feel that if they were brought up in this way, then that's how they expect their children to behave. In the twenty-first century, society recognises the rights of the child and has the expectation that all parents should be more caring and responsive to their children's needs by using positive methods such as praise, encouragement, negotiation and rewards to achieve appropriate behaviour.

Children and young people learn what their parents consider to be appropriate behaviour and will bring these expectations to the play setting. They also observe their parents' behaviour, which may be:

- ★ assertive – sensitive to their own *and* other people's needs
- ★ passive – too sensitive to other people's needs so *ignores own needs*
- ★ aggressive – obsessed with own needs so *ignores other people's needs*.

Other influences on children's behaviour

Playworkers should be aware of negative or traumatic family incidents (such as bereavement, serious illness or abuse) that may be experienced by the children or young people with whom they work, and the impact these might have on their cognitive and physical abilities, behaviour and emotional responsiveness.

Peer pressure may have a negative influence on children's behaviour as others may:

☆ persuade them to participate in dangerous activities including 'dares'

☆ pressure them into socially unacceptable behaviour (e.g. lying, stealing or bullying)

☆ exclude or threaten them if they do not conform

☆ encourage them to act in ways they never would as an individual (e.g. 'mob rule').

However, playworkers can use peer pressure to encourage positive behaviour by highlighting the positive benefits of certain behaviour for the group or the setting.

The media (TV, magazines, comics) and computer games can have positive or negative influences on children's behaviour, depending on what the children see and how they are affected by it. Children exposed to violent images may see aggressive behaviour as an acceptable way to deal with others. Children who observe more assertive behaviour (with its emphasis on negotiation and compromise) are likely to demonstrate similar positive behaviour. Television programmes, characters and personalities provide powerful role models for children's behaviour. Just consider the effectiveness of advertising!

Encouraging positive behaviour

What is considered to be positive or acceptable children's behaviour depends on each adult's tolerance levels. An adult's tolerance for different kinds of children's behaviour depends on the expectations for children's behaviour in relation to age/level of development, the particular social context in which the behaviour is demonstrated, and how the adult feels at that particular time.

Examples of positive children's behaviour include:

☆ sharing resources and adult's attention

☆ working co-operatively (e.g. taking turns)

☆ being friendly (e.g. helping or comforting others)

☆ following instructions and complying with adult requests

☆ being an active participant (e.g. contributing creative ideas)

☆ expressing self effectively (e.g. speaking clearly, calmly and quietly)

☆ being polite and an attentive listener

☆ being responsible for own actions

☆ being independent

☆ being flexible

☆ being aware of danger.

Examples of negative children's behaviour include:

★ not sharing; attention-seeking; jealousy
★ disrupting activities (e.g. taking things without asking, fighting or arguing)
★ being aggressive/abusive (e.g. upsetting or hurting others, bullying)
★ being defiant and refusing reasonable adult requests
★ overriding or ridiculing other people's ideas
★ expressing self inappropriately (e.g. emotional outbursts, whining or nagging)
★ being rude, cheeky or interrupting others
★ blaming others or lying about own actions
★ being easily led or too dependent on others
★ resisting change or being overly upset by change
★ having no sense of danger; being too compulsive.

Behaviour policy

The behaviour policy helps to shape and reflect the values of the play setting. Positive behaviour is an essential building block for creating a welcoming and pleasant play environment in which all members of the setting feel respected, safe and secure. A behaviour policy should include:

★ the play setting's aims and underlying principles for behaviour
★ the roles and responsibilities of playworkers
★ ground rules for children/young people
★ how positive behaviour will be promoted
★ strategies for dealing with unacceptable behaviour, including bullying
★ how the policy will be implemented
★ the use of rewards and sanctions
★ monitoring and reviewing procedures for the policy.

The policy should ensure consistency by providing clear guidelines for playworkers on its implementation as well as practical advice to parents and carers on how they can help. This information could be included in documents such as the staff handbook and the setting's brochure. The policy must be based on clear values (e.g. respect, fairness and inclusion) that are also reflected in the setting's aims and equal opportunities policy.

 KEY TASK

1. Find out about the behaviour policy for your setting.
2. List the key points of the policy.
3. Describe how you have developed and improved the setting's behaviour policy.

NVQ links – Level 2: PW1.2; Level 3: PW8.3, PW6.2

The benefits of positive behaviour

Promoting positive behaviour can bring many benefits to children, young people and playworkers. These include:

- ☆ the security and stability of a welcoming and pleasant play environment
- ☆ positive social interaction between children and staff
- ☆ encouraging children's independence, confidence and positive self-esteem
- ☆ providing consistent care for children, with clear rules and boundaries
- ☆ creating a positive framework with realistic expectations for children's behaviour
- ☆ positive motivation through praise, encouragement and rewards
- ☆ encouraging staff confidence in supporting children's play
- ☆ a positive atmosphere that makes working with children more enjoyable.

There are also potential benefits for society, such as:

- ☆ more positive social interactions including friendships, clubs, etc.
- ☆ re-development of community spirit and belief in citizenship
- ☆ positive attitudes towards others (e.g. equal opportunities, racial harmony)
- ☆ research shows that children who have positive early years experiences are less likely to go on to experience 'juvenile delinquency' and adult unemployment (Ball, 1994).

Praise and encouragement are essential components when promoting positive behaviour. All children need immediate and positive affirmations or rewards to show that their behaviour is progressing in accordance with expectations. You should emphasise the *positive* aspects of each child's attempts at demonstrating appropriate behaviour. Children must be praised and/or rewarded for *effort* not just achievement. Use praise to encourage children and young people to behave in acceptable ways and to raise their self-esteem.

Praise and encouragement promote positive behaviour in children by encouraging emotional well-being and high self-esteem, strong motivation for behaving in positive ways, positive attitudes to behaviour and learning, and effective communication and social interaction.

Rewards

Rewards can provide incentives for positive behaviour. Children and young people can be motivated by rewards such as:

- ☆ being given verbal praise
- ☆ choosing a favourite activity
- ☆ having a special responsibility
- ☆ receiving smiley faces, stars or stamps
- ☆ receiving stickers or badges.

Rewards are most effective when they:

- ★ provide positive feedback about a specific behaviour, effort or achievement
- ★ are sincere and given with maximum attention
- ★ recognise effort not just achievement, especially with difficult activities or goals
- ★ encourage children to focus on their *own* individual behaviour or achievement
- ★ show the adult's positive expectations for the child's behaviour.

EXERCISE: What methods do you use to provide praise and encouragement for children's behaviour in your setting? Give examples from your own experiences of promoting positive behaviour.

Seven ways to promote positive behaviour

1. **Keep rules to a minimum**. Children will often keep to a few rules if they have some freedom. Explain why certain rules are necessary (for safety, say). All children should learn to understand the need for rules, but they also need to develop their own self-control and to make their own decisions regarding behaviour.

2. **Be proactive**. This means preparing things in advance, including having the correct materials and equipment ready for play activities. You should also be clear about the behaviour guidelines for the children you work with and what your responsibilities are for dealing with any problems that might occur.

3. **Be positive**. Once ground rules have been set, encourage children to keep them through rewards. Reward positive behaviour using verbal praise and other positive incentives. Keep smiling! A sense of humour goes a long way.

4. **Ignore certain behaviour**. It may be appropriate to ignore some unwanted behaviour, especially attention-seeking or behaviour that is not dangerous or life-threatening. Sometimes it is not possible or appropriate to ignore unwanted behaviour (if a child is in danger, say). With younger children it may be more effective to distract the child (perhaps by playing a game) or to divert their attention to another activity.

5. **Be consistent**. Once rules, goals and boundaries have been negotiated and set, stick to them. Children need to know where they stand; they feel very insecure if rules and boundaries keep changing for no apparent reason. They need to understand that 'no' always means 'no', especially where safety is concerned.

6. **Know the children you work with**. An awareness of a child's home background, previous behaviour in school or other play setting, including any special needs, influences the way you respond to potentially disruptive children. Use a variety of techniques; different children respond differently to different methods (for example, a reminder of a ground rule may be sufficient or you may need to give a specific warning).

7. **Keep calm!** Be calm, quiet, firm and in control; shouting only makes matters worse. If you feel you are losing control, count to five and then proceed calmly. You may need to use strategies like time out to give the child a chance to calm down, but keep it short (just a few seconds) until the child is a little calmer.

Dealing with negative behaviour

The adult response to a child's behaviour is as important as the behaviour itself. Different people have different attitudes to what is or is not acceptable behaviour. The social context also affects adult attitudes towards children's behaviour (see above). All adults should consider certain types of behaviour unacceptable; these include behaviour that causes physical harm to others, self-harm, emotional/psychological harm to others, and destruction to property.

Key indicators of unwanted behaviour include having:

* ☆ limited attention span and concentration levels
* ☆ restricted range of communication skills
* ☆ hostile, uncaring or indifferent attitude towards others
* ☆ negative self-image and low self-esteem
* ☆ behaviour patterns that are inconsistent with expected development.

Children whose unwanted behaviour is demonstrated through aggressive or disruptive behaviour are usually the ones to attract the most adult attention, as they are easily identified and hard to ignore. Children who demonstrate unwanted behaviour in a withdrawn manner may be overlooked, especially by inexperienced adults or in a very busy setting.

Contributing factors that can affect children's behaviour include environmental, social or emotional factors such as bereavement or prolonged illness, divorce or separation, domestic violence or child abuse, moving house, changing school, and negative experiences in previous settings. Adults working in play settings may have little or no control over these contributing factors. But they *do* have control over additional factors such as their response to children's unwanted behaviour, insensitivity or inflexibility towards individual needs, inappropriate play opportunities, unwarranted disapproval from staff or other children in the setting, children who are being bullied.

Sanctions

While the emphasis should be on promoting positive behaviour through encouragement, praise and rewards, there may be times when these do not work. Sometimes it is necessary to impose sanctions for children or young people whose behaviour goes beyond acceptable boundaries or who break the ground rules of the play setting.

The setting should have a scale of sanctions for inappropriate behaviour. The behaviour policy should explain why these are necessary. Effective sanctions should be designed to discourage inappropriate behaviour rather than to punish children or young people who break the rules. Consistency in the application of sanctions is essential, and staff should use reprimands sparingly and fairly. Sanctions are more likely to discourage inappropriate behaviour if children and young people see them as being fair.

Fifteen ways to respond to persistent unwanted behaviour

1. **Consider past experiences**. Children learn about behaviour through their early relationships and experiences. No one's behaviour is static; they can acquire new behaviour patterns and discard behaviour that is ineffective or inappropriate.

2. **Remember adult influences on children's behaviour**. Adults working with children have a major influence on their behaviour. Adult responses to children's behaviour can make things better or worse. You may need to modify your own behaviour and responses.

3. **Be patient**. Changing children's behaviour takes time, so do not expect too much all at once. Take things one step at a time. Remember that behaviour may get worse before it gets better because some children will demonstrate even more challenging behaviour, especially if minor irritations are being ignored.

4. **Establish clear rules, boundaries and routine**. Children need to understand rules and the consequences if they do not follow them. They need clear boundaries as to what is or is not acceptable behaviour, with frequent reminders about these.

5. **Be consistent**. Adults should be consistent when responding to children with persistent unwanted behaviour or the children will become confused. Adults need to discuss and agree on responses to the child's behaviour. Playworkers should, where possible, work with the child's parents/carers so the child sees that everyone is working together to provide a consistent framework for behaviour.

6. **Use diversionary tactics**. You can sometimes divert the child from an emotional or aggressive outburst or self-damaging behaviour. Be aware of possible triggers to unwanted behaviour and intervene or divert the child's attention *before* difficulties begin. Being offered alternative choices or being involved in decision-making can also divert children.

7. **Encourage positive social interaction**. Help children develop their social skills so they can join in play activities with other children. Start off with one to one, then small groups and then larger groups. Play tutoring can help (e.g. using adult involvement to develop and extend social play).

8. **Help children find more positive ways to gain attention**. Most children want adult attention – it is the *way* they behave to gain attention that may need changing. Instead of being disruptive, children need to be encouraged to use more positive ways to get adult attention by asking or showing the adult that they have something to share.

9. **Help children to express their feelings**. Encourage children to express strong feelings such as anger, frustration or fear in positive ways (e.g. through play and communication). Young people need opportunities to express their grievances.

10. **Look at the play environment**. Identify, and where possible change, aspects of the play environment and routines within the setting that may be contributing towards the child's unwanted behaviour.

11. **Label the behaviour not the child**. Make sure any response to unwanted behaviour allows the child to still feel valued without any loss of self-esteem (e.g. 'I like you, Tom, but I don't like it when you …').

12 **Be positive**. Emphasise the positive and encourage children to be positive too. Phrase ground rules in positive ways (e.g. 'do' rather than 'don't'). Encourage children to focus on positive aspects of the setting (e.g. playing with friends, favourite activities).

13. **Use praise more than punishment**. Use regular positive feedback to encourage children to behave in acceptable ways and raise their self-esteem. Find out which kinds of rewards matter to them and use these. Rewarding positive behaviour is more effective than punishing unacceptable behaviour. Quiet reprimands are more effective than a public 'telling off', which only causes humiliation in front of others and increases the child's resentment towards the adult.

14. **Avoid confrontation if at all possible**. Use eye contact and the child's name to gain/hold their attention. Keep calm, sound confident and stay in control. If the child is too wound up to listen, give them a chance to calm down (e.g. 'time out').

15. **Give individual attention and support**. This encourages children to share their worries or concerns with a trusted adult. Time in involves giving children special individual attention to reinforce positive behaviour and decreases the need for them to gain adult attention through unwanted behaviour. It involves children talking with an adult about their day, including reviewing its positive aspects.

Sanctions are most effective when they:

- ★ balance against appropriate rewards
- ★ are reasonable and appropriate to the child's action so that major sanctions do not apply to minor lapses in acceptable behaviour
- ★ apply only to the child or children responsible and not the whole group
- ★ discourage unwanted/unacceptable behaviour without damaging the child's self-esteem
- ★ are used as a last resort; every effort should be made to be positive and to encourage acceptable behaviour through *positive* rather than negative reinforcement.

Sanctions for inappropriate behaviour may include:

- ★ staff registering disapproval and explaining why to children
- ★ staff warnings to children that their behaviour is unacceptable
- ★ 'time out' involving isolation of the child for a short period
- ★ child losing opportunity to do a favourite activity
- ★ child making a formal apology to those affected by their unacceptable behaviour
- ★ parents/carers being told at the end of the day or a letter being sent home outlining a serious incident
- ★ parents being invited in to the setting to discuss a serious incident
- ★ child being referred to the senior playworker.

Physical or corporal punishment is *not* an acceptable sanction (see page 158).

KEY TASK

1. Find out about your setting's policy for sanctions relating to children and/or young people's behaviour.
2. Describe why and how you have intervened when children and/or young people have demonstrated unwanted behaviour within the setting.

NVQ links – Level 2: PW1.2; Level 3: PW8.3

Helping children to deal with conflict themselves

Many young children may find it difficult to co-operate with other children in group activities. Disputes are frequent among young children. Often these disputes are short-lived; early friendships are easily broken but just as quickly mended. Learning to deal with these disputes is an important part of children's social and emotional development. Very young children will use physical force to maintain ownership of a toy, but by 3 to 4 years they begin to use language to resolve disputes (e.g. 'That's mine!'). By 5 to 6 years children continue to use language to resolve disputes and co-operate with others (e.g. 'After Shafiq's turn, it's my go'). Older children will use language to negotiate and compromise when there are disagreements (e.g. 'Let me borrow your blue felt-tip and you can use my red gel pen'). However, even some older children may sometimes find it difficult to share with others.

When working with children and young people it is inevitable that conflicts will arise involving arguments and fights between them. All children and young people will experience situations where they feel that life is not fair. They will have disagreements and disputes with others. Initially children rely on adults to help resolve these disputes, but gradually they learn how to deal with these for themselves. They need to learn how to use language to reach agreements so that as far as possible their needs and other people's can be met fairly.

There are only three possible ways to resolve conflicts:

1   to fight or bully – being aggressive ('I win so you lose')
2   to submit or retreat – being submissive or passive ('I lose because you win')
3   to discuss and negotiate – being assertive ('I win and you win').

Children and young people need to learn that the best way to resolve conflicts does not mean getting your own way all the time (being aggressive) or allowing others to get their own way all the time (being submissive or passive). The best way to resolve conflicts is to reach a satisfactory compromise by being assertive.

Point out to children and young people that shouting/physical violence never resolves conflicts but usually make matters worse and only demonstrates who is the loudest or strongest or has more power. Conflicts need to be discussed in a calm manner so that a mutually agreed compromise can be reached.

You can use books, stories and videos that depict potential conflict situations such as:

★ sharing play equipment or borrowing toys
★ deciding on rules for a game or choosing a game
★ choosing partners or teams fairly
★ knocking over models or spoiling activities *accidentally*
★ disrupting other children's play activities *deliberately*.

You could discuss the following with the children afterwards.

★ What was the cause of the conflict?
★ How was the conflict resolved?
★ What were the best solutions?
★ How would *they* resolve a similar conflict?

Younger children can do this type of activity with appropriate situations and guidance from sensitive adults. Using puppets and play people can also help. Where children and young people are used in role play or drama, adults can get them to act out how to resolve conflicts in peaceful ways.

You need to be aware of the setting's policy for dealing with conflicts, and be clear about your own responsibilities (for example, when and how to intervene, remembering children's and your own safety, procedures for reporting incidents, use of sanctions).

KEY TASK

1. Look at the conflict situations listed below. Suggest how children could deal with these themselves:
   - sharing play equipment
   - deciding on rules for a game or choosing a game
   - disrupting other children's play activities.
2. Describe how you have encouraged and supported children and/or young people in dealing with conflict for themselves.

NVQ links – Level 2: PW1.2; Level 3: PW8.3

Further reading

Burton, G. and Dimbleby, R. (1995) *Between Ourselves: An Introduction to Interpersonal Communication* (rev. edn). Arnold.

Elliott, M., Shenton, G. and Eirew, R. (1999) *Bully-free: Activities to Promote Confidence and Friendship*. Kidscape.

Houghton, D. and McColgan, M. (1995) *Working with Children*. Collins Educational.

Kamen, T. (2000) *Psychology for Childhood Studies*. Hodder & Stoughton.

Lindenfield, G. (1994) *Confident Children*. Thorsons.

Lyus, V. (1998) *Management in the Early Years*. Hodder & Stoughton.

Masheder, M. (1989a) *Let's Co-operate*. Peace Education Project.

Masheder, M. (1989b) *Let's Play Together*. Green Print.

Matthews, A. (1990) *Making Friends: A Guide to Getting Along with People*. Media Masters.

Petrie, P. (1989) *Communicating with Children and Adults: Interpersonal Skills for Those Working with Babies and Children*. Hodder Arnold.

Train, A. (1996) *ADHD: How to Deal with Very Difficult Children*. Souvenir Press.

Yeo, A. and Lovell, T. (1998) *Sociology for Childhood Studies*. Hodder & Stoughton.

9 Working with parents and carers

Key points

- ✿ The importance of good working relationships with parents and carers
- ✿ Helping parents and carers feel welcome and valued in the play setting
- ✿ Identifying the needs and expectations of parents and carers
- ✿ Effective communication with parents and carers
- ✿ Being sensitive to communication difficulties with parents and carers
- ✿ Handling conflicts with parents and carers
- ✿ Encouraging parents and carers to become involved in the play setting

The importance of good working relationships with parents and carers

Everyone benefits when the playworker develops an effective and positive working relationship with each parent or carer. Children and young people thrive when there is continuity of care from the adults who are most important in their lives, and parents' trust in you grows when the partnership is working well. A harmonious working relationship also enables you to promote children's and young people's physical and emotional well-being fully and gives you better job satisfaction.

To develop positive relationships with parents and carers you need to:

- ★ work co-operatively with parents and carers
- ★ perform your duties well

★ communicate openly and effectively

★ show sensitivity to family situations

★ seek constructive solutions to problems

★ maintain a consistent, positive attitude.

Four ways to develop positive relationships with parents and carers

The following guidelines may help you to foster positive relationships with parents and carers.

1. **Exchange information with parents and carers.**
   - Communication is the key to fostering a good relationship with parents and carers.
   - Keep the lines of communication open and deal with any problems as they occur, before they get out of hand.

2. **Respect each family's right to privacy.**
   - All matters relating to children and their families should be treated as private and confidential (see Chapter 10).
   - Parents/carers need to feel that you are trustworthy and will not gossip about them.
   - In the rare circumstance that you are concerned about a child's welfare, you should follow the setting's child protection procedures (see Chapter 6).

3. **Support parents' and carers' individuality and cultural/social background.**
   - Acknowledge the values, needs, expectations and ideas of parents, especially when there are disagreements (see below).
   - Your professional expertise must not be used to impose your ideas on parents, instead try to work *with* them to reach a reasonable compromise.

4. **Develop a partnership with parents and carers.**
   - A partnership between you and the parents/carers helps strengthen the playworker/parent relationship and provides the children with consistency.
   - Children may become confused when they receive contradictory messages from you and their parents or carers.

Helping parents and carers feel welcome and valued in the play setting

As a playworker, you should have a strong commitment to children and their parents or carers. At all times, you should behave towards parents and carers in a manner that shows personal courtesy and integrity. This includes:

★ helping them feel welcome and valued in the setting

★ seeking to establish a friendly and co-operative relationship with them

★ never distorting or misrepresenting the facts concerning any aspect of their child's play and development

- ✪ respecting the joint responsibility that exists between the setting and parents/carers for the development and well-being of their children
- ✪ respecting parental rights to enquiry, consultation and information with regard to the development of their children.

The setting should recognise that working in partnership with parents and carers is an important part of developing positive relationships between itself and the local community. Wherever possible, you should encourage parents to become actively involved in the life of the setting (see below). The setting should provide them with regular newsletters giving useful information on events or developments. Letters should also be sent to communicate specific information – about outings, say, or special visitors to the setting.

Welcome sign.

You should appreciate the difficulty experienced by some parents who are not in daily personal contact with the setting (for example, those whose children are brought or collected by a childminder). Ideally, the setting should operate an 'open door' policy, which means that parents are welcome to come and discuss any concerns with staff at any time.

Identifying the needs and expectations of parents and carers

Many parents and carers have expectations of the play setting that may not necessarily coincide with its own aims and values. Many parents may not even be aware of the importance of play to their children's development. The majority of parents rely on play settings to provide childcare when their children are not in school (for instance, at out-of-school clubs and holiday play schemes). Their choice of setting may not be determined by their children's play needs but by their own needs and expectations (for example, affordable quality childcare, availability and accessibility, hours that suit their work patterns, peace of mind that their children are being cared for in a safe environment).

When identifying the needs and expectations of parents and carers you should consider the family's cultural and social background as well as the expressed wishes of the parents. However, you must also follow the agreed policies and procedures with regard to the way you provide care and support for children and young people within the setting.

You may need to give parents positive reassurance about what their children are doing in the play setting (such as explaining the benefits of play to their child's development). Any concerns or worries expressed by a parent/carer should be passed immediately to the appropriate person in the setting. If a parent makes a request to see the senior playworker, then you should follow the relevant policy and procedures of the setting.

 KEY TASK

Describe how your setting establishes and develops positive working relationships with parents and carers, including:

- helping them feel welcome and valued in the setting
- respecting their individuality and cultural/social background
- identifying their needs and expectations
- respecting their wishes, as long as they are consistent with children's rights and the policies of the setting.

NVQ links – Level 2: PW1.3; Level 3: PW14.1, PW8.4

Effective communication with parents and carers

Parents usually know a lot about their children and their children's needs so it is important to listen to what they have to say. You should actively encourage positive relationships between parents (or designated carers) and the setting. Some parents may find you more approachable if you live in the local community and your own children attend the same setting.

When communicating with parents (or carers) use their preferred names and modes of address (the correct surname, for example). This is especially important when a woman has changed her name following divorce or remarriage. Only give information to a parent that is consistent with your role and responsibilities within the setting. Any information shared with parents must comply with the confidentiality requirements of the setting. When sharing information about a child with their parents ensure that it is relevant, accurate and up to date.

Sharing information is an essential part of working with children and their parents or carers. Playworkers will need essential information *from* parents including:

- ☆ routine information (e.g. medical history/conditions such as allergies; cultural or religious practices that may have implications for the care of the child, such as special diets; who delivers and collects the child, if applicable)
- ☆ emergency information (e.g. contact telephone numbers at work and home for parents/carers, GP)
- ☆ other information (e.g. factors that may adversely affect the child's behaviour, including family difficulties and crises such as divorce, serious illness or bereavement).

Remember to pass on information from parents to the relevant member of staff. Always remember *confidentiality* with regard to information provided by parents or carers (see Chapter 10).

Playworkers will also need to *give* parents information on:

- ☆ the main aims and objectives of the setting
- ☆ the age range of the children and/or young people
- ☆ adult/child ratios
- ☆ staff names, roles and qualifications
- ☆ the setting's opening hours
- ☆ admission and settling-in procedures
- ☆ record-keeping
- ☆ an outline of approaches to children's play and development
- ☆ the facilities for indoor and outdoor play
- ☆ arrangements for children with special needs, including the administration of medicines
- ☆ behaviour management, including sanctions for inappropriate behaviour
- ☆ procedures regarding food, drink, meal/snack times.

Five ways to encourage effective communication with parents and carers

You can encourage effective communication with parents and carers in the following ways.

1. **Being welcoming** and creating an environment that provides opportunities to talk with parents. Use a weekly newsletter to share information with parents and carers.
2. **Being clear** about the aims and objectives of the setting and sharing these with parents and carers.
3. **Being sensitive** when talking with parents and carers; being willing to share positive information about the child's play and development, not just the negative.
4. **Being tactful** when talking with parents and carers.
5. **Being attentive** and listening carefully to the parents' views and any particular concerns *they* may have concerning their child. Showing parents that their involvement in their child's care, play and development is respected and valued.

This information is usually given to parents and carers in the setting's brochure, prospectus or information pack. Information can also be communicated to parents and carers via letters, noticeboards, newsletters and open days.

KEY TASK

1. Give examples of how your setting provides clear and accurate information for parents and carers (e.g. copies of the setting's information pack or newsletters).
2. Find out about your setting's policy regarding confidential information from parents and carers.
3. What are your setting's policy and procedures for parents wishing to discuss the care, play and development of their children with the senior playworker?

NVQ links – Level 2: PW1.3; Level 3: PW14.1, PW8.1, PW8.4

Being sensitive to communication difficulties with parents and carers

You should use language that parents and carers are likely to understand. Try to avoid jargon or technical language – especially if you are not clear about its meaning! Requests for information that are beyond your role and responsibilities, or any difficulties in communicating with parents or carers, should be referred to the appropriate person, such as the senior playworker. You may need guidance on how to handle sensitive situations regarding your interactions with some parents and carers. This is especially the case where a parent or carer makes derogatory remarks about a particular playworker or setting policy. (There is more detailed information on communication difficulties with adults in Chapter 10.)

Playworkers who have additional communication skills may be very useful in the setting (say, being able to use sign language to communicate with a parent who has a hearing impairment, or bilingual playworkers who can liaise with parents whose community language is not English). Playworkers who share local community languages may help parents and carers feel more welcome and help to avoid possible misinterpretations concerning cultural differences. In multi-cultural Britain, playworkers with good local language skills can be a real asset to play settings.

EXERCISE: Describe how you have handled any communication difficulties with parents or carers in your setting. Remember: *confidentiality*.

Handling conflicts with parents and carers

You need to be able to recognise and respond to any problems that affect your ability to work effectively. This includes dealing appropriately with difficulties and conflict situations that affect your working relationships with parents and carers.

Conflicts and difficulties are part of everyone's working lives. If communication and working relationships break down, then conflict situations can arise that seriously damage the atmosphere in the setting. Conflicts can occur between: you and the children or young people; you and your colleagues; you and the children's or young people's parents/carers.

Most conflicts involving parents or carers arise due to:

☆ concerns about duties and responsibilities
☆ disagreements about children's behaviour
☆ clashes concerning different lifestyle choices.

Conflicts can also arise due to prejudice or discrimination. Evidence of such attitudes or behaviour must be challenged, as they are not only undesirable but also unlawful. Most difficulties and conflicts can be resolved through open and honest discussion. This will involve arranging a mutually convenient time to talk to the parents about the problem and will usually include the senior playworker.

Remember the following important points.

1. Focus on the facts by stating the exact nature of the problem.
2. Avoid making personal comments – be tactful!
3. Suggest a possible and practical solution.
4. Be prepared to compromise if at all possible.

The best way to resolve conflicts or disagreements is to be assertive by discussing and negotiating a compromise that suits everyone, to bring about a win/win solution to the problem. Remember, again, 'compromise equals wise'! (For more information on dealing with conflicts and complaints, including grievance procedures, see Chapter 10.)

KEY TASK

1. What are your setting's procedures for dealing with complaints from parents or carers?
2. Describe how you have handled a disagreement or misunderstanding with a parent or carer. Remember: *confidentiality*.

NVQ links – Level 2: PW1.3; Level 3: PW14.1, PW8.4

Encouraging parents and carers to become involved in the play setting

Encouraging parents and carers to get involved is an important part of developing links with the local community. You can encourage them to be more involved by ensuring that the setting is friendly, welcoming and accessible. You should encourage them to become actively involved in the day-to-day life of the setting – for example, as parent helpers or volunteers, or as participants in play committees, special events, outings and other activities.

You should actively encourage parents and carers to:

☆ engage in sport and play activities with their children (e.g. cycling, swimming, walking, playing board games)

☆ help in the setting (e.g. with play opportunities, with the provision of food and drinks, with administration, with preparation for trips and outings)

☆ share their expertise (arts and crafts, bilingual storytelling, and so on)

☆ join in with outings (e.g. visits to parks, playgrounds and sports facilities)

☆ participate in special events (e.g. puppet shows, theatre groups; fundraising for the setting, the local community, local and national charities)

☆ promote play services for their local community (see Chapter 12).

A parent getting involved in the play setting.

KEY TASK

1. List four ways to encourage parents and carers to become involved in the work of the play setting. Give examples from your own experiences of working with parents and carers.

2. Describe how you have supported parents and carers involved in the work of the setting, including:

   - ensuring they meet legal and organisational requirements
   - ensuring they understand and support the values of the setting
   - providing information on ground rules and setting procedures
   - finding opportunities appropriate to their needs and skills
   - monitoring their involvement, and providing guidance and support.

NVQ links – Level 3: PW14.2

Further reading

Meggit, C. and Sunderland, G. (2000) *Child Development: An Illustrated Guide*. Heinemann Educational.

O'Hagan, M. and Smith, M. (1999) *Early Years Child Care and Education: Key Issues*. Bailliere Tindall.

Petrie, P. (1997) *Communicating with Children and Adults: Interpersonal Skills for Early Years and Playwork*. Hodder Arnold.

Ramsey, R.D. (2002) *How to Say the Right Thing Every Time: Communicating Well with Students, Staff, Parents, and the Public*. Corwin Press.

Whalley, M. (1997) *Working with Parents*. Hodder & Stoughton.

Woolfson, R. (1994) *Understanding Children: A Guide for Parents and Carers – A Practical Guide to Child Psychology*. Caring Books.

10 Professional practice

Key points

- ✪ The importance of good working relationships with colleagues
- ✪ Carrying out agreed duties and responsibilities
- ✪ Effective teamwork
- ✪ Effective communication with colleagues
- ✪ Sharing information with colleagues
- ✪ Participating effectively in team meetings
- ✪ Providing support for colleagues
- ✪ Following organisational procedures for dealing with conflict
- ✪ The Children Act 1989 and play provision
- ✪ Equal opportunities and anti-discriminatory practice in the play setting
- ✪ Record-keeping
- ✪ The play setting's requirements regarding confidentiality
- ✪ Reflective practice
- ✪ Professional development and training opportunities

The importance of good working relationships with colleagues

Establishing and developing good working relationships with colleagues is important because this helps to maintain a positive play environment that benefits the children, young people and staff. Good working relationships also reflect the play setting's aims, such as:

- ★ providing a caring environment that fosters co-operation and respect
- ★ encouraging the children's development through play
- ★ delivering play opportunities in stimulating and appropriate ways
- ★ working in partnership with parents and the local community.

All playworkers should have a strong commitment to children, young people, colleagues, parents and the local community. You and your colleagues should behave at all times in a manner that demonstrates personal courtesy and integrity. You should actively seek to develop your personal skills and professional expertise.

With regard to colleagues in the play setting you should:

★ have a duty of care towards them
★ demonstrate an awareness of the work-related needs of others
★ remember confidentiality in discussions with colleagues concerning problems associated with their work
★ respect the status of colleagues, particularly when making any assessment or observations of their work
★ never denigrate a colleague in the presence of others
★ if relevant to your role, use maximum frankness and good faith in all matters relating to appointments to posts, and provide references that are fair and truthful (see Chapter 11).

With regard to your work commitments in the setting you should:

★ always have proper regard for the health, safety and well-being of children and/or young people, colleagues and yourself (see Chapter 5)
★ respect and fulfil your contractual obligations
★ respect the right of an individual to hold religious or political beliefs and do not seek to impose your own personal opinions in such matters
★ never misrepresent your professional qualifications and work experience
★ never canvass directly or indirectly in order to secure a post
★ ensure that other commitments (e.g. part-time employment or study) do not hinder your capacity to fulfil your contractual obligations
★ make careful and appropriate use of all resources provided.

Carrying out agreed duties and responsibilities

To function in an effective and professional manner you need to be clear about your role and responsibilities as a playworker. These will depend on the type of setting and your experience and/or qualifications. You should not be required to perform general duties or specific tasks that you are either not qualified or not allowed to do (for example, give first aid or administer medicines). However, do not refuse to perform a duty or task just because it is not in your job description as sometimes it may be necessary for everyone to help out (clearing away, cleaning up after a mess, and such like).

General duties

Here are some examples of the general duties you may be expected to do as part of your responsibilities as a playworker:

* ✭ check play equipment for safety
* ✭ set out and put away play equipment
* ✭ help with the administration of the setting
* ✭ provide drinks, meals and/or snacks for children.

Specific tasks

Here are some examples of the specific tasks you may be expected to do as part of your responsibilities as a playworker:

* ✭ plan and support play activities
* ✭ read or tell a story
* ✭ play a game with a group of children or young people
* ✭ provide appropriate assistance during a play activity
* ✭ report any problems or concerns to the senior playworker
* ✭ contribute to planning and review meetings
* ✭ escort children to/from the setting.

> EXERCISE: List examples of your own general duties and specific tasks.

Contract of employment

By law, most employees who are employed for a month or more must receive a written statement of employment within eight weeks of starting a job. The written statement or contract of employment must include the start date, the period of employment and notices, main duties, working hours, salary, holidays, sick pay and grounds for dismissal. You should make sure your contract of employment includes a job description that specifies your exact duties and responsibilities in detail. (See Chapter 11 for more information on employment rights.)

The responsibilities of the playworker

You need to know and understand what your exact responsibilities are. When you have this information, you will be clear about what is required from you when carrying out agreed duties and responsibilities. Details should be set out in your job description if you are already employed as a playworker. (See Chapter 11, page 230, for sample job description.)

KEY TASK

1. Draw up a job description for your ideal playwork job.
2. If you are already employed as a playworker, make sure you have a copy of your contract, including a job description specifying your exact duties and responsibilities.

NVQ links – Level 2: A52.1; Level 3: PW11.1

Effective teamwork

Much of adult life involves working with other people, usually in a group or team. Individuals within a team affect each other in various ways. Within the team there will be complex interactions involving different personalities, roles and expectations, as well as hidden agendas that may influence the behaviour of individual members of the team. Teamwork is essential when working closely and regularly with other people over a period of time.

Effective teamwork (which you can remember using the mnemonic 'TEAMWORK', below) is important because it helps all members of the team to:

* **T**ake effective action when planning and/or assigning agreed work tasks
* **E**fficiently implement the agreed work tasks
* **A**gree aims and values that set standards of good practice
* **M**otivate and support each other
* **W**elcome feedback about their work
* **O**ffer additional support in times of stress
* **R**eflect on and evaluate their own working practices
* **K**now and use each person's strengths and skills.

To be an effective team member you need to know and understand:

* the organisational structure of the setting
* your role and responsibilities
* the roles and responsibilities of other team members
* how to contribute to effective team practice
* how to participate in team meetings
* key policies, including anti-discriminatory practice, record-keeping, confidentiality
* your role and responsibilities in relation to these policies.

The organisational structure of the play setting

You need to know and understand the different roles of the team members in your setting and the process of decision-making within the team. Depending on the type of setting, you may be working as part of a team that includes some or all of the following:

- ✩ playwork manager, play centre manager or play scheme manager
- ✩ senior playworker, co-ordinator or supervisor
- ✩ other playworkers, including assistant playworkers
- ✩ parent helpers and/or other volunteers
- ✩ students on placement from college
- ✩ pupils on work experience from secondary school.

> EXERCISE:
> 1. Draw a diagram to show the organisational structure of your setting, including where you and your colleagues fit into this structure.
> 2. Outline the role and main responsibilities of each member of your particular team.

Effective communication with colleagues

Effective communication is essential for developing effective team practice. Look back at the list in Chapter 8 of interpersonal skills needed for effective communication with children and young people. Effective lines of communication are also important to ensure that all members of the team receive the necessary up-to-date information to enable them to make a full contribution to the life of the setting. Make sure you check any noticeboards, newsletters and/or staff bulletins for important information. You can also use informal opportunities such as breaks or lunchtimes to share information, experiences and ideas with other playworkers. You may find that a communications book or file is useful to complement regular meetings with other playworkers. If you are a new (or student) playworker you may benefit from the knowledge and understanding of existing playworkers; if you are an experienced playworker you can make a valuable contribution to the induction or ongoing training of new playworkers, possibly acting as a mentor.

Being sensitive to communication difficulties with colleagues

As a playworker you should use language that your colleagues (including parent helpers, volunteers and students) are likely to understand. Try to avoid jargon or technical language unless you are sure that they, too, understand its meaning. Any requests for information from colleagues that are beyond your knowledge and expertise, or any difficulties in communicating with colleagues should be referred to the appropriate person (the senior playworker, say). You may need guidance on how to handle sensitive situations regarding your interactions with some colleagues, especially where a colleague makes derogatory remarks about another playworker or disregards setting policy (see the section below on dealing with conflict).

KEY TASK

1. List examples of how you communicate with colleagues in your play setting.
2. Describe how you have handled any communication difficulties with colleagues in your setting. Remember: *confidentiality*.

NVQ links – Level 2: A52.1; Level 3: PW8.4

Sharing information with colleagues

You will be working as part of a team with other playworkers, including the senior playworker. Your colleagues will need regular information about your work (for example, feedback about play opportunities and updates about children's participation and/or developmental progress). Some of this information may be given orally (for instance, outlining a child's participation and developmental progress during a particular play activity or commenting on a child's behaviour). Even spoken information needs to be given in a professional manner – that is, to the appropriate person (the senior playworker, say) in the right place (not in a corridor where confidential information could be overheard) and at the right time (urgent matters need to be discussed with the senior playworker immediately while others may wait until a team meeting). Some information will be in written form (activity plans, noticeboards, newsletters, staff bulletins and records, and so on. (See the section on record-keeping, below.)

Serious concerns about a child's persistent unwanted behaviour should be discussed with colleagues, including the senior playworker. Remember confidentiality (see below). However, all adults working with children have a legal duty to report serious concerns about a child's welfare (for example, possible child abuse). Every play setting should have guidelines about child protection issues (see Chapter 6), as well as clear structures for sharing concerns about children's behaviour with colleagues, and appropriate ways to deal with these concerns. Be aware of your own role and responsibilities within this structure. You may need specialist advice, guidance or support to provide the best possible approaches to responding to some children's behavioural and/or emotional difficulties. (There is detailed information in Chapter 8 on dealing with children's unwanted behaviour.)

KEY TASK

1. List the methods you use to share information with colleagues in your setting.
2. Describe the method(s) you would use to share serious concerns with a colleague.

NVQ links – Level 2: A52.1 Level 3: PW11.1, PW11.2

Participating effectively in team meetings

You will be involved in regular staff or team meetings with other playworkers in the setting, including the senior playworker or playwork manager. These meetings will enable you to make relevant contributions to provide more effective support for children and/or young people, and to assist in the efficient organisation of the setting.

At these staff or team meetings you may discuss:

- ★ specific plans for children's play opportunities
- ★ the developmental progress made by children, including their achievements
- ★ any difficulties children may have in accessing play opportunities
- ★ appropriate resources and play approaches
- ★ plans for special events (e.g. visitors to the setting, outings, open days)
- ★ review and develop the policies of the setting.

You need to prepare for meetings carefully, especially if you have been asked to provide information (on a particular play opportunity, say, or on the progress of a child/young person with whom you work). Even if you are not required to make a specific contribution you still need to look at the meeting agenda and any relevant information in advance so that you can participate in discussions during the meeting. At team meetings, participate in ways that are consistent with your role and responsibilities in the setting. Ensure your contributions are relevant and helpful to the work of the team. Express your opinions in a clear, concise manner and demonstrate respect for the contributions made by other team members. Make notes during the meeting to remind yourself of any action you need to take as a result of the issues discussed and decisions made by the team.

KEY TASK

1. Participate in a staff or team meeting relevant to your role in the setting (for example, a meeting to discuss weekly or monthly plans for play opportunities for the children and/or young people who use the setting). (When doing this task, for reasons of confidentiality, you should avoid referring to meetings where problems concerning specific children or young people are discussed in detail.)

2. Make notes on the key points discussed at the meeting. With your team leader's (e.g. the senior playworker) permission, include a copy of the agenda.

3. Then consider the following points:
   - What preparation did you need to do before the meeting?
   - What was your contribution to the meeting?
   - What action did you need to take as a result of the meeting (e.g. were you set specific tasks and, if so, what were they)?

NVQ links – Level 2: A52.1; Level 3: PW11.1

Providing support for colleagues

As a member of a team, you need to relate positively to your colleagues by:

☆ being supportive towards them
☆ helping to reduce sources of stress
☆ challenging discrimination and prejudice (see the section on anti-discriminatory practice, below)
☆ improving your own performance (see the section on reflective practice, below).

To provide effective support for colleagues you need to know:

☆ the setting's expectations for children's play and development
☆ the aims and objectives for children's play
☆ the setting's expectations for behaviour
☆ the inclusion policy for children with disabilities.

You can also be supportive towards colleagues by being an attentive listener. Listening carefully to colleagues will enable you to recognise possible signs of stress. You can then respond by being sympathetic and understanding, offering to help directly if you can and/or giving information on sources of help and advice, such as:

★ help available within the setting

★ national and local advice lines

★ the Citizens Advice Bureau

★ counselling services such as Relate.

Ten ways to provide support for colleagues
1. working with other members of staff as part of a team
2. working in partnership with them to prepare and maintain the play environment
3. working in partnership with parents and carers
4. knowing and following relevant setting policies and procedures
5. attending staff or team meetings
6. helping to monitor and evaluate children's participation and developmental progress
7. providing feedback about children's play and behaviour
8. helping with play resources and setting administration
9. recognising and using personal strengths and abilities
10. developing skills through work-based training and other courses.

If you have concerns about a colleague with a serious problem ask the senior playworker about what to do next, but *always* remember to maintain confidentiality, especially if your colleague has told you something in confidence.

 KEY TASK

1. Describe how you have asked for help, information or support from your colleagues.
2. Give examples of how you have offered support to colleagues, including:
   - playworkers working at the same level as you
   - your line manager (e.g. the senior playworker)
   - staff for whom you are responsible.

NVQ links – Level 2: A52.1; Level 3: PW11.1, PW11.2

Following organisational procedures for dealing with conflict

You need to be able to recognise and respond to issues that affect the team's ability to work effectively. This includes dealing appropriately with difficulties and conflict situations that affect your working relationships with colleagues. This may mean taking direct action and/or reporting your concerns to someone who has the authority to deal with these difficulties (the senior playworker, say, or playwork manager) if you cannot resolve them or they are outside your role/beyond your capabilities.

Conflicts are a part of everyone's working lives. Most are usually minor and resolved quickly, especially when people work together effectively as a team. If communication and working relationships break down, then conflict situations can arise that seriously damage the atmosphere of the setting. Conflicts can occur between: colleagues; staff and senior management; staff and parents/carers; the play setting and the local authority.

Most conflicts at work arise due to:

- ★ concerns about workloads
- ★ disputes over pay and conditions
- ★ disagreements about management issues
- ★ clashes between personalities.

Conflicts can also arise due to prejudice or discrimination. Incidents of such attitudes or behaviour must be challenged, as they are not only undesirable but also unlawful. However, it is essential to follow the setting's policy and procedures, together with any relevant legal requirements, when dealing with these issues.

Many difficulties and conflicts within the setting can be resolved through open and honest discussion. Sometimes another person can act as a mediator to help those involved to reach a satisfactory agreement or compromise. Where serious difficulties or conflict situations cannot be resolved, then the setting should have a grievance procedure to deal with them. This usually involves talking in the first instance to your line manager (e.g. senior playworker) about the problem; they will then refer the matter to the senior manager (e.g. playwork manager). If the problem concerns your line manager, then you may need to talk to the playwork manager directly. You may also be asked to put your concerns in writing. If the matter cannot be resolved at this stage then, depending on the nature of the conflict, the setting's committee, the local authority or voluntary agency and relevant trades unions may be involved. Check with your line manager or the staff handbook for the exact procedures in your setting. (See the section in Chapter 11 on grievance and disciplinary procedures.)

KEY TASK

1. Outline you setting's procedures for dealing with conflict.
2. Describe how you have responded (or would respond) to a conflict situation in the play setting. (Be tactful and remember *confidentiality*!)

NVQ links – Level 2: A52.1; Level 3: PW11.3

The Children Act 1989 and play provision

You need to be aware of the Children Act 1989 in relation to play provision. The Act stresses the importance of play to children's all-round development:

> Children's need for good quality play opportunities changes as they grow up, but they need such opportunities throughout childhood in order to reach and maintain their optimum development and well-being. Under fives develop knowledge of themselves and their world through play… For school age children play is a means whereby they can develop a broader range of interests, complementary to subjects learned during school time, and a positive approach to use of leisure time.
>
> (DOH, 1997, Section 5.6)

The Act also highlights the importance of local authorities, the private sector and voluntary organisations providing a range of services for children and their families, including day care facilities and services for children's play. For example:

* drop-in centres
* family centres
* full and sessional day care
* open-access facilities
* parent and toddler groups
* playbuses
* playgroups
* toy libraries.

The Children Act provides guidance and regulations for standards of good practice in day care and other services for young children and their families. Under the terms of the Act, local authorities are required to regulate the day care and supervised activities provided for children aged under 8, including full and sessional day care, holiday play schemes, out-of-school clubs and open-access facilities. These standards have now been updated and are set out in the day care national standards.

The day care national standards

Depending on the type of play provision and the age of the children using the play facility the **Day Care and Childminding (National Standards) (England) Regulations 2003** may apply to your setting. There are 14 national standards, which are accompanied by supporting criteria for the five categories of day care and childminding provision (full day care, sessional day care, crèches, out-of-school care, childminding). Regulations under the Children Act 1989 require providers to meet the 14 standards and relevant supporting criteria. The national standards do not supersede other relevant legislation such as health and safety, food hygiene, fire and planning requirements.

The 14 national standards are as follows:

- **Standard 1 – Suitable person:** Adults providing day care, looking after children or having unsupervised access to them are suitable to do so.

- **Standard 2 – Organisation:** The registered person ensures that required adult:child ratios and training and qualifications requirements are met, and organises space and resources to meet the children's needs effectively.

- **Standard 3 – Care, learning and play:** The registered person meets children's individual needs and promotes their welfare. They plan and provide activities and play opportunities to develop children's emotional, physical, social and intellectual capabilities.

- **Standard 4 – Physical environment:** The premises are safe, secure and suitable for their purpose. They provide adequate space in an appropriate location, are welcoming to children and offer access to the facilities for a range of activities which promote their development.

- **Standard 5 – Equipment:** Furniture, equipment and toys are provided which are appropriate for their purpose and help to create an accessible and stimulating environment. They are of suitable design and condition, well maintained and conform to safety standards.

- **Standard 6 – Safety:** The registered person takes positive steps to promote safety within the setting and on outings and ensures proper precautions are taken to prevent accidents.

- **Standard 7 – Health:** The registered person promotes the good health of children and takes positive steps to prevent the spread of infection and appropriate measures when they are ill.

- **Standard 8 – Food and drink:** Children are provided with regular drinks and food in adequate quantities for their needs. Food and drink is properly prepared, nutritious and complies with dietary and religious requirements.

- **Standard 9 – Equal opportunities:** The registered person and staff actively promote equality of opportunity and anti-discriminatory practice for all children.

- **Standard 10 – Special needs (including special educational needs and disabilities):** The registered person is aware that some children may have special needs and is proactive in ensuring that appropriate action can be taken when such a child is identified or admitted to the provision. Steps are taken to promote the welfare and development of the child within the setting in partnership with the parents and other relevant parties.

- **Standard 11 – Behaviour:** Adults caring for children in the provision are able to manage a wide range of children's behaviour in a way which promotes their welfare and development.

- **Standard 12 – Working in partnership with parents and carers:** The registered person and staff work in partnership with parents to meet the needs of the children, both individually and as a group. Information is shared.

- **Standard 13 – Child protection:** The registered person complies with local child protection procedures approved by the Area Child Protection Committee and ensures that all adults working and looking after children in the provision are able to put the procedures into practice.

- **Standard 14 – Documentation:** Records, policies and procedures which are required for the efficient and safe management of the provision, and to promote the welfare, care and learning of children are maintained. Records about an individual child are shared with the child's parent.

(DfES, 2003: 6–8)

Equal opportunities and anti-discriminatory practice in the play setting

It is important to show sensitivity to the needs of all children and young people in the setting. They all need to feel valued and accepted by others, especially if they might feel different from the rest of the group due to a disability or because of their race/culture. As a playworker, you must have a positive attitude and be able to learn how to encourage children and young people, including those with disabilities, to maximise their individual potential.

Legislation relating to equal opportunities and disability discrimination

As a playworker you must know and understand the basic requirements of legislation relating to equal opportunities and disability discrimination. The **Sex Discrimination Act 1975** and the **Race Relations Act 1976** made it unlawful to discriminate on the grounds of sex, race, colour, ethnic or national origin. These acts, with subsequent amendments, established statutory requirements to:

- ✰ prevent discrimination
- ✰ promote equality of opportunity
- ✰ provide redress against discrimination.

Amendments to these acts and the recent **Disability Discrimination Act 1995** have developed and extended anti-discrimination legislation. The **Race Relations (Amendment) Act 2000** introduced new statutory duties for the public sector, including actively promoting race equality. Under a new EU directive the grounds for discrimination will go beyond the three main areas of gender, race and disability (discussed in this chapter) to include age, religious belief and sexual orientation. Individual rights are also protected by the **Data Protection Act 1998**, **Human Rights Act 1998** and **Freedom of Information Act 2000**.

Useful websites with summaries of equal opportunities and disability discrimination include:

- ✰ Commission for Racial Equality – www.cre.gov.uk
- ✰ Disability Rights Commission – www.drc-gb.org
- ✰ Equal Opportunities Commission – www.eoc.org.uk.

Challenging discrimination and prejudice

All play settings have an equal opportunities policy with procedures to ensure that it is implemented. You must follow the setting's policy and procedures, together with any relevant legal requirements when dealing with these issues.

As a playworker, you should:

★ challenge discrimination or prejudice when necessary (for example, if a colleague makes a derisory comment about a person's race, culture or disability, you should tell them why it is unacceptable to express their views in this way)

★ state that you will not condone views that discriminate against another person

★ provide support for children, young people and adults who experience discrimination or prejudice by encouraging them to respond with positive action

★ follow the relevant setting policy and procedures.

 KEY TASK

Describe how you have challenged (or would challenge) discrimination or prejudice in the play setting. Remember: *confidentiality*.

NVQ links – Level 3: PW11.2

Diversity and inclusion in the play setting

As a playworker you must know and understand the importance of diversity and inclusion in the setting. You must never express stereotyped views relating to a person's culture, race, gender or disability.

Cultural diversity

Children and young people are influenced by images, ideas and attitudes that create prejudice and lead to discrimination or disadvantage. Research shows that by the age of 5, many white children believe black people are inferior; while many black children believe that they are viewed with less respect than white people. Children are not born with these attitudes – they learn them. Unfortunately, racism *does* exist in both urban and rural communities. All play settings, even those with few or no ethnic minority children and young people, must take action to challenge and prevent racism. Adults in play settings have an important role to play in promoting children's and young people's positive attitudes towards themselves, other people and other cultures.

Adults working with children and young people must not have stereotyped views about their potential or have low expectations of those from particular ethnic or cultural groups. Many ethnic-minority families have a strong commitment to their local communities and their children's well-being. Different child-rearing practices are evident in different cultures, but differences are also apparent in different families within the same culture.

You need to:

- ★ recognise and eliminate racial discrimination
- ★ maximise each child's motivation and potential
- ★ encourage each child to feel a positive sense of identity
- ★ ensure the play environment reflects children and their cultures in positive ways.

Gender issues

Research shows that by the age of 5, gender identity is clearly established. Children think that girls are more polite, easily hurt and open about showing their feelings, and boys are more capable, stronger and aggressive. The origins of these perceived differences between boys and girls can be difficult to work out, because social conditioning begins from birth, especially the expectations for female and male behaviour. These expectations are reinforced throughout childhood by parents, siblings, and other family members, as well as by other adults and children in the following ways: the clothes and toys given to children; comments on children's behaviour; expectations for children's play and learning. Stereotyped gender expectations are also reinforced through advertising, TV programmes, magazines, comics and books. Gender stereotyping is especially damaging to the self-image and identity of girls because it can lessen their confidence and lower their self-esteem. Boys, too, can be limited by gender stereotypes by being forced to behave in tough or less caring ways in order to conform and be accepted by others.

As a playworker, you should:

- ★ challenge gender stereotypes in the media, literature and everyday life
- ★ give all children and young people opportunities to play with a wide variety of toys, games and play equipment
- ★ provide role-play opportunities (including dressing-up clothes), especially for younger children, which allow them to explore different roles
- ★ ensure that neither gender thinks they are superior to the other
- ★ expect the same standards of behaviour from all children regardless of gender.

Disability awareness

Children and young people with disabilities can also be affected by stereotypical images. For example, seeing stereotyped images of disability in the media (or the total absence of disabled people, especially in magazines); being labelled by their disability rather than viewed as an individual; having restricted or limited choices; being viewed as 'handicapped'; being seen as disabled and therefore having to fit into the 'able' world.

The medical model of disability

The medical model of disability sees people with disabilities as having the problem. They have to adapt to fit into the world as it is. If this is not possible, then they are excluded in specialised institutions or isolated in their homes. The medical model of disability emphasises the person's impairment and provides support for stereotypical views of disability that evoke pity, fear and patronising attitudes towards disabled people. The medical model creates a cycle of dependency and exclusion. In addition, the design of the physical environment (such as play, leisure, school and work facilities) presents disabled people with many barriers, making it very difficult or sometimes impossible for their needs to be met, and limiting their day-to-day activities (Disability Equality in Education, www.diseed.org.uk).

The social model of disability

The social model of disability views the barriers that prevent disabled people from participating in any situation as what disables them. The social model suggests that disabled people are individually and collectively disadvantaged by a complex form of institutional discrimination as fundamental to our society as sexism and racism. Disabled people are often made to feel that it is their fault that they are different. The only difference is that they have an impairment that limits their physical, mental or sensory functions. Restructuring physical environments and accepting people with disabilities for who they are, without fear, ignorance or prejudice, would benefit everyone (Disability Equality in Education, www.diseed.org.uk).

As a playworker, you should:

★ recognise the disabled child/young person as an individual, not by their condition or impairment (e.g. child *with* autistic tendencies not autistic child)

★ provide positive role models of people with disabilities

★ recognise the potential of *all* children and young people

★ have high but realistic expectations for *all* children and young people

★ encourage the 'able' world to adapt to children and young people with disabilities, not the other way round.

MEDICAL MODEL THINKING	SOCIAL MODEL THINKING
Child is faulty	Child is valued
Diagnosis	Strengths and needs defined by self and others
Labelling	Identify barriers and develop solutions
Impairment becomes focus of attention	Outcome-based programme designed
Assessment, monitoring, programmes of therapy imposed	Resources are made available to ordinary services
Segregation and alternative services	Training for parents and professionals
Ordinary needs put on hold	Relationships nurtured
Re-entry if normal enough *or* permanent exclusive	Diversity welcomed: child is included
Society remains unchanged	Society evolves

The differences between the medical and social models of disability.
(From Disability Equality in Education website.)

Twelve ways to promote equal opportunities and anti-discriminatory practice

1. Books and stories about real-life situations with people the children can identify with.

2. Posters, pictures, photographs, displays, jigsaws, puzzles, toys and other play materials that reflect positive images of race, culture, gender and disability.

3. Activities that encourage children to look at their physical appearance in a positive light (e.g. games looking in mirrors, self-portraits (ensuring paints provided for all skin tones), drawing round each other to create life-size portraits).

4. Activities that encourage children to focus on their skills and abilities in positive ways (e.g. an 'I can ...' tree, with positive statements about what each child *can* do).

5. Activities that encourage children to express their likes and dislikes, plus confidence in their own name and who they are (e.g. circle games such as 'The Name Game', where each child takes it in turn to say 'My name is ... and I like to ... because ...', or 'Circle Jump', where each child takes a turn at jumping into the circle, making an action that they feel expresses them and saying 'Hello, I'm ...'; then the rest of the children copy the action and reply 'Hello ... [repeating the child's name]').

6. Sharing experiences about themselves and their families through topics like 'All About Me', and by inviting family members such as parents/grandparents to come in to the setting to talk about themselves and their backgrounds.

7. Providing opportunities for imaginative/role play that encourages children to explore different roles in positive ways (e.g. dressing-up clothes, cooking utensils, dolls and puppets that reflect different cultures).

8. Visiting local shops, businesses and community groups that reflect the cultural diversity of the setting and the local community.

9. Inviting visitors in to the setting to talk positively about their roles and lives (e.g. (female) police officer or fire-fighter, (male) nurse, people with disabilities or from ethnic minorities). (Note: avoid tokenism, include these visitors as part of ongoing topics.)

10. Celebrating cultural diversity by celebrating the major festivals of the faiths in the local community (e.g. Diwali (Hindu), Channuka (Jewish), Christmas (Christian)).

11. Valuing language diversity by displaying welcome signs and other information in community languages (see page 183).

12. Providing positive examples of:
    - black/Asian people and women from all ethnic groups in prominent roles in society (e.g. politicians, doctors, lawyers, business people, teachers)
    - black/Asian people's past contributions to politics, medicine, science, education, and so on; look at important historical figures like Martin Luther King, Mahatma Gandhi and Mary Seacole
    - people with disabilities participating fully in modern society, such as Stephen Hawking, David Blunkett and Marlee Matlin, as well as famous people from the past like Louis Braille, Helen Keller and Franklin D. Roosevelt.

KEY TASK

1. Compile a resource pack that promotes equal opportunities. You might include the following information and resources:
   - posters, wall charts, photographs and pictures
   - booklets and leaflets
   - suggested activities
   - list of relevant children's books and stories
   - list of useful organisations and addresses.
2. Plan, implement and evaluate at least one activity suggested in your resource pack.

NVQ links – Level 3: PW6.3, PW8.1

Inclusion

You should know how to judge whether your setting is inclusive and supportive of diversity, and should be able to demonstrate that you support inclusion and diversity through your words, actions and behaviours in the setting. You must know and understand the importance of promoting the setting to children and young people who may experience barriers to participation (for example, children and young people with disabilities or those from other minority groups).

Inclusion is about children's and young people's right to:

★ attend their local mainstream settings
★ be valued for who they are
★ be provided with all the support they need to thrive in a mainstream setting.

Inclusive provision should be seen as an extension of the play setting's equal opportunities policy and practice. It requires a commitment from the whole staff, parents, children and young people to include the full diversity of children and young people in the local community. This may require planned restructuring of the whole setting.

Disabled child in a play setting.

You must know and understand how to identify good inclusive provision and practice in the play setting. Kidsactive defines inclusive provision as: 'provision that is open and accessible to all, and takes positive steps in removing disabling barriers, so that disabled and non-disabled people can participate' (Douch, 2004). The inclusion indicators listed in the accompanying box may help you to identify whether inclusion is being put into practice in your setting.

Inclusion indicators

1. **Visitors can see:**
   - nobody makes a fuss about the presence of disabled children
   - activities are designed around the interests and enthusiasms of all children who attend, and with regard to any dislikes or impairments they may have
   - each person, adult or child, is welcomed on arrival
   - all children, including disabled children, have choices and are able to exercise those choices

2. **The leader/manager:**
   - has sought out families, schools and services for disabled children, and built links to promote the involvement of disabled children
   - runs regular staff meetings that are designed to enable staff to reflect on their practice together and develop good future practice
   - can identify action taken and progress made towards inclusion, and also the things s/he still needs and plans to do to make the setting more inclusive.

3. **The staff:**
   - have received disability equality training and/or attitudinal training and continue to undertake other training relating to inclusion
   - feel that they are consulted and informed by the leader/manager.

4. **Disabled and non-disabled children:**
   - report being involved in making rules/policies or 'having a say in what goes on'
   - say they are generally happy with the setting.

5. **Parents of disabled and non-disabled children:**
   - feel welcome and valued
   - say they are consulted about how best to meet their children's needs.

6. **Policies and paperwork indicate that:**
   - a commitment to inclusion is explicit in public and internal documentation
   - staff who have particular support roles with individual disabled children are full members of the team and have job descriptions that stress the inclusion of the child rather than just one-to-one support.

(Douch, 2004)
(Copyright Philip Douch and Kidsactive, 2004.)

You should also know the types of support that children and young people may need to access, and make the best use of play opportunities within the setting (for example, adapting activities, equipment, materials and timing as necessary to meet individual needs).

You can show that you support inclusion and diversity by:

- ✮ providing a positive role model for diversity and inclusion by treating all children, parents and colleagues with courtesy and respect
- ✮ acknowledging and celebrating diversity within the setting
- ✮ portraying people from diverse cultural and social backgrounds in positive ways
- ✮ ensuring that the play opportunities and resources available are accessible to everyone
- ✮ providing appropriate forms of support to children and young people who may experience barriers to participation within the setting
- ✮ encouraging self-confidence and self-esteem in children and young people
- ✮ challenging and dealing with inappropriate words and behaviour
- ✮ promoting diversity and inclusion to children, young people, parents and colleagues.

KEY TASK

1. Find out about your setting's policies and procedures for diversity and inclusion, including:
   - cultural diversity
   - disability awareness
   - equal opportunities.
2. What is *your* role in promoting diversity and inclusion?

NVQ links – Level 3: PW6.3, PW8.1, PW11.2

Record-keeping

Every play setting keeps a variety of records, including essential personal information for each child or young person using the facility. The setting will also have contact details for the person responsible for the setting, staff and volunteers. Play settings also have records relating to administrative duties (such as permission slips for outings and requisition forms for play resources). Records may also include observations and assessments of the children's participation and developmental progress (see Chapter 3), and activity plans, with evaluations of the effectiveness of the play opportunities (see Chapter 4). There will also be staff records relating to job applications and appointments (see Chapter 11).

The importance of record-keeping

It is essential to keep records in order to:

- ☆ monitor children's participation and developmental progress
- ☆ provide accurate and detailed information regarding play and behaviour
- ☆ determine the effectiveness of the play activities
- ☆ determine the effectiveness of adult support or intervention
- ☆ give constructive feedback to children and/or young people
- ☆ share information with parents, colleagues and sometimes other professionals
- ☆ identify and plan for new play opportunities
- ☆ facilitate effective administration in the setting.

Collecting and organising records

The types of record you will need to keep will depend on the type of play setting. Where, when and how to record information should be as directed by the senior playworker. Personal information about the children and/or young people who use the play facility is usually collected from the parents/carers as part of the registration process. The registration form should include the following information for each child or young person:

- ☆ home address and telephone number
- ☆ emergency contact details (e.g. names and telephone numbers for parents/carers, GP)
- ☆ medical history/conditions such as allergies and dietary needs
- ☆ cultural or religious practices that may have implications for the care of the child, such as special diets
- ☆ who collects the child (if applicable) including the transport arrangements (such as taxi or minibus) for a child with disabilities.

Examples of other records and key information include:

- ☆ accident/incident forms
- ☆ administration of medicines
- ☆ attendance registers
- ☆ fire drill records
- ☆ infectious, notifiable diseases
- ☆ insurance documents
- ☆ forms for outings
- ☆ record of visitors
- ☆ risk assessments.

Requests for records or information from colleagues should be dealt with professionally and handed in on time. This is particularly important if the information is needed for a meeting or review as any delay may stop others

GREEN FIELDS OUT-OF-SCHOOL CLUB
Registration Form

Personal Details:

Child's Name: _____ Date of Birth: _____

Home Address: _____

_____ Home Telephone No.: _____

School's Name and Address: _____

_____ School Telephone No.: _____

Contact Details:

1. Parent's Name and Address: _____

Home Telephone No.: _____ Work Telephone No.: _____

2. Parent's Name and Address: _____

Home Telephone No.: _____ Work Telephone No.: _____

Emergency Contact Details:

1. Name: _____ Telephone No.: _____

2. Name: _____ Telephone No.: _____

3. Name: _____ Telephone No.: _____

Medical Details:

GP's Name and Address: _____

_____ GP Telephone No.: _____

Please state any known medical conditions or allergies: _____

Please state any special dietary requirements including the child's food preferences:

_____

I give my consent to any emergency treatment required for my child while at the

Green Fields Out-of-School Club.   Yes/No

Signed _____ Dated _____

All records are confidential and kept in accordance with the Data Protection Act 1998.

Record sheet – registration form.

from performing their responsibilities effectively. Remember to maintain confidentiality as appropriate to your setting's requirements (see below).

It is important that records are complete, legible and updated on a regular basis. Emergency contact information must always be up to date. How often updating is necessary depends on the different types of record that you make a contribution towards.

Storing records

You need to know the exact policy and procedures for storing records in the play setting. You should also know what your own roles and responsibilities are regarding the storage of records. Most records relating to children and staff should be stored and locked away, but should be kept where playworkers can reach them easily.

You must maintain the safe and secure storage of the setting's records at all times. You should not leave important documents lying around; always put them back in storage after use. As well as the physical security of records, you need to be aware of levels of staff access to information. You should never give out the passwords to the setting's equipment (e.g. computers) unless you have permission from the member of staff responsible for the record-keeping systems.

Accessing information

Confidentiality is important with regard to record-keeping and the storing of information. Only the appropriate people should have access to confidential records. Except where a child is potentially at risk, information should not be given to other agencies unless previously agreed. Where the passing of confidential information is acceptable, then it should be given in the agreed format. Always follow the setting's policy and procedures regarding confidentiality and the sharing of information. Check with the senior playworker if you have any concerns about these matters. (See below for more information on confidentiality.) You should also be aware of any legal requirements with regard to record-keeping and accessing information in your setting (for instance, the Data Protection Act 1998 – see below).

The basic provisions of the Data Protection Act 1998 relevant to the playworker

Under the Data Protection Act 1998, settings processing personal information must comply with the following enforceable principles of good practice. Personal data must be:

1. fairly and lawfully processed
2. processed for limited purposes
3. adequate, relevant and not excessive
4. accurate
5. not kept longer than necessary
6. processed in accordance with the data subject's rights
7. stored securely.

The Act safeguards the storage of data kept on computers, including hard drives and floppy disks. All records relating to personal information must be kept securely within the setting, and the person to whom the records refer should have access to them.

Under the Data Protection Act 1998:

... an individual is entitled:

(a) to be informed by any data controller whether personal data of which that individual is the data subject are being processed by or on behalf of that data controller,

(b) if that is the case, to be given by the data controller a description of –

(i) the personal data of which that individual is the data subject,

(ii) the purposes for which they are being or are to be processed, and

(iii) the recipients or classes of recipients to whom they are or may be disclosed,

(c) to have communicated to him in an intelligible form –

(i) the information constituting any personal data of which that individual is the data subject, and

(ii) any information available to the data controller as to the source of those data ...

(Data Protection Act, 1998, Section 7(1))

KEY TASK

1. Give examples of the types of record used in your setting.
2. Outline the record-keeping systems and procedures used within your setting.
3. What is your setting's policy for the storage and security of records containing personal information about children, including confidentiality requirements?
4. What are your responsibilities concerning record-keeping?

NVQ links – Level 2: A52.1; Level 3: PW8.4, PW15.1, PW15.2

The play setting's requirements regarding confidentiality

You may find that the parents or carers of the children and/or young people you work with will talk to you about their problems or give you details about their family. Senior staff at your setting may also tell you confidential information to help you understand the needs of particular children or young people and so enable you to provide more effective support. Whether it is a parent or colleague that gives you confidential information, you must not gossip about it. However, you may decide to pass on information to colleagues on a 'need to know' basis – for example, to enable other members of staff to support a child's play and development more effectively or where a child might be in danger.

If you think that a child is at risk then you must pass on confidential information to an appropriate person (such as the senior playworker or the playworker in your setting who is responsible for child protection issues). If you decide to pass on confidential information then you should tell the person who gave you the information that you are going to do this and explain that you have to put the needs of the child first. (For information on confidentiality in child protection matters see Chapter 6.) Remember that every family has a right to privacy and you should only pass on information in the genuine interests of the child or to safeguard their welfare.

Reflective practice

In this chapter we have seen how being an effective team member involves making an individual contribution through your participation in team meetings and working with your colleagues to provide better support for the children and/or young people who use your setting. Here we look at how having a reflective attitude will help you to review and develop your professional practice as a playworker.

Looking after yourself

In order to make a more effective contribution to the work of the setting you need to:

- ★ develop and maintain confidence in your own abilities
- ★ maintain or improve your self-esteem
- ★ practise assertiveness techniques
- ★ take care of your emotional well-being.

Self-esteem is developed from childhood; some children and adults have feelings of low self-esteem that have negative effects on their confidence in their own abilities. You may need to develop your own feelings of self-worth to improve your self-esteem (see Chapter 7 and the 'Further reading' section at the end of this chapter).

Assertive people gain control over their lives by expressing personal feelings and exerting their rights in such a way that other people listen. Assertive individuals also show respect for other people's feelings. Practising assertiveness techniques involves:

- ☆ being aware of your own feelings
- ☆ putting your feelings into words
- ☆ connecting how you feel with the actions of others
- ☆ being aware of the other person's feelings
- ☆ arranging a specific time and place for a discussion
- ☆ making a statement showing you are aware of their feelings
- ☆ listening actively to their feedback.

(Houghton and McColgan, 1995)

Working with children or young people is a rewarding but often challenging or even stressful occupation. You need to take responsibility for your own emotional well-being and take the necessary action to tackle or reduce stress in your life. For example:

- ☆ develop assertiveness techniques
- ☆ take regular exercise including relaxation
- ☆ have a healthy diet
- ☆ manage your time effectively (see below).

Time management

Effective time management involves being clear about what you need to do and that you are able to do it. Unrealistic work goals lead to work tasks piling up, unnecessary stress, feeling overwhelmed, and time being wasted in unnecessary disagreements due to tempers flaring.

Ten essential steps to effective time management
1. Decide to use your time more effectively.
2. Check what you need to do, then prioritise: urgent/essential down to unimportant.
3. Make 'to do' lists in order of priority.
4. Estimate the time needed for tasks realistically.
5. Say 'No' or delegate if you cannot do a task in the time specified.
6. Forward-plan using a good diary.
7. Organise how you intend to do each task.
8. Do it!
9. Monitor or revise plans if necessary.
10. Value other people's time by being punctual for meetings and appointments.

Efficient organisation of the play environment can also contribute to more effective time management. For example:

- ★ a chalkboard or whiteboard may be used to indicate where people are in the setting
- ★ check that cupboards, desk drawers, filing cabinets, and so on, are clearly labelled
- ★ keep everything you need for specific tasks in one place
- ★ store items you use regularly in accessible places
- ★ throw away rubbish!
- ★ find out if there is a quiet room/area for undisturbed work or discussions.

EXERCISE:
1. How do you plan your time to include work duties, study requirements and home/family commitments?
2. Make a list of the ways you could manage your time more effectively.

Evaluating personal effectiveness

You need to know and understand clearly the exact role and responsibilities of your work (see the section on carrying out agreed duties and responsibilities, on page 191 of this chapter). Review your professional practice by making regular and realistic assessments of how well your working practices match your role and responsibilities. Share your self-assessments with those responsible for managing and reviewing your work performance (during your regular discussions/meetings with other playworkers, say, or with your line manager). You should ask other people for feedback about how well you fulfil the requirements and expectations of your role. You can also reflect on your own professional practice by making comparisons with appropriate models of good practice (for example, the work of more experienced playworkers within the setting).

Self-evaluation

Self-evaluation is needed to improve your own professional practice and to develop your ability to reflect upon activities and modify plans to meet the needs of the children and/or young people you work with. When evaluating your own practice, consider the following points.

- ★ Was your own contribution appropriate? Did you choose the right time, place and resources? Did you intervene enough or too much?
- ★ Did you achieve your goals (e.g. objectives/outcomes for the children and yourself)? If not, why not? Were the goals too ambitious or unrealistic?

- ★ What other strategies/methods could have been used? Suggest possible modifications.
- ★ Who can you ask for further advice (e.g. the senior playworker)?

Developing personal development objectives

To develop your effectiveness as a playworker, you should be able to identify your own personal development objectives, which are 'SMART' – that is:

- ★ **S**pecific
- ★ **M**easurable
- ★ **A**chievable
- ★ **R**ealistic
- ★ **T**ime-bound.

You should discuss and agree these objectives with those responsible for supporting your professional development. For example, you may consider that some of your work tasks require modification or improvement, and discuss possible changes with your line manager. Or you may feel that you lack sufficient knowledge and skills to implement particular activities and need to discuss opportunities for you to undertake the relevant training. To achieve your personal development objectives you should make effective use of the people, resources and other professional development or training opportunities available to you.

A professional portfolio highlighting your existing experience and qualifications can form the basis for assessing your training needs. This portfolio will also be a tangible record of your professional development and will help to boost your self-esteem. (See Chapter 1 for information on compiling a professional portfolio.)

KEY TASK

1. Describe how you review and improve your own work performance. Include:
   - your existing strengths and skills
   - skills and knowledge you need to improve
   - plans for improving your work and preparing for future responsibilities.
2. Identify your own SMART personal development objectives.
3. Compile your own professional portfolio if you do not already have one.

NVQ links – Level 2: A52.2; Level 3: PW10.1, PW10.2

Professional development and training opportunities

When assessing your personal development and training needs you should consider:

- ☆ your existing experience and skills
- ☆ the needs of the children and/or young people you work with
- ☆ any problems with how you currently work
- ☆ any new or changing expectations for your role.

Possible professional development and training opportunities for playworkers include:

- ☆ play and child development
- ☆ strategies for dealing with challenging behaviour
- ☆ best practice in play provision
- ☆ first aid training
- ☆ child protection
- ☆ equal opportunities workshops
- ☆ disability and inclusion training
- ☆ conflict resolution
- ☆ working with parents
- ☆ arts and crafts workshops
- ☆ drama and storytelling workshops
- ☆ games workshops.

Specific training and recognised qualifications for playworkers are also available (such as NVQ/SVQ Levels 2 and 3 in Playwork). (See Chapter 1 for detailed information on the playwork qualifications available, from introductory level through to degree level.) Funding for vocational courses in playwork may be available from your local authority. Training courses and qualifications can have a positive influence on improving the status of playworkers as well as enabling them to share examples of good practice with other playworkers. Play settings also benefit from having playworkers who are able to improve their expertise and increase their job satisfaction.

KEY TASK

1. Give examples of your participation in training and development opportunities.
2. Find out about the professional development and training opportunities for playworkers in your local area.

NVQ links – Level 2: A52.2; Level 3: PW10.2

Further reading

British Red Cross (2004) *Count Me In!* National Youth Agency and the British Red Cross. (A disability awareness training resource pack aimed at 13–25-year-olds. Suitable for youth work and other educational settings, the pack was developed by young Red Cross volunteers.)

Burton, G. and Dimbleby, R. (1995) *Between Ourselves: An Introduction to Interpersonal Communication* (rev. edn). Arnold.

Dare, A. and O'Donovan, M. (1997) *Good Practice in Caring for Children with Special Needs*. Stanley Thornes.

Houghton, D. and McColgan, M. (1995) *Working with Children*. Collins Educational.

Hughes, B. (2001) *Evolutionary Playwork and Reflective Analytic Practice*. Routledge.

Johnstone, D. (2001) *An Introduction to Disability Studies*. David Fulton Publishers.

Lindenfield, G. (2000) *Self Esteem: Simple Steps to Developing Self-Reliance and Perseverance* (rev. edn). HarperCollins.

Lindon, J. (1998) *Equal Opportunities in Practice*. Hodder & Stoughton.

Mortimer, H. (2002) *Special Needs Handbook*. Scholastic.

Roet, B. (1998) *The Confidence to be Yourself*. Piatkus.

Sallis, E. and Sallis, K. (1990) *People in Organisations*. Palgrave.

Siraj-Blatchford, I. (1994) *The Early Years: Laying the Foundations for Racial Equality*. Trentham Books.

Steiner, B. *et al.* (1993) *Profiling, Recording and Observing – a Resource Pack for the Early Years*. Routledge.

Tilstone, C. *et al.* (1998) *Promoting Inclusive Practice*. Routledge Falmer.

Woolfson, R. (1991) *Children with Special Needs – a Guide for Parents and Carers*. Faber & Faber.

Yeo, A. and Lovell, T. (1998) *Sociology for Childhood Studies*. Hodder & Stoughton.

11 Managing a play setting

Key points

- ⚙ The management role
- ⚙ Management skills
- ⚙ Managing a budget
- ⚙ Recruitment
- ⚙ Employment rights
- ⚙ Taking appropriate action to retain colleagues
- ⚙ Effective planning and fair allocation of work within your area of responsibility
- ⚙ Monitoring the progress and quality of work of individuals/teams
- ⚙ Identifying learning needs and providing learning opportunities for colleagues
- ⚙ Developing the work of the organisation

The management role

As a playwork manager or member of the senior management team, you may be responsible for managing one of these types of play setting: after-school club, breakfast club, out-of-school club, holiday play scheme or community project. The setting may be:

- ★ privately owned or voluntary managed
- ★ 'not for profit' or profit making
- ★ a charity, co-operative organisation, private company or social enterprise
- ★ a childcare setting providing play opportunities for school-aged children.

(SureStart, 2003a)

The people in a management team usually share the management of a play setting, with one person having overall responsibility. There should be a clear management structure with management duties carried out by different members of the management team. Members should know what their key responsibilities are within the team.

Management skills

To manage a play setting effectively you need to know and understand basic management skills, leadership styles and leadership skills. Basic management skills can be divided into four main categories:

1. **Managing resources:** securing funding, organising finances, managing a budget (including preparing, submitting and agreeing a budget for a set period), obtaining and/or creating appropriate resources.

2. **Managing people:** recruiting and retaining colleagues, motivating staff, providing training opportunities, working with parents and carers, working with difficult children, managing difficult team members and dealing with personality clashes, dealing with disciplinary issues.

3. **Managing activities:** effective planning and organisation (e.g. activity plans, work rota, holidays), monitoring children's play, development and participation in play activities.

4. **Managing information:** registration (including following legal requirements), day-to-day administration (e.g. daily attendance register), monitoring the progress and quality of work of individuals or teams.

Leadership styles

Leadership style affects the behaviours, beliefs and attitudes of people who work together as a team. It is also important in creating a positive atmosphere in the workplace by reducing work stress and promoting job satisfaction. There are three different leadership styles: autocratic, laissez-faire and democratic.

1. **Autocratic leadership:** this style of leadership demonstrates a lack of confidence and trust in colleagues. The team leader imposes decisions without consulting or involving other team members. There is little effective communication and few opportunities to be involved in the decision-making process within the setting. Team members feel that they are expected to follow instructions on their working practices without being critical or reflective.

2. **Laissez-faire leadership:** this style of leadership involves allowing colleagues to make their own decisions but providing some support as required. The whole team is responsible for day-to-day management, including budgeting and evaluating the effectiveness of the work in the setting. Team members may feel stressed and under pressure especially if there is a lack of guidance and support.

3. **Democratic leadership:** this style of leadership involves encouraging team members to contribute to the development of the setting's policies, procedures and practices, including the recruitment of staff. The team leader acknowledges and values the individual skills and contributions of each team member. Colleagues feel motivated and actively share their knowledge and experience for the mutual benefit and support of team members.

(Houghton and McColgan, 1995)

Leadership skills

A good team leader will have the ability to:

⭐ respond to the individual needs of team members

⭐ promote team spirit and co-operation between colleagues

⭐ motivate team members to carry out agreed tasks

⭐ allow team members to express their ideas and opinions

⭐ enable the team to devise action plans and effective strategies

⭐ direct the team towards making decisions

⭐ use the skills and experience of all team members effectively

⭐ be supportive to fellow team members

⭐ give positive feedback to team members.

(O'Hagan and Smith, 1993)

EXERCISE:
1. Make a list of your management skills. Are there any particular skills that you need to work on and improve?
2. What would you say is your leadership style? List your own leadership skills.

Group dynamics

As a manager or team leader, you should also know and understand how group dynamics affect the various stages of team development – that is, people's social interaction and their behaviour within social groups. Each individual has different personal characteristics that affect their ability to communicate effectively and work comfortably alongside others. From your experiences of working with colleagues you may have identified their differing characteristics that influence their willingness or reluctance to interact within the team. You also need to be aware of the stages in the development of a team and how these affect group dynamics. Research suggests that groups and teams grow and develop through a four-stage cycle, as outlined below.

1. **The forming stage:** a team starts by learning about its members. First impressions are important and the team leader should assist colleagues in this early stage by providing appropriate introductions, 'ice breaking' activities and an induction programme. They should also ensure participation by all team members.

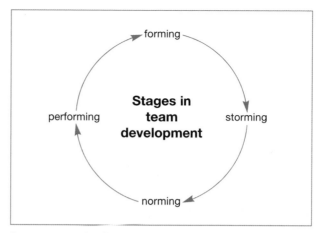

Stages in team development.

2. **The storming stage:** team members establish their positions within the team and decide on group functions. There may be arguments and personality clashes between certain members. The team leader can assist by providing opportunities for group discussion that tackle these matters in an open and positive manner, helping colleagues to sort minor disagreements between themselves and acting as an impartial referee if necessary. This can be a difficult stage but it is essential to the healthy development of the team, as more serious conflicts may emerge later if the team does not work through this stage.

3. **The norming stage:** team members reach agreement on how to work together, including establishing ground rules for the team and their individual responsibilities. They plan and organise the setting's working practices (e.g. ground rules for the children/young people using the setting, the timetable/provision of play activities and the rota for routine tasks such as tidying up, providing refreshments).

4. **The performing stage:** group trust is established and team members work well together. At this stage the team is usually positive, enthusiastic, co-operative and energetic, with team members supporting each other. There is a positive atmosphere within the setting.

(Houghton and McColgan, 1995)

Remember that colleagues will need to work through these stages again when changes arise (a person leaving or joining the team, say). You also need to be aware of the possible problems that can arise within a team and how to identify any signs of tension. These might include:

⭐ frequent arguments about differing views and ideas
⭐ uncertainty concerning team purpose or activity
⭐ confusion over roles and responsibilities within the team
⭐ lack of participation by some team members
⭐ lack of support for team members.

(See the section on page 243, on resolving conflicts.)

Managing a budget

As a playwork manager or member of the senior management team, you may be responsible for managing a budget, including:

☆ preparing, submitting and agreeing a budget for a set period

☆ monitoring actual performance against the agreed budget

☆ responding to identified variances and any unforeseen developments.

Preparing, submitting and agreeing a budget for a set period

As part of managing a play setting you will need to know how to prepare, submit and agree a budget for a set period (e.g. for each month). You can do this with a monthly budget report setting out the setting's *expected* income and expenditure. The monthly budget report also provides details of the setting's *actual* income and expenditure using information from the cash book (see below). The monthly budget reports provide the information for the setting's profit and loss statement at the end of the year. Monthly budget reports provide accurate figures for the play setting's cash flow forecast and they also form the basis for the next year's business forecast.

Using a computer you may be able to set up the setting's budget on a spreadsheet to enable income and expenditure to be updated easily on a daily basis. By law, all businesses have to keep records of their income and expenditure. Keeping such records will also help you to manage the finances of the setting more efficiently and help to prevent/detect fraud or theft.

You should keep records of all the setting's *income*, which may come from a variety of sources (for example, grants, funding, donations and, where applicable, payments from parents whose children use the play facility). You should also keep records of all the play setting's *expenditure*, such as:

☆ receipts of anything purchased by the play setting for the play setting

☆ details and receipts of costs (e.g. rent, rates and utility bills)

☆ details of wages paid to employees

☆ invoices for equipment repairs or replacements

☆ invoices for travel expenses

☆ invoices for training expenses.

(SureStart, 2003a)

Monitoring actual performance against the agreed budget

You should monitor the setting's actual financial performance against the agreed budget. The most common way to do this is to update and review the budget on a monthly basis. Record all transactions in a cash book so that you can see at a glance all the income and expenditure for the setting. Use the cash book on a daily basis to record transactions as they occur so that your records are always up to date. You should also have a petty cash book for staff to record the purchase of small items such as books, crayons and ingredients for cooking activities. You or a designated member of staff should be responsible for managing the petty cash system, including keeping all receipts and a locked box containing the petty cash 'float'. The petty cash box should be kept in one place and locked at all times (SureStart, 2003a).

Responding to identified variances and any unforeseen developments

A monthly budget will also show *variance* – that is, the difference between the expected expenditure and the actual expenditure for that point in the year. Monitoring and reviewing a monthly budget enables you to respond to variances (by, say, dealing with cash flow problems and taking action to prevent continual overspending). You will also be able to deal promptly with any unforeseen developments such as unexpected repairs, and falling numbers of children and/or young people using the play setting. If the financial position of the setting looks poor, you could try the following strategies.

- ★ **Increase sales:** focus on the specifics that will help you get more people using the play service and, therefore, more cash coming in (see Chapter 12).
- ★ **Collect money:** review your debtors and increase your efforts to collect overdue cash
- ★ **Negotiate different payment methods with suppliers:** change the way you pay bills and spread large bills over longer periods to help with cash flow, or change to lower-cost providers.
- ★ **Control costs:** unless a cost is absolutely necessary you do not have to incur it.

(SureStart, 2003a)

KEY TASK

Outline the methods you use to manage a budget in your setting. Include information on:

- preparing, submitting and agreeing a budget for a set period
- monitoring actual performance against the agreed budget
- responding to identified variances and any unforeseen developments.

NVQ links – Level 3: A27

Recruitment

As a playwork manager (or member of the senior management team) you will be involved in recruiting and selecting people to undertake specific activities or job roles within your area of responsibility. The staff recruitment procedures for the setting should reflect the values of playwork, which include anti-discriminatory practice, inclusion and positive attitudes. Good practice in staff recruitment involves finding the right person for the job. Any new employee should have the right skills and experience for the job, and must be a suitable person to work with children and/or young people. Good practice starts with the way in which you advertise the job and the information sent to potential applicants (SPRITO/SkillsActive Playwork Unit, 2001).

Advertisements

There are many places where you can place advertisements for job opportunities at your setting, including advertisements in newspapers or specialist magazines, local schools and colleges, local shops, libraries, community centres, leisure/sports centres and the Internet. (See the section in Chapter 1 on finding employment as a playworker.)

Advertisement checklist

Ensure you include:

- ☆ a brief description of what the job involves
- ☆ the hours of work and rate of pay
- ☆ location of the job
- ☆ job-share opportunities (especially for full-time jobs)
- ☆ closing date for applications
- ☆ contact details
- ☆ phone number that potential applicants can call for more information
- ☆ interview date.

(SPRITO/SkillsActive Playwork Unit, 2001)

Application packs

It is a good idea to compile an application pack with all the relevant information, including a letter for applicants, a job description, a person specification, an application form and details about the play setting.

You may ask applicants to send a covering letter outlining why they have applied for this particular post and their suitability for the job, with a copy of their CV as well as the completed application form.

Sample application form

Personal details

Name: _____

Date of birth: _____ Age: _____

Address: _____

_____

_____

Telephone no.: _____

Mobile no.: _____

E-mail address: _____

National Insurance no.: _____

Nationality: _____

Religion: _____

Emergency contact information

Name, address and telephone number of your next of kin (e.g. parent, spouse or partner): _____

_____

_____

_____

Please circle Yes or No for the following

- Do you have any special dietary requirements? Yes/No

- Would you consider yourself to be in good health? Yes/No

- Do you require any medication? Yes/No

  If yes, what? _____

- Do you have any known allergies? Yes/No

  If yes, what? _____

- Do you have any disabilities? Yes/No

  If yes, what? _____

- Are you a smoker? Yes/No

- Do you have a full, clean driving licence? Yes/No

- Are you a car owner? Yes/No

  If yes, is your car insured for business use? Yes/No

- Do you have an up-to-date first aid certificate? Yes/No

- Are you a qualified playworker? Yes/No

  If yes, how many years' experience do you have? _____

- What ages of children/young people have you worked with (please circle):

  under-5s/4 to 7 years/8 to 12 years/13 to 16 years/16+ years

Education and qualifications

Secondary school: _____

GCSEs/O levels/CSEs: _____

A levels: _____

College/university: _____

Course(s) studied: _____

Qualifications achieved: _____

Employment history

Please give details of your current position and your previous three positions. If you are a newly qualified playworker please state your current/final college work placement and any other relevant playwork and/or childcare experience (e.g. babysitting, holiday play schemes, voluntary work with children and/or young people).

From	To	Position held and ages of children	Main duties and salary	Reason for leaving

Have you given/been given notice to leave your current employer? Yes/No

If yes, when? _____ If no, what notice period is required? _____

What is the earliest date you are able to start a new position? _____

References

Please give details of the names, addresses (including postcode) and telephone numbers of your two referees, stating what position you held, duties involved, number and ages of children and/or young people, and how long your service for them lasted.

Name of referee	Address and telephone number	Position held and ages of children and/or young people	From	To

Disclosures

Do you have a criminal record? Yes/No

Do you have a disclosure from the Criminal Records Bureau? Yes/No

If yes, please state type and date of issue: _____

An enhanced disclosure is required for all applicants. If you do not have one already, do you consent to completing the necessary form? Yes/No

Additional information

Do you sing and/or play any musical instruments? Yes/No

Do you speak any other languages? Yes/No

Do you swim? Yes/No

What do you like to do in your spare time?

_____

_____

_____

Signed: _____

Date: _____

Job description and person specification

Applicants will need to know the exact duties and responsibilities of the position as well as the skills and qualities they will need to do the job. Duties and responsibilities should be set out in a job description, while skills and qualities should be set out in a person specification.

Sample job description and person specification

Job description

Job title: Playworker

Location: Green Fields Out-of-School Club

Responsible to: Senior Playworker

Main purpose of job: To support the senior playworker with the day-to-day organisation of the out-of-school club. You will be responsible for assisting with planning and supporting the play and development of children aged 5 to 11 years through the provision of appropriate play opportunities.

Duties and responsibilities

1. Supporting the children
   - To assist in preparing and maintaining a stimulating play environment
   - To provide support for children's self-directed play
   - To ensure the safety of the children and to assist in their general welfare
   - To facilitate children's social, physical, intellectual, communication and emotional development
   - To promote and reinforce the self-esteem of all the children
   - To encourage acceptance and inclusion of children with disabilities
   - To assist with sick children and administer first aid as appropriate
   - To establish and develop positive working relationships with the children

2. Supporting the senior playworker
   - To assist the senior playworker with the planning and preparation of play activities
   - To support the senior playworker in providing for the safe supervision of children in the play setting
   - To provide general help including preparation of rooms, materials and equipment (e.g. changing/mixing paint, cutting card/paper, setting up play equipment, putting away materials/equipment correctly, checking materials)
   - To assist with the provision of refreshments
   - To assist with relevant paperwork and administration (e.g. record-keeping)

3. Supporting the work of the play setting
   - To be aware of and follow the play setting's policies and procedures, especially those relating to health and safety, child protection and equal opportunities
   - To understand own role and responsibilities in relation to the play setting's policies
   - To maintain confidentiality in accordance with the play setting policy
   - To attend staff meetings and training sessions as appropriate
   - To acquire the full range of skills and knowledge needed to satisfy job requirements (e.g. playworkers without a playwork qualification will be required to undertake a NVQ Level 2 or 3 in Playwork after appointment)
   - To establish and develop positive working relationships with colleagues and parents
   - To encourage and support parents and carers involvement in the play setting
   - To assist in marketing and promoting the play setting in the local community.

▶

Person specification

Essential criteria
- Must be over 18 years old
- Must be able to provide challenging, stimulating and safe play opportunities
- Must have a commitment to equal opportunities and inclusive practice
- Must have some experience of working with 5- to 11-year-olds
- Must be able to meet children's individual needs
- Must be able to communicate effectively with children and adults
- Must be able to work as part of a team

Desirable criteria
- Should have up-to-date first aid qualification
- Should have some previous experience of administration
- Should have attended a playwork training course
- Should have a valid driving licence
- Should be able to use common sense and work using own initiative
- Should be able to speak a community language or use sign language

 KEY TASK

Compile an application pack for the post of playworker at your setting. Include the following:

- an advertisement for the job
- a letter for applicants
- a job description with details of the duties and responsibilities of the job
- a person specification listing the skills and qualities needed for the job
- an application form
- brief details about the setting.

NVQ links – Level 3: A319

Shortlists and interviews

After the closing date for applications, you need to decide which applicants to invite for interview. If you are not going to interview all applicants, you will need to draw up a shortlist of suitable applicants. Prepare a shortlist by identifying which applicants meet the criteria in the person specification. If an applicant meets all the essential criteria, then invite them for an interview.

The interview panel should consist of at least three people, including one who knows about recruitment and someone who understands playwork. Select someone to chair the interview. The chair will greet the applicant, introduce the other interviewers, explain about the structure of the interview, watch the time and keep the interview on track. The panel should decide beforehand who will ask which questions and when. Remember to allow time for presentations (if applicable) and for applicants to ask questions. Have a 10- to 15-minute break between interviews so that the panel can make notes and discuss any points about each interview (SPRITO/SkillsActive Playwork Unit, 2001). (See the section in Chapter 1 on finding employment for details of questions and important issues to discuss at interviews.)

The completed application forms and any notes made during shortlisting and interviews are confidential (see the section on confidentiality in Chapter 10). They must be kept locked away when not in use. Keep information relating to the successful applicant and also unsuccessful applicants, in case they contact you about why they were not successful in gaining the post.

When you offer the job to the successful applicant remember to:

☆ allow time for a reply before rejecting the other applicants in case the chosen applicant does not accept the job

☆ clarify that the job offer is subject to satisfactory references and disclosure (see below)

☆ explain the length of the probationary period and how it will be monitored.

(SPRITO/SkillsActive Playwork Unit, 2001)

If no applicants meet all the essential criteria, either at the shortlisting stage or after the interviews, then you should not appoint anyone to the post. Review the recruitment procedures and start again (SPRITO/SkillsActive Playwork Unit, 2001).

References

You will need to take up references for the successful applicant. The purpose of references is to validate the information given by the applicant on the application form, to find out if they are of good character and to see if the referee thinks the applicant is a suitable person to work with children and/or young people. (See the section on references in Chapter 1.)

Legislation affecting recruitment

You need to be aware of relevant legislation affecting recruitment, including the laws to protect children and young people. The following are some examples.

☆ The **Children Act 1989**: this covers a number of issues regarding the care of children. The part relevant to recruitment relates to the description of a 'fit' person.

☆ The **Day Care and Childminding (National Standards) (England) Regulations 2003**: regulations under the Children Act 1989 require providers to meet the 14 standards and the relevant supporting criteria (see page 201). The relevant standard for recruitment is 'Standard 1 – Suitable person: Adults providing day care, looking after children or having unsupervised access to them are suitable to do so'.

☆ The **Protection of Children Act 1999**: this reinforces the duty of care and is linked to checks by the Criminal Records Bureau (see below).

You also need to be aware of relevant legislation designed to protect people applying for jobs from being unfairly treated in the recruitment process. The following are some examples.

- ✯ The **Sex Discrimination Act 1975** (amended 1986): this makes it unlawful to discriminate against a person on the grounds of sex or marital status in employment, training or the provision of goods, facilities and services.
- ✯ The **Race Relations Act 1975** (amended 2000): this makes it unlawful to discriminate against a person in relation to employment or training on the grounds of race, colour, ethnic origin, nationality or national origin.
- ✯ The **Disability Discrimination Act (1995)**: this makes it unlawful to discriminate against a disabled person in employment or for an employer to fail to provide the necessary reasonable adjustments for disabled employees and applicants, or to offer less favourable terms to disabled employees, including those with mental illness.
- ✯ The **Employment Rights Act 1996**: this entitles employees to a written statement of employment. (See below for more information on employment rights.)

Criminal Records Bureau and disclosures

The Police Act 1997 (Part V) was introduced to protect certain vulnerable groups. The Act makes applicants for certain posts 'exempt' from declining to give employers details of their past criminal history. These posts include those involving access to children, young people, the elderly, disabled people, alcohol or drug users, and the chronically sick. Organisations that include exempt posts are legally entitled to ask applicants for details of all convictions, whether they are 'spent' or 'unspent', under the Rehabilitation of Offenders Act 1974. Registered organisations are now authorised to obtain details of an applicant's criminal history from the Criminal Records Bureau (CRB), an executive agency of the Home Office. The details of this information are set out in a disclosure. There are three types of disclosure: basic, standard and enhanced.

Basic disclosures

Basic disclosures are *not* suitable for applicants intending to work with children, young people, the elderly and other vulnerable groups. A basic disclosure includes only information held on central police records that are unspent according to the Rehabilitation of Offenders Act 1974.

Standard disclosures

Standard disclosures include information about spent and unspent convictions, cautions, warnings and reprimands. Standard disclosures are available for applicants applying for posts involving regular contact with children, young people and/or other vulnerable groups. A standard disclosure also checks information held by the Department of Health and Department for Education and Skills (List 99). A standard disclosure can only be obtained through a body registered to the CRB and not by the individuals themselves.

Enhanced disclosures

Enhanced disclosures are for posts listed in Section 115 of the Police Act 1997, such as those involving unsupervised contact with children, young people and vulnerable groups. It is the most comprehensive and appropriate check that is available to organisations and gives thorough information on all records held on:

- ✩ the police national computer for convictions
- ✩ the Department of Health and Department for Education and Skills (List 99)
- ✩ the POCA list (Protection of Children Act)
- ✩ the POVA list (Protection of Vulnerable Adults).

These are lists of adults who are considered not suitable to work with children, but who may not have been prosecuted. The Chief Officer of Police may also release information for inclusion in an enhanced disclosure, and additional information may be sent that is not released to the applicant. An enhanced disclosure can only be obtained through a body registered to the CRB and not by the individuals themselves.

The Protection of Children Act 1999 and the Criminal Justice and Court Services Act 2000 make it an offence for any organisation to offer employment involving regular contact with children to anyone who has been convicted of certain offences or included on lists of people considered unsuitable for such work. It is also a criminal offence for someone who knows they are banned from working with children to apply for, accept or undertake such work.

 KEY TASK

1. Give a reflective account of your involvement in the recruitment and selection process at your setting.
2. Review your setting's recruitment and selection process, and suggest possible improvements.

NVQ links – Level 3: A319

Employment rights

By law, most employees who are employed for a month or more must receive a written statement of employment within eight weeks of starting a job. The written statement of employment or contract must include: the start date, the period of employment and notices, main duties, working hours, salary, holidays, sick pay and grounds for dismissal.

Contents of the written statement of employment

As well as what is required by law, it is helpful for a playworker to have a written statement of employment that also includes more detailed information so that you and the employee are both clear about exactly what you expect from each other. You should make sure the written statement of employment covers all aspects regarding the care of children and/or young people, and the employee's conduct in the play setting. Although the law says that an employee must have a written statement of employment within eight weeks of starting, ideally you should provide a written contract after you have made an offer of employment and before the new employee starts work.

To avoid misunderstandings and possible problems, make sure the written statement of employment or contract includes the following:

- name and address of the employer
- employee's name and address
- hours of work
- job description, with exact duties and responsibilities in detail
- details of the salary and salary review
- details of extra pay (or time off in lieu) for extra hours
- holiday entitlement and holiday pay
- rules about absence, sickness and sick pay entitlements
- maternity/paternity rights
- pension arrangements
- disciplinary and grievance procedures
- notice periods
- probationary period (see below).

The probationary period

After an offer of employment has been accepted, you should agree a probationary period. This will allow you and the new employee to try out arrangements before you both commit yourselves to a more permanent agreement. You should ensure that any agreed probationary period is clearly stated in the written statement of employment or contract and includes the period of notice required during this period. For example, a probationary period of four weeks or one month is quite usual, with either party being able to terminate the employment by giving one week's notice in writing.

Other statutory employment rights

In addition to the written statement of employment, a playworker is also entitled to a number of statutory employment rights that apply to all employees as soon as they start work. These include protection against:

* unlawful deductions from their salary
* adverse treatment on the grounds of sex, race or disability
* dismissal for seeking to enforce their statutory employment rights.

Other statutory employment rights that apply to working as a playworker include the following.

* **Maximum working hours:** a playworker is covered by the Working Time Directive, which regulates the hours an employee can be expected to work. An employer cannot insist that an employee work more than 48 hours per week.

* **National Minimum Wage:** an employer must pay employees at least £4.10 per hour if they are aged between 18 and 21 years old (increasing to £4.25 from 1 October 2005 and £4.45 from 1 October 2006), and £4.85 per hour if they are aged 22 years or over (increasing to £5.05 from 1 October 2005 and £5.35 from 1 October 2006).

* **Statutory Sick Pay (SSP):** an employer must pay employees SSP if they are sick for four days in a row or more.

* **Paid annual holiday:** an employee, whether full- or part-time, is entitled to four weeks' annual paid leave.

* **Notice of termination of employment:** a playworker is entitled to one week's notice if their employer terminates their employment when they have been working for more than one month. When an employee has been employed for two years, they are entitled to two weeks' notice. This continues (one week for each year worked) until they have worked for the same employer for 12 years. The notice period can be over-ridden by a longer period if it is included in the contract of employment. For example, it is usual practice for an employee to give at least four weeks' notice (after the probationary period) to enable the employer to make alternative arrangements to maintain adult/child ratios.

Other statutory employment rights apply on completion of a qualifying period of service. Here are some examples.

* **Protection against unfair dismissal:** if an employee has been in continuous employment (with the same employer) for at least one year they are automatically protected against unfair dismissal.

* **Statutory Maternity Pay (SMP):** if a female employee becomes pregnant and has been working for the same employer for at least nine months prior to the baby's due date, they are entitled to SMP and maternity leave.

* **Statutory Paternity Pay (SPP):** as from April 2003 new fathers are entitled to two weeks' SPP, with a right to a further 13 weeks' unpaid leave. To qualify the employee must have been in continuous employment for at least six months.

* **Redundancy pay:** an employee is entitled to redundancy pay if they have been in continuous employment for a minimum of two years, as long as they are not employed on a fixed-term contract.

Taking appropriate action to retain colleagues

Taking appropriate action to retain colleagues is an important challenge when managing a play setting, especially when you need to maintain the relevant adult/child ratios. Staff members are one of the most important resources of a setting. You need to know how to retain colleagues who have the knowledge, experience and skills that are the greatest assets to the setting. If colleagues keep leaving, not only do you lose their knowledge, experience and skills, but the setting will also incur extra recruitment costs. High staff turnover is detrimental to children and/or young people, who will miss out on continuity of care. Planning appropriate play opportunities can also be more difficult when there are uncertainties about staffing. There can also be an adverse effect on the atmosphere of the setting where constant staff changes mean there is little time to develop and maintain positive working relationships with both children and adults. High staff turnover can also put pressure on remaining staff and can lead to absenteeism or low morale.

Twelve ways to retain colleagues

1. Communicate with colleagues and ensure they have up-to-date information.
2. Talk to your colleagues and learn what demotivates them.
3. Talk to your colleagues and learn what motivates them.
4. Eliminate as many demotivating factors as you can and maintain these changes.
5. Listen to your colleagues' ideas (e.g. introduce a suggestion scheme).
6. Consider implementing some of the ideas suggested by your colleagues.
7. Identify the learning needs of your colleagues, including consulting them about the learning opportunities they feel they need to do their work more effectively.
8. Ensure that colleagues have the knowledge and skills they need for work (e.g. providing access to appropriate training courses and qualifications).
9. Provide accessible support systems (e.g. mentoring, 'buddy' system).
10. Have an 'open door' policy so that colleagues know that you are approachable.
11. Provide consistent, supportive leadership and give constructive feedback on performance.
12. Recognise staff achievement and celebrate success. Remember to say 'Thank you'!

Effective planning and fair allocation of work within your area of responsibility

Staff meetings are essential for effective planning. Such meetings also provide regular opportunities to share day-to-day information and to solve any problems. Staff meetings should be held regularly – about once every four to six weeks. Ensure that there is an agenda for the meeting and that the minutes of the meeting are recorded and can be easily accessed by staff. Encourage colleagues to share best practice, knowledge and ideas on developing appropriate play opportunities in the setting. As well as general staff meetings you should have regular team meetings for the more detailed planning of play opportunities and allocation of work within your area of responsibility.

You can allocate work and responsibilities in a variety of ways. Here are some examples:

- ✫ **Responsibility for a play area:** each playworker (or group of playworkers) is responsible for a specific area of the setting and for developing play opportunities within that area. The playworker(s) will provide support for the individual needs of the children/young people in that area, including appropriate adult supervision or intervention as and when necessary.

- ✫ **Responsibility for a play activity:** each playworker is responsible for a specific play activity. The adult stays with the same activity throughout the day/week and is responsible for: selecting and setting out materials or helping the children to access these for themselves; encouraging the children's interest and participation in the activity; providing appropriate adult supervision or intervention as required; helping children to clear away afterwards.

- ✫ **Responsibility for a group of children/young people:** each playworker is responsible for a small group of children as their key worker. The playworker helps them to settle into the play setting and is responsible for: greeting their group of children on arrival; encouraging the children's play and development in the setting; establishing and maintaining a special relationship with each child and their family.

- ✫ **Responsibility for an individual child/young person:** a playworker may have special responsibility for a child or young person with disabilities. The playworker will be responsible for: ensuring that child's particular needs are met in an inclusive way within the setting; ensuring they have the necessary materials to participate in the play opportunities provided, including any specialist equipment; establishing and maintaining a special relationship with the child and their family.

Job rotation

Job rotation involves giving colleagues the opportunity to experience other roles within the setting. It can be an interesting and positive way for colleagues to gain varied work experience and to develop new skills. It can also be extremely useful when covering staff absences.

A staff rota can be a useful way to ensure the fair allocation of work within the setting. Use the rota to share out some of the more routine jobs within the play setting (e.g. washing paint pots). If you use a rota, make sure you give adequate notice of changes to it so that your colleagues know what areas and activities they are responsible for in, say, a particular week.

Use staff questionnaires to gain useful information about your colleagues' views on the planning and allocation of work within the play setting. Some example questions are listed below.

- ✯ Is the current staff rota system working?
- ✯ What difficulties (if any) do they have with balancing work and family needs?
- ✯ What do they believe you could offer to give them more support?
- ✯ What suggestions do they have to make the setting more effective?

Motivating colleagues

Motivating colleagues is essential part of your role as a manager. Motivation is a key factor in creating a positive play environment and maintaining good working relationships within the setting. Remember that everyone is an individual and your colleagues will all respond to different motivating factors. Find and use the motivating factors for the colleagues in your team.

Seven ways to motivate colleagues more effectively

1. Identifying and trying to understand the individual needs and personal goals of your colleagues.
2. Remembering that higher pay is not the only way to motivate colleagues. Other rewards may be more appropriate for getting them to work more effectively.
3. Setting work targets that are realistic and achievable but that also provide your colleagues with some challenges to prevent boredom and increase job satisfaction. Involve them in setting their own targets (e.g. using SMART objectives – see Chapter 10).
4. Always consulting your colleagues before changing agreed targets.
5. Always using praise or other rewards to acknowledge your colleagues' achievements.
6. Using group pressure to influence motivation in positive ways (e.g. involving your colleagues in group decision-making to strengthen their commitment).
7. Keeping your colleagues regularly informed about what is happening in the setting.

Effective delegation

Effective delegation is another important factor in managing a play setting. It involves motivating your colleagues to carry out specific tasks to enable you to focus on the jobs that you need to do. Delegation also enables you to make use of the particular strengths and skills of your colleagues. Developing effective delegation takes time and practice.

Guidelines for effective delegation

1. **Find the right person:** in terms of existing and potential abilities, attitude, personality.
2. **Consult first:** allow your colleagues to be involved in deciding what is to be delegated.
3. **Think ahead:** do not wait for a crisis to occur and then delegate. Try to delegate in advance.
4. **Delegate whole tasks:** where possible, delegate a complete task to a colleague, rather than just a small section of a task.
5. **Specify expected outcomes:** make it clear what outcomes are expected from your colleagues.
6. **Take your time:** especially if you have been under-delegating or are dealing with less experienced staff. A gradual transfer of responsibility will allow both you and your colleagues to learn what is involved.
7. **Delegate the good and the bad:** if you delegate the tasks that are pleasant to do and also those that are not so pleasant, your colleagues will have the opportunity to gain valuable, realistic experience of many types of job. Just as importantly, they will be able to see that you are not just passing on the 'not so nice' jobs you don't want to do yourself.
8. **Delegate, then trust:** when you delegate a task to a colleague, together with the responsibility for getting it done, you then need to trust that person to complete the job to your specified and mutually agreed requirements. Failing to trust usually involves constant interference on your part, with the result that your colleagues will come to believe that you do not consider them capable of carrying out the agreed tasks.

(Wandsworth EYDCP)

KEY TASK

1. Give examples of effective planning and fair allocation of work within your area of responsibility. You could include copies of planning sheets, minutes from a staff or team meeting and a work rota.
2. Describe how you motivate your colleagues.
3. Outline ways in which you could make use of effective delegation. Give examples from your experiences of managing a play setting.

NVQ links – Level 3: A320

Monitoring the progress and quality of work of individuals/teams

Monitoring and evaluation helps those working in the play setting to understand how the policies and procedures are working in practice, to check the quality of work and provision of play opportunities, and to plan for the future. It can also help to make day-to-day working within the setting more effective.

Identifying measurable standards and checks can be difficult in play settings. However, depending on the type of setting, there may be measurable standards and checks, including some that are set locally (such as local authority requirements) and some that are set nationally (like legislation relating to registration and inspection). (See Chapter 12 for more detailed information on evaluating play service provision.)

When monitoring the progress and quality of work of individuals or teams within your area of responsibility, you should encourage your colleagues to take responsibility for their own work tasks and to use existing feedback systems to keep you informed of work progress.

When establishing procedures for monitoring in the play setting include the following:

- ★ formal procedures (e.g. reports, formal meetings, mentoring, staff appraisals, supervision)
- ★ informal procedures (e.g. observations, informal meetings, conversations)
- ★ the type of information required (e.g. checklists, evaluation sheets, progress reports)
- ★ when the information will be delivered to you or others in the team (e.g. daily, weekly, monthly, termly, annually)
- ★ the form of the information (e.g. verbal, written, e-mail, audio-visual)
- ★ where and how the information will be delivered (e.g. meeting, face to face, presentation, electronic)
- ★ the amount of detail required.

(Wandsworth EYDCP)

Mentoring

Mentoring is a structured approach to supporting a colleague by pairing an experienced member of the team with a less experienced member of the team. It is a very effective way for colleagues to share knowledge, skills and experience. Mentoring involves:

- ★ 'shadowing' (e.g. watching the work of a more experienced colleague)
- ★ learning 'on the job' (e.g. developing new skills)
- ★ asking and answering everyday questions
- ★ introducing other people in the setting

* providing guidance and constructive criticism
* agreeing and setting daily objectives
* reviewing progress
* providing feedback to manager on progress
* identifying further training needs
* providing friendly and reassuring support.

Supervision

Supervision provides opportunities for your colleagues to reflect on their work performance and to review any difficulties they may have, as well as to discuss issues that it may not be appropriate to raise at a team meeting. Some people prefer to use terms like 'keep in touch' or 'one to one' instead of supervision. Plan regular sessions with each member of staff. Agree and set clear ground rules about supervision and confidentiality. Keep written records of supervision sessions and ensure that these are stored in a locked file.

A suggested format for a supervision session is:

* discuss current feelings about the job
* review work since last supervision, including any goals set
* discuss current work, including successes and difficulties
* provide support or training as required.

(Wandsworth EYDCP)

Staff appraisals

Staff appraisals or reviews are a formal way for you to keep up to date with the work performance of your colleagues and to identify their ongoing training needs. Staff appraisals usually take place once a year. They should have an agreed format (e.g. a form to be completed by the playworker prior to the appraisal meeting that will form the basis of discussion at the actual appraisal meeting).

KEY TASK

Outline the methods you use to monitor the progress and quality of work of the individuals and/or teams within your area of responsibility in the play setting. For example:
* staff and/or team meetings
* mentoring
* supervision sessions
* staff appraisals.

NVQ links – Level 3: A320

Resolving conflicts

Conflicts can arise in even the best-run play settings. The resolution of conflict situations within the setting requires the team leader to work with colleagues. Whenever possible it is better for colleagues to find their own solutions with the team leader acting as a facilitator or mediator. Sometimes a colleague may not make allowances for a parent's or carer's particular problems or does not show respect for the needs and rights of parents/carers. Conflicts need to be handled sensitively and resolved as quickly as possible to avoid creating a negative, unpleasant atmosphere for all those in the setting, which can have a detrimental effect on the well-being of the children and young people. (For further information see the section in Chapter 10 on dealing with conflict.)

Personal problems may affect a colleague's working relationships with others in the setting. The team leader should have a one-to-one discussion and suggest where sources of help might be found. (See the section in Chapter 10 on providing support for colleagues.)

Grievance and disciplinary procedures

The Employment Rights Act 1996 requires that all employees who work for more than 16 hours a week have a contract, a formal written agreement stating their terms and conditions of employment. This statement should also include information about the setting's grievance and disciplinary procedures. The Employment Act 2002, Sections 35–38, deals with changes to the rules concerning written particulars of employment, including ensuring the statement complies with the Act's requirements for minimum statutory internal grievance and disciplinary procedures.

Grievance procedure

If an employee has a grievance relating to their employment, they are entitled to invoke the setting's grievance procedure (which may be part of a local authority agreement) and should be included in the staff handbook. The grievance should be raised initially with their line manager (e.g. the senior playworker). The grievance should be raised orally in the first instance, although the employee may be requested to put it in writing. If the grievance relates to the employee's line manager, then the grievance should be referred to the line manager's line manager (e.g. the playwork manager).

Disciplinary procedure

The setting will expect reasonable standards of performance and conduct from all staff members. Details of the disciplinary procedure (which may be part of a local authority agreement) should be included in the staff handbook. If an employee is dissatisfied with a disciplinary decision they should in the first instance contact the senior manager, usually within five working days of the date of the decision.

1. Describe how you have responded (or would respond) to a conflict situation as the manager or team leader in a play setting. (Be tactful and remember *confidentiality!*)
2. Outline the grievance and disciplinary procedures for playworkers in the setting where you work.

NVQ links – Level 3: A320

Identifying learning needs and providing learning opportunities for colleagues

As part of managing a play setting, you need to be able to identify the learning needs of your colleagues and to provide appropriate learning opportunities for them. This includes: staff induction – welcoming and meeting the learning needs of new members of staff; and staff development – identifying and providing for the learning needs of existing staff.

Staff induction

Induction provides new members of staff with the opportunity to learn about the setting and what is expected of them. It can be helpful to compile an induction pack including:

- ☆ a 'welcome' letter
- ☆ copies of essential policies and procedures – for example, equal opportunities, health and safety, child protection, fire and emergency procedures
- ☆ information about the play setting's administration (e.g. registration and consent forms, monitoring forms, risk assessment, time sheets)
- ☆ names of staff and their main roles and responsibilities
- ☆ the management structure of the setting
- ☆ details of who to contact if they have any problems
- ☆ general information and publicity about the setting
- ☆ floor plan of the building.

Sometimes it may be appropriate to ask the playworker who is leaving to stay on during the new playworker's first week. The departing playworker can share the workload and help the new member of staff to familiarise themselves with their new working environment. They can also help the new member of staff to gain a better understanding of the exact duties and responsibilities expected of them in the play setting.

Staff development

Good-quality and appropriate staff development and training can have a huge, positive impact on workplace performance, which in turn can greatly enhance the play experiences of the children and/or young people using the setting. To be effective, staff development should take into account the needs of individual staff members and the needs of the setting as a whole.

When providing learning opportunities for your colleagues, you should start by identifying their learning needs (for example, what additional knowledge and skills do they need to work more effectively?). Staff appraisals can help you to identify these learning needs. Once these learning needs have been identified, you need to agree with your colleague(s) on an appropriate training course or qualification that will help to meet them. (See Chapter 1 for information about playwork qualifications; see Chapter 10 for information on training courses relevant to playwork.)

When considering staff development you will have a choice of training options, including:

☆ sending staff on existing training courses (as a group or individually)
☆ inviting trainers in to the setting to run sessions for you
☆ running in-house training.

Another aspect of staff development is to look at ways that your colleagues can pass on their knowledge, skills and experience to other playworkers (training as playwork trainers or playwork NVQ assessors, say).

Training opportunities should be also be offered to parents and carers as well as staff members, and should include meetings with speakers, discussion groups and reading materials (such as books, factsheets and information packs).

First aid training.

Encouraging your colleagues to take responsibility for their own learning

Each member of staff should have a Personal Development Plan or Continuing Professional Development Plan that includes training and personal development goals and how these relate to the aims of the play setting. (For more information see the section in Chapter 10 on professional development and training opportunities.)

KEY TASK

Describe how you identify the learning needs of your colleagues and provide learning opportunities to meet these needs.

NVQ links – Level 3: A321

Developing the work of the organisation

Working towards recognised benchmarks can have a positive impact on the play setting and help to develop the work of the organisation. Here are some examples.

- ✩ **Best Play:** includes a set of seven objectives that play provision should aim to achieve.
- ✩ **Playwork Quality Assurance Schemes:** there are three nationally accredited playwork quality assurance schemes – Kids Club Network 'Aiming High', Somerset and Torbay Early Years Team 'Flying High', and Northumberland Out of School Childcare Initiative (NOOSI) Quality Assurance Award.
- ✩ **Practical Quality Assurance System for Small Organisations:** a self-assessment tool for small voluntary organisations and projects to develop a practical quality-assurance system in order to provide better services for their users.
- ✩ **Investors In People:** an award for organisations to prove that they place value on their staff by following good practice in terms of staff development and management.

(SPRITO/SkillsActive Playwork Unit, 2001)

(For more detailed information on developing the work of the organisation see Chapter 12.)

Further reading

Adirondack, S. (1992) *Just About Managing: Effective Management for Voluntary Organisations and Community Groups.* London Voluntary Service Council.

Armstrong, M. (1999) *How to be an Even Better Manager.* Kogan Page.

Clegg, B. and Birch, P. (2002) *Crash Course in Managing People.* Kogan Page.

DTI (Department of Trade and Industry) (August 2001) *Contracts of Employment* (PL810 Rev 6) and (August 2000) *Written Statements of Employment Practice* (PL700 Rev 5). Both are available from your local JobCentre or the DTI website at www.dti.gov.uk.

DTI (July 2003) *Individual Rights of Employees* (PL 716 Rev 10) and (May 2003) *Redundancy Entitlement – Statutory Rights: A Guide for Employees* (PL808 Rev 6). These booklets can be obtained from your local JobCentre or the DTI website (see above).

DTI (July 2003) *Your Guide to the Working Time Regulations.* A free booklet is available from the DTI or the DTI website (see above).

Hobart, C. and Frankel, J. (1996) *Practical Guide to Childcare Employment.* Nelson Thornes.

Maddocks, J. (2002) *Playwork Training and Qualifications: Meeting the Daycare Standards.* SPRITO/SkillsActive Playwork Unit.

National Centre for Playwork Education (North East) (n.d.) *Training Playwork Trainers* (2nd edn). National Centre for Playwork Education (North East).

O'Hagan, M. and Smith, M. (1999) *Early Years Child Care and Education: Key Issues.* Bailliere Tindall.

Petrie, P. (1989) *Communicating with Children and Adults: Interpersonal Skills for Those Working with Babies and Children.* Hodder Arnold.

Sallis, E. and Sallis, K. (1990) *People in Organisations.* Macmillan.

Scott, J. and Rochester, A. (1984) *Effective Management Skills: Managing People.* Warner Books.

SPRITO/SkillsActive Playwork Unit (2001) *Recruitment, Training and Qualifications in Playwork – an Employer's Guide.* SPRITO/SkillsActive Playwork Unit.

SPRITO/SkillsActive Playwork Unit (2002) *Quality Training, Quality Play – The National Strategy for Playwork Education, Training and Qualifications 2002–2005.* SPRITO/SkillsActive Playwork Unit. (Currently being reviewed; new strategy document being developed: *Quality Training, Quality Play – New Horizons 2005–2010.*)

SPRITO/SkillsActive Playwork Unit (2003) *Playwork Induction Standard for People Working with Children in the Holidays.* SPRITO/SkillsActive Playwork Unit.

SureStart (2003) 'Team Steps to Success' guides: *Managing your Childcare Business and Managing Finance.* Available free from the Business Success for Childcare website at www.surestart.gov.uk/support4business.

There are two types of evaluation method.

1. **Quantitative:** something measured or measurable by, or concerned with, quantity and expressed in numbers or quantities.
2. **Qualitative:** something that is not summarised in numerical form, such as minutes from meetings and general notes from observations. Qualitative data normally describe people's knowledge, attitudes or behaviours and are often more subjective.

(SkillsActive, 2004a)

When evaluating play service provision, you need to consider the following points:

1. Does the current play service provision:
   ☆ meet the needs of the local community
   ☆ reflect mobility and access within the local community
   ☆ meet children's and/or young people's play needs
   ☆ help and support parents'/carers' interests
   ☆ contribute to sound community development objectives
   ☆ sustain the interest, involvement and support of children and/or young people
   ☆ reflect differing needs – age groups, gender, ethnic/cultural and disability acceptance
   ☆ meet all safety requirements (e.g. child protection, accident prevention)
   ☆ have regular reviews?
2. Do the play resources:
   ☆ meet the needs of children/young people and the communities in which they live
   ☆ reflect the principles of the UN Convention on the Rights of the Child, especially Article 31 – all children have a right to relax and play, and to join in a wide range of activities
   ☆ benefit children and/or young people as a first priority
   ☆ enable adjustment to changing circumstances
   ☆ receive regular reviews?
3. Do the play service's training opportunities:
   ☆ have a child-centred focus
   ☆ have adequate resources
   ☆ support parents and volunteers as well as employees
   ☆ include management needs
   ☆ meet community and voluntary-sector requirements
   ☆ reflect the views of those seeking or needing training
   ☆ receive regular reviews?

(Fair Play for Children)

Developing evaluation methods and identifying appropriate criteria

When evaluating play service provision you will need to develop evaluation methods and identify appropriate criteria. For example, you could use the 'play objectives' in *Best Play: What Play Provision Should do for Children* and the 'characteristics of VITAL play opportunities' from *Getting Serious About Play: A Review of Children's Play*. (See the 'Further reading' section at the end of this chapter.)

The play objectives

Best Play sets out seven play objectives that should apply to any play service provision that respects the rights of children and aims to offer children and/or young people appropriate play opportunities that will enable them to grow and learn. The play objectives set out how the definition of play and the underpinning values and principles of playwork should be put into practice. They also provide useful criteria for evaluating play service provision. *Best Play* is neither a quality-assurance scheme nor a set of standards. However, its seven play objectives can form the basis for quality-assurance systems for any play service provision (National Playing Fields Association, Children's Play Council and Playlink, 2000). (For further information see the section in Chapter 4 on using objectives to evaluate play provision.)

Your evaluation methods should help you to assess whether the play service provision meets the play needs of the children and young people in practice. You could use the characteristics of VITAL play opportunities from *Getting Serious About Play* as the basis for appropriate criteria – for example:

- ☆ **V**alue-based
- ☆ **I**n the right place
- ☆ **T**op quality
- ☆ **A**ppropriate
- ☆ **L**ong-term

(DCMS, 2004)

(See the details of characteristics of VITAL play opportunities in Chapter 4.)

Collecting, recording, analysing and reporting evaluations

When evaluating play service provision, you will need to collect, record and analyse information using the agreed evaluation methods and criteria. After you have analysed the information you have gathered, you will need to report the results to the relevant colleague, including any recommendations for changes or improvements to the play service provision. You should remember to follow your setting's policies and procedures for collecting, recording, reporting and storing information (see the sections on record-keeping and confidentiality in Chapter 10).

When collecting, recording and analysing information, consider the following important questions.

☆ What is the purpose of the evaluation process?

☆ What are the questions to be asked?

☆ What data are required?

☆ How can the data be obtained?

☆ What do the data mean?

☆ What needs to be done now?

(Bullen, 1996)

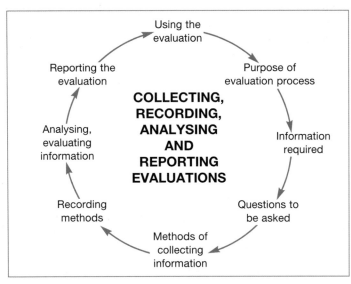

Collecting, analysing and reporting evaluations.

KEY TASK

1. Outline the resources and organisational policies that are relevant to evaluating the play service provision.

2. Briefly describe how you discuss and agree evaluation methods and criteria with the relevant member of staff, and how you report the evaluation results.

3. Which evaluation methods and criteria do you use to evaluate the play service provision?

4. Give examples of how you collect, record, analyse and store information using these evaluation methods, including any recommendations for changes or improvements to the play service provision.

NVQ links – Level 3: B227.1

Using feedback from people in the community about play initiatives

An important aspect of promoting play services is to find out what children, young people, parents, carers and others in the local community think about the play setting and the play opportunities provided. You should know how to gain and use feedback from people in the local community about play initiatives. Feedback can be gained *informally*, through discussions with individuals or small groups, or *formally* using meetings or questionnaires. Ensure that you listen and respond to the views and experiences of people in the local community, especially those of children and young people. Try to include their suggestions when planning to make changes or improvements to the play service. (See the section in Chapter 2 on consulting and involving children and young people in decision-making.)

When gathering and using feedback, remember the following important points.

★ Respond immediately to what children, young people and adults have to say.
★ Inform them of how their ideas will be taken forward.
★ Inform them of how their ideas are taken into account.
★ Inform them if they did not influence change, and say why.
★ Have feedback discussions and provide opportunities to ask questions.

(Kirby *et al.*, 2003)

 KEY TASK

Give examples of how you have gained and used feedback about play initiatives from:

- children and/or young people
- parents and carers
- other people in the local community.

NVQ links – Level 2: A52.3; Level 3: B226.1

Developing and improving play services

You should be aware of the available research and resources relevant to developing and improving play services (for example, Play Councils or Play Forums and the SkillsActive Playwork Unit). Play Councils or Play Forums have been established in many areas, and provide a central focus for consultation, sharing of information and resources relating to play service provision. The SkillsActive Playwork Unit (formerly SPRITO) leads the development of playwork education and training through consultation, developing an education and training infrastructure, setting standards, maintaining quality, fostering innovation and offering information, support and guidance (SkillsActive, 2004a). (See the 'Further reading' section at the end of this chapter.)

The SkillsActive Playwork Unit website has very useful and up-to-date information, including:

✰ the Code of Practice for Playwork Training Providers
✰ endorsed training courses
✰ register of playwork trainers
✰ approval of products for training materials and publications
✰ playwork news and events
✰ research on play, playwork and playworkers
✰ downloadable publications relevant to playwork
✰ the National Occupational Standards for Playwork.

You should know and understand the legal requirements relevant to developing and improving play services. For example:

✰ the Disability Discrimination Act 1995
✰ the Children Act 1989
✰ the UN Convention on the Rights of the Child 1989
✰ the Health and Safety at Work Act 1974
✰ Management of Health and Safety at Work Regulations 1992
✰ European Standards BSEN 1176 and 1177.

The legal requirements under the **Disability Discrimination Act 1995** are of particular importance to developing and improving play services. Since 1996, the Disability Discrimination Act (DDA) has made it unlawful for service providers to treat disabled people less favourably. Since 1999, there has been a duty to make reasonable adjustments in certain circumstances. From October 2004, this was extended to cover adjustments in relation to any physical features that create a barrier for disabled people. The DDA must be taken into account when developing and improving play services (for example, making play spaces fully accessible). In addition, the **Disability Discrimination Act Code of Practice on Rights of Access to Goods**, **Facilities**, **Services and Premises** provides guidance for service providers on how the duties under the DDA might apply in practice, including recommendations for an inclusive approach to service development involving consultation with disabled people and those representing them. Another important legal requirement under the **Management of Health and Safety at Work Regulations 1992** is for play service providers to carry out risk assessments of children's play facilities. Interpretations and understandings of risk are essential to the development and improvement of accessible play spaces (Dunn *et al.*, 2004).

You should also know and understand the organisational policies and procedures relevant to developing and improving play services – for example, play provision, health and safety, inclusion and anti-discriminatory practice. In particular, the policy for play provision should include information on the following.

✰ **The aims and objectives of the policy:** what play provision is required; why the play provision is required; how the play provision will be supported; how the play provision relates to Article 31 and other relevant legislation and strategies.

✰ **A review of current provision and resources:** where and how play opportunities are currently provided; quality issues; resources; community involvement.

✰ **Evaluation of play provision:** monitoring and evaluation; feedback from children, young people, parents and others in the local community; inter-agency liaison.

✰ **Development and improvement of play provision:** fixed equipment provision; informal community resources; organised play activities; networking needs; access.

✰ **Support processes and resources:** equal opportunities and inclusion; health and safety; child protection; funding and resources; training and education (e.g. skills-based, NVQ-related).

KEY TASK

1. Describe how you have been involved in developing and improving play services. Include examples of:
   - using available research and resources
   - meeting legal requirements
   - following the relevant organisational policies and procedures.
2. Summarise your setting's procedures for developing and improving play service provision.

NVQ links – Level 2: A52.3; Level 3: B227.2

Consulting other people in the development of play services

You may be responsible for consulting other people on the development and improvement of the play service, including representative groups and individuals (for instance, current and potential new users of the setting, individuals who may experience barriers to access – such as those with disabilities – and relevant colleagues within the play setting). You should contribute to the development and improvement of play services by:

- ☆ consulting the relevant colleagues about possible improvements to the setting
- ☆ getting your colleagues' approval to try out these improvements
- ☆ working with colleagues, representative groups and individuals to develop specific plans for improvements to the play service
- ☆ testing the feasibility and desirability of the improvements with representative groups and individuals
- ☆ using their feedback to make appropriate adjustments to the plans
- ☆ agreeing with the relevant colleague a full implementation plan for improvements.

(SkillsActive, 2004a)

Developing suggestions for play services based on research and consultation

Access to relevant market research is an essential tool for developing suggestions for improvements to play services. Market research provides a valuable insight into the play service market, its trends, and its current and potential new users. Local market research includes looking at the existing play services, children's and young people's play needs and preferences for play provision, and the requirements of the parents/carers in the community. These needs and requirements may be satisfied by your setting and other play services in the local area or may as yet be unmet. Needs and requirements are constantly changing, so market research should be updated regularly (using, say, short questionnaires or customer surveys). Market research also helps the play service to plan more effectively and to set realistic and achievable objectives (SureStart, 2003b).

An awareness of the existing play opportunities in your local area will help you to:

- ☆ identify any gaps in your setting and/or other play services in the community
- ☆ learn about your setting's strengths and weaknesses
- ☆ develop and improve play services for existing users
- ☆ promote the setting and encourage new users.

You also need to develop suggestions for play services based on consultation with children, young people and their parents/carers, as well as individuals and organisations in the voluntary, community and statutory sectors. You should consult children and/or young people about their views, ideas, wishes, aims, objectives and hopes for play services in their local area. The need to consult and listen to children about their play is important. (See the section in Chapter 2 on consulting and involving children and young people in decision-making.)

Your consultations should also involve the community and voluntary sectors – not just play-based organisations but other organisations, including the Council for Voluntary Service, rural community councils, disability organisations, equal opportunities and community relations bodies.

Consultations should also involve the statutory sector (such as the local authority, social services, health authority, local education authority, the housing department, planning department, police, youth service and any organisation with an interest in some aspect of play or play service provision).

KEY TASK

Give a detailed example of how you have contributed to the development and improvement of the play service. Include information on how you:

- consulted the relevant colleagues about possible improvements to the setting
- obtained your colleagues' approval to try out these improvements
- worked with colleagues, representative groups and individuals to develop specific plans for improvements to the play service
- tested the feasibility and desirability of the improvements with representative groups and individuals
- used their feedback to make appropriate adjustments to the plans
- agreed with the relevant colleague a full implementation plan for improvements.

NVQ links – Level 2: A52.3; Level 3: B227.2

The importance of networking

When developing suggestions for improving play service provision you need to understand the importance of networking. Establishing and maintaining effective links with other organisations and individuals can help you to develop play opportunities in the local community. For example, you can establish and maintain links with other organisations and individuals such as local Learning and Skills Councils, further and higher education colleges, and other local networks including parents/carers, disability groups, out-of-school clubs, community centres, leisure and sports centres.

You can help to develop network opportunities with other organisations and individuals by:

- ☆ identifying potential links
- ☆ establishing contact
- ☆ responding to approaches
- ☆ exploring the benefits of future links
- ☆ agreeing on methods of contact and exchange of information
- ☆ exchanging relevant information for the benefit of those involved.

Your play setting may be involved in a local Play Partnership aimed at improving children and young people's play environments, facilities, resources and awareness. If you do not have a Play Partnership in your local area, you might like to consider starting one by contacting relevant organisations such as local Play Councils or Play Forums, the local Early Years Development and Childcare Partnership (EYDCP), SureStart, the local Children's Trust, Children's Councils, Youth Councils, Regional Play Networks, Regional Centres for Playwork and Education, leisure services, local education authority, social services, health authority, GP Trusts, community councils, Council for Voluntary Service, and the like.

Members of the Play Partnership should agree and develop a common aim and philosophical base. Fair Play for Children (see 'Further reading') has a number of models available that can be adapted. Articles 31, 12, 13 and 14 from the UN Convention on the Rights of the Child should be adopted as the basic principles for working as a partnership. (See the information in Chapter 2 on the UN Convention on the Rights of the Child.)

KEY TASK

Give examples of how you have helped to develop network opportunities with other organisations and individuals, including information on how you have:

- identified potential links
- established contact
- responded to approaches
- explored the benefits of future links
- agreed on methods of contact and exchange of information
- exchanged relevant information for the benefit of those involved.

NVQ links – Level 3: B226.2

Promoting own area of playwork and the work of the play setting

You should be able to promote your own area of playwork and the work of the setting. You can make people in the local community aware of the range of play opportunities, including the benefits of play and playwork, by:

⭐ identifying opportunities to promote your area of playwork
⭐ identifying opportunities to promote the work of the setting

★ communicating the purpose, values and methods of playwork

★ presenting information about local play opportunities in appropriate ways

★ emphasising the benefits of playwork to the wider community

★ following the setting's policies and procedures for promoting play services.

(SkillsActive, 2004a)

Opportunities for promoting your own area of playwork and the work of the play setting include:

1. visual and written presentations
2. children's councils and youth forums
3. social action groups
4. community groups and meetings
5. advisory groups (e.g. for the organisation, playwork projects and research)
6. creative youth groups (e.g. videos, newsletters, drama, arts)
7. conferences and presentations (verbal, written, visual)
8. research and consultation
9. open days and other special events focused on play
10. advocacy with and for children and young people.

(Kirby *et al.*, 2003)

KEY TASK

Give examples of how you promote your own area of playwork and the work of the play setting. Include information on how you have:

- identified opportunities to promote your area of playwork
- identified opportunities to promote the work of the setting
- communicated the purpose, values and methods of playwork
- presented information about local play opportunities in appropriate ways
- emphasised the benefits of playwork to the wider community
- followed your setting's policies and procedures for promoting play services.

NVQ links – Level 3: B226.1

Contributing to the promotion of play services

One of your responsibilities may include contributing to the promotion of the play setting. You should be aware of the available resources, any legal requirements (e.g. Trades Descriptions Act) and the setting's policies and procedures relevant to promoting play services. You can make an effective contribution to promoting the services of the play setting by:

- ★ making suggestions for appropriate promotional methods
- ★ discussing and agreeing a promotional strategy with the relevant colleague
- ★ developing promotional methods and materials
- ★ implementing the promotional methods as agreed.

(SkillsActive, 2004a)

Developing promotional materials for play services

A promotional strategy involves a formal plan of where, how and when you intend to promote the play service. Whenever you contribute to the promotion of the services provided by the setting, it should be part of an overall promotional strategy.

Promotional methods include:

- ★ leaflet distribution and mail shots
- ★ media features (e.g. local newspapers, local radio/television)
- ★ advertising in newsletters, newspapers and magazines
- ★ links with local JobCentres
- ★ cards in newsagents and other shop windows, and on health centre or public noticeboards
- ★ posters in libraries or on noticeboards
- ★ open days and visits to the play setting
- ★ special events (e.g. local fairs, play events)
- ★ incentive schemes
- ★ advertising on the Internet, including creating own website.

When developing promotional methods and materials, remember the following important points.

- ★ Select the most effective way to reach your target audience.
- ★ Know how much money, if any, is available for advertising.
- ★ Try and make the play service stand out by including points that make it unique (for example, staff who are fluent in more than one language, flexible opening hours, outdoor play areas, activities for young people).
- ★ Try different styles to appeal to different target groups (for example, advertising aimed at children and/or young people will be different to that aimed at their parents/carers).

- ☆ Keep the message short but include key points such as age range, opening hours, examples of play opportunities and, if applicable, the cost of using the play facility.
- ☆ Inspire confidence and trust by mentioning that the play setting is registered and run by qualified and experienced playworkers.

(SureStart, 2003b)

An information pack

A well-presented information pack can be a useful way to provide potential users with all the information they need about the play setting. The pack should be attractive, simple and to the point. Present the pack in a distinctive, fun and professional way. Use a good printer and lay out the pages well. Put the pages in a good-quality folder or plastic binder. Include the following:

- ☆ front cover with the play setting name, logo or picture
- ☆ contact details (e.g. name, address, telephone number, e-mail address and website if the setting has one)
- ☆ brief history of the play setting (e.g. how long it has operated)
- ☆ the play service (e.g. full details of the play service being offered, such as age range, hours, prices (if applicable), facilities, play opportunities)
- ☆ experience and qualifications (e.g. details of the experience and qualifications of the playworkers)
- ☆ references (e.g. references from past and present users of the setting, including children's and/or young people's comments)
- ☆ 'good news stories' (e.g. press clippings, children's drawings, and possibly photos of play activities or outings)
- ☆ registration and documentation (e.g. copies of any relevant memberships, registrations and other professional/local authority certification).

(SureStart, 2003b)

KEY TASK

Describe how you have made a contribution to promoting the services of your setting. Include information on how you have:

- made suggestions for appropriate promotional methods
- discussed and agreed a promotional strategy with the relevant colleague(s)
- developed promotional methods and materials
- implemented the promotional methods as agreed.

NVQ links – Level 3: B227.3

Further reading

Children and Young People's Unit (2002) *Building a Strategy for Children and Young People*. CYPU.

Children's Play Council (2002) *Making the Case for Play: Building Policies and Strategies for School-aged Children*. National Children's Bureau.

DCMS (Department for Culture, Media & Sport) (2004) *Getting Serious About Play: A Review of Children's Play*. DCMS.

Fair Play for Children (n.d.) *Play Action Guide: Local Play Partnerships – a Grass Roots Exercise in Developing Children's Rights* and *Play Action Guide: Formulating a Local Play Policy*. (Both available free from the Fair Play for Children website at www.arunet.co.uk/fairplay/pubs.htm.)

Kirby, P. *et al.* (2003) *Building a Culture of Participation: Involving Children and Young People in Policy, Service Planning, Delivery and Evaluation – Handbook*. DfES.

National Playing Fields Association, Children's Play Council and Playlink (2000) *Best Play: What Play Provision Should do for Children*. NPFA.

Office of the Deputy Prime Minister (2003) *Developing Accessible Play Space: A Good Practice Guide*. ODPM. (Available free from the ODPM website at www.odpm.gov.uk.)

Playlink (2003) *Making Sense: Playwork in Practice*. Playlink.

SkillsActive (2004) *What can the Playwork Unit do for You?* National Network of Playwork Education and Training. (Available free from the SkillsActive Playwork Unit website at www.playwork.org.uk.)

SureStart (2003) *Marketing your Childcare Business*. (A 'Business Success for Childcare' guide, available free from the SureStart website at www.surestart.gov.uk/support4business.)

APPENDIX

A

A–Z of useful contacts and information

A

Advisory Conciliation and Arbitration Service (ACAS)

Head office: Brandon House, 180 Borough High Street, London SE1 1LW
Tel: 020 7210 3613 Helpline: 08457 47 47 47
Website: www.acas.org.uk

All4KidsUK Ltd

14 The Service Road, Potters Bar, Hertfordshire EN6 1QA
Tel: 01707 659383
Website: www.all4kidsuk.com
(A comprehensive children's directory for parents and carers.)

Amateur Swimming Association

Head office: ASA, Harold Fern House, Derby Square,
Loughborough LE11 5AL
Tel: 01509 618700
Website: www.britishswimming.org

Anti-Bullying Network

Moray House School of Education, University of Edinburgh,
Holyrood Road, Edinburgh EH8 8AQ
Tel: 0131 651 6100
Website: www.antibullying.net
(Provides information about bullying and anti-bullying strategies.)

Article 12

8 Wakley Street, London EC1V 7QE
Tel: 01305 880059
Website: www.article12.com
(An organisation run by children and young people aged under 18 years
for children and young people.)

B

Barnardo's

Head office: Tanners Lane, Barkingside, Ilford, Essex IG6 1QG
Tel: 020 8550 8822
Website: www.barnardos.org.uk

Bar Pro Bono Unit

7 Gray's Inn Square, London WC1R 5AZ
Tel: 020 7831 9711
Website: www.barprobono.org.uk
(Provides free legal advice and representation for people in England
and Wales who cannot afford legal assistance or where legal aid is not
available.)

British Red Cross
9 Grosvenor Crescent, London SW1X 7EJ
Tel: 020 7235 5454
Website: www.redcross.org.uk

British Youth Council
The Mezzanine 2, 2nd Floor, Downstream Building, 1 London Bridge,
London SE1 9BG
Tel: 0845 458 1489
Website: www.byc.org.uk
(A charity run by young people for young people.)

Bully Online
9 Knox Way, Harrogate, North Yorkshire HG1 3JL
Website: www.bullying.co.uk
(A registered charity providing information for children, parents and teachers.)

C
Child Accident Prevention Trust (CAPT)
18–20 Farringdon Lane, London EC1R 3HA
Tel: 020 7608 3828
Website: www.capt.org.uk

Children's Law Centre (for Northern Ireland)
Tel: 0808 808 5678 (for young people), 028 9043 4242 (for adults)
Website: www.childrenslawcentre.org

Children's Legal Centre (for England and Wales)
University of Essex, Wivenhoe Park, Colchester, Essex CO4 3SQ
Tel: 01206 873820 (general legal advice)
Website: www.childrenslegalcentre.com
(Offers free legal advice and information on the law in relation to children.)

Children Now
Haymarket Professional Publications, 174 Hammersmith Road, London W6 7JP
Tel: 020 8267 4706
Website: www.childrennow.co.uk
(Weekly magazine for people working with children and their families. The
website includes job vacancies and access to a free newsletter via e-mail.)

Children's Play Council
National Children's Bureau, 8 Wakley Street, London EC1V 7QE
Tel: 020 7843 6016
Website: www.ncb.org.uk

Children's Play Information Service
National Children's Bureau, 8 Wakley Street, London EC1V 7QE
Tel: 020 7843 6303
Website: www.ncb.org.uk

Children's Rights Alliance for England
94 White Lion Street, London N1 9PF
Tel: 020 7278 8222
Website: www.crae.org.uk

Commission for Racial Equality (CRE)
Head office: St Dunstan's House, 201–211 Borough High Street, London SE1 1GZ
Tel: 020 7939 0000 (general enquiries)
Website: www.cre.gov.uk

Council for Awards in Children's Care and Education (CACHE)
8 Chequer Street, St Albans, Hertfordshire AL1 3XZ
Tel: 01727 847636
Website: www.cachc.org.uk

Criminal Records Bureau (CRB)
Information line: 0870 909 0811
Website: www.crb.gov.uk
Disclosures website: www.disclosure.gov.uk

D
Department for Education and Skills (DfES)
Sanctuary Buildings, Great Smith Street, London SW1P 3BT
Tel: 0870 000 2288
Website: www.dfes.gov.uk

Disability Rights Commission (DRC)
Freepost MID 02164, Stratford-upon-Avon CV37 9BR
Helpline: 08457 622 633 (Textphone: 08457 622 644)
Website: www.drc-gb.org

Disability Information Centre
Middlesbrough General Hospital, Ayresome Green Lane, Middlesbrough TS5 5AZ
Tel: 01642 827471

E
Edexcel
Head office: Stewart House, 32 Russell Square, London WC1B 5DN
Tel: 0870 240 9800 (customer services)
Website: www.edexcel.org.uk

Equal Opportunities Commission
Arndale House, Arndale Centre, Manchester M4 3EQ
Tel: 0845 601 5901 (general enquiries)
Website: www.eoc.org.uk

F
4children (formerly Kids Club Network)
Bellerive House, 3 Muirfield Crescent, London E14 9SZ
Tel: 020 7512 2112
Website: www.4children.org.uk

Fair Play for Children
35 Lyon Street, Bognor Regis, West Sussex PO21 1BW
Tel: 0845 330 7635
Website: www.arunet.co.uk/fairplay

G
Games For Kids
Website: www.links4kids.co.uk
(Contains links to websites with educational games and fun activities for children.)

H
Healthy Living
Helpline: 0845 2 78 88 78
Website: www.healthyliving.gov.uk
(Scotland's healthy living campaign website.)

I
Institute of Leisure and Amenity Management (ILAM)
ILAM House, Lower Basildon, Reading, Berkshire RG8 9NE
Tel: 01491 874800
Website: www.ilam.co.uk

J
Justice for Children
Website: www.childline.org.uk/extra/campaigns-childwitnesses.asp
(A coalition of more than 60 organisations campaigning for child-centred changes to the justice system.)

K
Kidscape
2 Grosvenor Gardens, London SW1W ODH
Tel: 020 7730 3300
Website: www.kidscape.org.uk
(The national charity to help prevent bullying and child abuse.)

L
The Law Centres Federation
Duchess House, 18–19 Warren Street, London W1T 5LR
Tel: 020 7387 8570
Website: www.lawcentres.org.uk
(Free and independent professional legal advice.)

Learndirect
Tel: 0800 100 900 (free advice line)
Website: www.learndirect.org.uk

Learning and Skills Council
Head office: Cheylesmore House, Quinton Road, Coventry CV1 2WT
Tel: 0845 019 4170, Helpline: 0870 900 6800
Website: www.lsc.gov.uk/national/default.htm

M
Mind
Granta House, 15–19 Broadway, London E15 4BQ
Tel: 020 8221 9666 (publications), 08457 660 163 (Mind info line)
Website: www.mind.org.uk
(Provides mental health support and information on mental health issues.)

N
National Children's Bureau
8 Wakley Street, London EC1V 7QE
Tel: 020 7843 6000
Website: www.ncb.org.uk/home.php

National Institute for Health and Clinical Excellence (NICE)
MidCity Place, 71 High Holborn, London WC1V 6NA
Tel: 020 7067 5800
Website: www.nice.org.uk

National Playing Fields Association (NPFA)
Stanley House, St Chad's Place, London WC1X 9HH
Tel: 020 7833 5360
Website: www.npfa.co.uk

National Society for the Prevention of Cruelty to Children (NSPCC)
Weston House, 42 Curtain Road, London EC2A 3NH
Tel: 020 7825 2500
NSPCC Child Protection Helpline: 0808 800 5000 (24-hour)
Website: www.nspcc.org.uk/html/home/home.htm

National Youth Agency
Eastgate House, 19–23 Humberstone Road, Leicester LE5 3GJ
Tel: 0116 242 7350
Website: www.nya.org.uk

O
Office for Standards in Education (Ofsted)
Alexandra House, 33 Kingsway, London WC2B 6SE
Tel: 020 7421 6800, Helpline: 08456 014771
Website: www.ofsted.gov.uk

Out of School
Nursery World, Admiral House, 66–68 East Smithfield, London E1W 1BX
Tel: 020 7782 3000
Website: www.nurseryworld.co.uk
(Monthly supplement included in *Nursery World* magazine.)

P

PlayBoard
59–65 York Street, Belfast, Northern Ireland BT15 1AA
Tel: 028 9080 3380 (head office)
Website: www.playboard.org

Playlink
72 Albert Palace Mansions, Lurline Gardens, London SW11 4DQ
Tel: 0207 720 2452
Website: www.playlink.org.uk

Play Wales
Baltic House, Mount Stuart Square, Cardiff CF10 5FH
Tel: 029 2048 6050
Website: www.playwales.org.uk

Pre-school Learning Alliance
Unit 213–216, 30 Great Guildford Street, London SE1 0HS
Tel: 020 7620 0550
Website: www.pre-school.org.uk

Q

Qualifications and Curriculum Authority (QCA)
83 Piccadilly, London W1J 8QA
Tel: 020 7509 5555
Website: www.qca.org.uk
(Useful information on the qualification and training framework for playwork, as well as early years care and education.)

Queen Elizabeth's Foundation for Disabled People
Leatherhead Court, Woodlands Road, Leatherhead, Surrey KT22 0BN
Tel: 01372 841100
Website: www.qefd.org

R

Rainer
Rectory Lodge, High Street, Brasted, Kent TN16 1JF
Tel: 01959 578200
Website: www.raineronline.org
(Provides comprehensive services for under-supported young people, including aftercare projects for young people leaving care or young offenders' institutions, employment projects, counselling and mentoring.)

Royal Society for the Prevention of Accidents (RoSPA)
Edgbaston Park, 353 Bristol Road, Birmingham B5 7ST
Tel: 0121 248 2000 (general information)
Website: www.rospa.com

S

St John Ambulance
27 St John's Lane, London EC1M 4BU
Tel: 08700 10 49 50
Website: www.sja.org.uk

Save the Children
1 St John's Lane, London EC1M 4AR
Tel: 020 7012 6400
Website: www.savethechildren.org.uk

Scottish Child Law Centre
54 East Crosscauseway, Edinburgh EH8 9HD
Tel: 0131 667 6333 (information helpline), 0800 328 8970 (free legal advice for under-18s)
Website: www.sclc.org.uk
(Provides information on Scottish law and children's rights.)

SkillsActive Playwork Unit
6th Floor, Castlewood House, 77–91 New Oxford Street, London WC1A 1PX
Tel: 020 7632 2000
Website: www.playwork.org.uk

SureStart Unit
2C, Caxton House, Tothill Street, London SW1H 9NF
Tel: 0870 000 2288 (Public Enquiry Unit)
Website: www.surestart.gov.uk
SureStart working with children and young people
Website: www.childcarecareers.gov.uk

T
Trades Union Congress (TUC)
Congress House, Great Russell Street, London WC1B 3LS
Tel: 020 7636 4030 (general enquiries), 0870 600 4882 (rights line)
Website: www.tuc.org.uk
(For comprehensive information on many work-related issues.)

Traveline
Public transport information
Tel: 0870 608 2 608
Website: www.pti.org.uk
(Impartial information on planning your journey, by bus, coach or train.)

U
UNICEF UK – The Rights Site
UNICEF UK, Education Department, Africa House, 64–78 Kingsway, London WC2B 6NB
Tel: 020 7312 7611
Website: www.therightssite.org.uk

V
Voice for the Child in Care
Unit 4, Pride Court, 80–82 White Lion Street, London N1 9PF
Tel: 0808 800 5792 (for young people)
Website: www.vcc-uk.org/vcc_public/default.asp
(Provides advocates for young people who are in care, have left care or are involved with social services.)

Volunteering England
Regents Wharf, 8 All Saints Street, London N1 9RL
Tel: 0800 028 3304
Website: www.navb.org.uk

W
Winston's Wish
Clara Burgess Centre, Bayshill Road, Cheltenham GL50 3AW
Tel: 0845 2030405
Website: www.winstonswish.org.uk
(Support for bereaved children, young people, families and professionals.)

Women's Aid Federation of England
PO Box 391, Bristol BS99 7WS
Helpline: 0808 2000 247 (Freefone 24-hour)
website: www.womensaid.org.uk
(A national charity offering support, advice and information on domestic violence.)

X
Xchange
Website: www.bbc.co.uk/xchange/index.shtml
(Contains games and fun activities for children, plus links to other BBC websites for children.)

Y
Young Minds
102–108 Clerkenwell Road, London EC1M 5SA
Tel: 020 7336 8445
Website: www.youngminds.org.uk
(Information on children's mental health for young people, parents and professionals.)

Young People Now
Haymarket Professional Publications, 174 Hammersmith Road, London W6 7JP
Tel: 020 8267 4793
Website: www.ypnmagazine.com/home/index.cfm
(Weekly magazine for those working with young people aged 11 to 25 years. The website includes job vacancies and access to a free newsletter via e-mail.)

Z
Zoo directory
Website: www.ukwebfind.co.uk/dispzoos.html
(Lists zoos, safari parks, wildlife parks, Sea Life Centres, theme parks, castles, museums, art galleries and other attractions suitable for children.)

B Record of key tasks

KEY TASK	Date completed
Chapter 2: The play environment	
• Find out more about the UN Convention on the Rights of the Child.	
• Investigate the rights of children/young people in your local community.	
• Make a list of the existing policies and procedures that relate to the rights of children and young people in your play setting.	
• Design a booklet (for parents, students or volunteers) outlining how your play setting promotes children's and young people's rights.	
• Working with children and young people, develop suggestions for meeting their rights in the play setting.	
• Outline the ways your play setting consults and involves children and/or young people in decision-making.	
• Explain your role and responsibilities in developing, implementing and reviewing policies and procedures.	
Chapter 3: Play and child development	
• Collect information on the play needs and preferences of the children and/or young people in your play setting.	
• Observe a child during a play activity.	
Chapter 4: Planning and supporting play	
• List the range of existing play spaces or play environments in your local area.	
• Describe how you plan and support children's and/or young people's play in your play setting.	
• List the main play resources available in your setting.	
• List the ways in which you provide appropriate support for children's and/or young people's self-directed play.	
• Describe how you have observed and responded to a child's/young person's play cues.	
• Give two examples of how you have supported children's and/or young people's play frames.	

KEY TASK	Date completed
Chapter 4 (continued)	
• List examples of each play type based on your experiences of providing play opportunities for children and/or young people.	
• Observe children and/or young people involved in a play activity.	
• Outline the play setting's policies and procedures that are relevant to risk-taking during play activities	
• Describe how you have ended a play session.	
Chapter 5: Health and safety in the play setting	
• Find out about the statutory and regulatory requirements that apply to your play setting.	
• Find out about the legal and organisational requirements for the toilet and wash areas in your play setting.	
• Find out about your play setting's policy and procedures for responding to children's illnesses or allergies in the setting.	
• Find out about your play setting's policy and procedures for dealing with accidents and injuries, including the provision of first aid.	
• Find out about your play setting's fire and evacuation procedures.	
• Outline the procedures for risk assessment and dealing with hazards in your play setting.	
• Find out about your play setting's policy and procedures relating to health and safety and maintaining children's safety during play.	
• Give a reflective account of your involvement in an outing or trip.	
Chapter 6: Child protection	
• What are your play setting's procedures for reporting the signs of possible abuse?	
• What are your role and responsibilities for reporting information on possible abuse to a senior colleague or external agency?	
• Give a reflective account of how you have handled a child's personal disclosure.	
• Find out about your setting's policy and procedures with regard to the confidentiality of information in child protection matters.	
• Outline your play setting's anti-bullying policy and main strategies for dealing with bullying behaviour.	
Chapter 7: Children's health and well-being	
• Find out what information on healthy lifestyles for children and young people is available in your local area.	

KEY TASK	Date completed
Chapter 7 (continued)	
• Working with a group of children and/or young people, design a poster that illustrates the importance of personal hygiene.	
• What are your play setting's procedures for the preparation and storage of food?	
• Describe how you have encouraged and supported children's and/or young people's emotional well-being.	
• What are the procedures in your play setting for welcoming and settling in children and/or young people new to the setting?	
Chapter 8: Promoting positive relationships and behaviour	
• List four ways in which you have shown that you value children's individuality, ideas and feelings.	
• Listen to adults talking with children and/or young people.	
• Describe how you have involved children and/or young people in decision-making and encouraged them to make choices within the play setting.	
• Think about the goals and boundaries that might be appropriate to the children and/or young people you work with in your play setting.	
• Devise and implement an activity that could encourage children and/or young people to play together in a positive way.	
• Find out about the behaviour policy for your play setting.	
• Find out about your play setting's policy for sanctions relating to children's and/or young people's behaviour.	
• Suggest how children could deal with potential conflict situations themselves.	
Chapter 9: Working with parents and carers	
• Describe how your play setting establishes and develops positive working relationships with parents and carers.	
• Give examples of how your play setting provides clear and accurate information for parents and carers.	
• What are your play setting's procedures for dealing with complaints from parents or carers?	
• List four ways to encourage parents and carers to become involved in the work of the play setting.	

KEY TASK	Date completed
Chapter 10: Professional practice	
• Draw up a job description for your ideal playwork job.	
• List examples of how you communicate with colleagues at your play setting.	
• List the methods you use to share information with colleagues at your play setting.	
• Participate in a staff or team meeting relevant to your role at the play setting.	
• Describe how you have asked for help, information or support from your colleagues.	
• Outline your play setting's procedures for dealing with conflict.	
• Describe how you have challenged (or would challenge) discrimination or prejudice in the play setting.	
• Compile a resource pack that promotes equal opportunities.	
• Find out about your play setting's policies and procedures for diversity and inclusion.	
• Give examples of the types of record used in your play setting.	
• Describe how you review and improve your own work performance.	
• Give examples of your participation in training and development opportunities.	
Chapter 11: Managing a play setting	
• Outline the methods you use to manage a budget in your play setting.	
• Compile an application pack for the post of playworker at your play setting.	
• Give a reflective account of your involvement in the recruitment and selection process at your play setting.	
• Give examples of effective planning and fair allocation of work within your area of responsibility.	
• Outline the methods you use to monitor the progress and quality of work of individuals and/or teams within your area of responsibility in the play setting.	
• Describe how you have responded (or would respond) to a conflict situation as the manager or team leader in a play setting.	
• Describe how you identify the learning needs of your colleagues and provide learning opportunities to meet them.	

KEY TASK	Date completed
Chapter 12: Promoting play services	
• Outline the resources and organisational policies that are relevant to evaluating the play service provision.	
• Give examples of how you have gained and used feedback about play initiatives.	
• Describe how you have been involved in developing and improving play services.	
• Give a detailed example of how you have contributed to the development and improvement of the play service.	
• Give examples of how you have helped to develop network opportunities.	
• Give an example of how you promote your own area of playwork and the work of the play setting.	
• Describe how you have made a contribution to promoting the services of your play setting.	

Glossary

activity: play and learning opportunity that involves active participation and discussion.

adult/child ratio: the number of adults in relation to children within the setting (e.g. three adults with a group of thirty children would be shown as a ratio of 1:10).

anti-discriminatory practice: taking positive action to challenge discrimination.

behaviour: a person's actions, reactions and treatment of others.

bullying: behaviour that is deliberately hurtful or aggressive.

carer: any person with responsibility for the care/education of a child during the parent's temporary or permanent absence.

child abuse: a person's actions that cause a child to suffer *significant harm* to their health, development or well-being.

cognitive: intellectual abilities involving processing information received through the senses.

community language: main language spoken in a child's home.

concepts: the way people make sense of and organise information.

conflict situations: verbal or physical disagreement (e.g. arguments, fighting, disputing rules).

consultation: actively involving other people in a two-way process of sharing information and ideas and decision-making.

disclosure: details of a person's criminal history obtained from the Criminal Records Bureau in order to check their suitability to work with children, young people and other vulnerable groups.

diversity: a mix of people from various ethnic, cultural and social backgrounds.

egocentric: preoccupied with own needs; unable to see another person's viewpoint.

emotional outburst: uncontrolled expression of intense emotion (e.g. rage or frustration).

enhanced disclosure: comprehensive check of a person's criminal history for those having unsupervised contact with children, young people and other vulnerable groups.

equal opportunities: the provision and promotion of equal chances and choices (e.g. equal access to a full range of play opportunities for all children and young people regardless of race, gender or disability).

facilitator: person who makes things easier by providing the appropriate environment and resources.

ground rules: the agreed rules for play opportunities.

group dynamics: people's social interaction and their behaviour within social groups.

holistic: the holistic approach means looking at the 'whole' child (i.e. *all* aspects of the child's development).

inclusion: the principle whereby all children and young people, including those with disabilities or from minority groups, have full and open access to mainstream settings, including play facilities.

IQ or intelligence quotient: a person's mental age in comparison to their chronological age.

key factor: an essential aspect affecting play, learning and development.

mediator: a person who acts as an intermediary between parties in a dispute.

milestones: significant skills that children and young people develop in and around certain ages as part of the usual or expected pattern of development.

modes of language: the different ways to communicate with other people, e.g. thinking, speaking, listening, reading, writing and non-verbal communication.

norm: the usual pattern or expected level of development/behaviour.

parent: person with parental responsibility (as defined in the Children Act 1989).

peers: children or young people of similar age within the setting.

personality: distinctive and individual characteristics that affect each person's view of themselves, their needs, feelings and relationships with others.

play cues: facial expressions, language or body language that communicate the child's or young person's wish to play or invite others to play.

play environments: environments with resources to stimulate children's and young people's play.

play frame: material or non-material boundary that keeps the play intact.

play needs: are the individual needs of children and young people for play.

play settings: anywhere where children and young people can play.

play spaces: areas that support and enrich the potential for children and young people to play.

problem-solving: activities that involve finding solutions to a difficulty or question.

psychological: relating to the study of the mind and behaviour, including language, cognitive, social and emotional development.

quality: standard of care and play opportunities provided in the play setting (ideally high/excellent).

resources: the range of equipment and materials needed to stimulate play.

role models: significant people whose actions, speech or mannerisms are imitated by a child.

sensory: relating to the senses; sensory experiences enable children to make sense of their environment.

sequence: development following the same basic pattern but not necessarily at fixed ages.

social context: any situation or environment where social interaction occurs (e.g. home, play setting, local community).

socialisation: the process of developing social and emotional skills to enable children to relate positively to others.

special needs: all children have individual needs, but some children may have additional needs due to physical disability, sensory impairment, learning difficulty or emotional/behavioural difficulty.

specialist: person with specific training/additional qualifications in a particular area of development (e.g. speech and language therapist, educational psychologist).

stages: development that occurs at fixed ages.

stereotyped: simplistic characterisation or expectation of a person based on perceived differences or prejudices relating to their race, culture, gender, disability or age.

temperament: person's disposition or personality, especially their emotional responses.

time in: giving each child or young person special individual attention to reinforce positive behaviour.

time out: a short break or suspension of an activity that allows a cooling-off period for all involved but that, especially, gives the child or young person a chance to calm down.

transition: the process of adjusting to a new situation or new people.

References

Association of Teachers and Lecturers (2000) ATL guide to children's attitudes, in *Report*, June/July issue. ATL.

Ball, C. (1994) *Start Right: The Importance of Early Learning*. RSA

Bartholomew, L. and **Bruce**, T. (1993) *Getting to Know You: A Guide to Record-Keeping in Early Childhood Education and Care*. Hodder & Stoughton.

Bethea, L. (1999) Primary prevention of child abuse, *American Family Physician* 5(6).

Brennan, W.K. (1987) *Changing Special Education Now*. Open University Press.

British Nutrition Foundation (2003) *The Balance of Good Health*. British Nutrition Foundation.

Brown, F. (ed.) (2002) *Playwork: Theory and Practice*. Open University Press.

Bruce, T. (2001) *Learning Through Play*. Hodder & Stoughton.

Bullen, P. (1996) Evaluating human services, *Evaluation News and Comment: The Magazine of the Australasian Evaluation Society*, June.

Burton, G. and **Dimbleby**, R. (1995) *Between Ourselves: An Introduction to Interpersonal Communication* (rev. edn). Arnold.

Child Accident Prevention Trust (2002a) *Taking Chances: The Lifestyles and Leisure Risks of Young People*. CAPT.

Child Accident Prevention Trust (2002b) *Factsheet: Home Accidents*. CAPT.

Child Accident Prevention Trust (2002c) *Factsheet: Toys and Accidents*. CAPT.

Child Accident Prevention Trust (2003) *Factsheet: Child Accident Facts*. CAPT.

Child Accident Prevention Trust (2004a) *Factsheet: Children and Accidents*. CAPT.

Child Accident Prevention Trust (2004b) *Factsheet: Playground Accidents*. CAPT.

Children and Young People's Unit (2001) *Learning to Listen: Core Principles for the Involvement of Children and Young People*. DfES.

Children and Young People's Unit (2002) *Building a Strategy for Children and Young People*. CYPU.

Commission for Racial Equality (1989) *From Cradle to School: A Practical Guide to Race Equality and Childcare*. CRE.

Dare, A. and **O'Donovan**, M. (1997) *Good Practice in Caring for Children with Special Needs*. Stanley Thornes.

Davenport, C. (1994) *An Introduction to Child Development*. Collins Educational.

Davie, R. (1994) Social development and social behaviour, in D. Fontana (ed.) *The Education of the Young Child*. Blackwell.

Davy, A. (1998) *Playwork: Play and Care for Children 5–15* (rev. edn). Macmillan.

DCMS (Department for Culture, Media & Sport) (2004) *Getting Serious About Play: A Review of Children's Play*. DCMS.

DfEE (Department for Education and Employment) (1998a) *Guidance on First Aid for Schools: A Good Practice Guide*. DfEE.

DfEE (1998b) *Health and Safety of Pupils on Educational Visits: A Good Practice Guide*. DfEE.

DfEE/DOH (1996) *Supporting Pupils with Medical Needs: A Good Practice Guide*. DfEE.

DfES (Department for Education and Skills) (2000) *Bullying: Don't Suffer in Silence – an Anti-bullying Pack for Schools*. DfES.

DfES (2002) *Transforming Youth Work: Resourcing Excellent Youth Services*. DfES/Connexions.

DfES (2003) *National Standards for Under 8s Daycare and Childminding: Out of School Care*. DfES.

DfES (2004a) *Need a Nanny? A Guide for Parents*. DfES.

DfES (2004b) *Every Child Matters: Change for Children*. DfES.

DOH (Department of Health) (1991) *The Children Act 1989: Guidance and regulations, Volume 2: Family Support, Day Care and Educational Provision and Young Children*. HMSO.

DOH (1997) *The Children Act 1989 – Guidance and Regulations*. HMSO.

DOH (2003) *What to do if You're Worried a Child is Being Abused*. HMSO.

DOH (2004) *Choosing Health: Making Healthier Choices Easier*. The Stationery Office.

DOH, Home Office and Department for Education (1999) *Working Together to Safeguard Children*. HMSO.

Donaldson, M. (1978) *Children's Minds*. Fontana.

Douch, P. (2004) What does inclusive play actually look like?, *Playtoday* 42, May/June.

Dunn, K. *et al.* (2004) *Research on Developing Accessible Play Space: Final Report*. HMSO.

Early Years National Training Organisation (2003) *Wanting to Work in Early Years Education, Childcare and Playwork* and *Get that job in Early Education, Childcare and Playwork*. Both available from the Early Years NTO website at www.early-years-nto.org.uk.

Einon, D. (1986) *Creative Play*. Penguin.

Fontana, D. (1994) Personality and personal development, in D. Fontana (ed.) *The Education of the Young Child*. Blackwell.

Foster-Cohen, S. (1999) *Introduction to Child Language Development*. Longman.

Goleman, D. (1996) *Emotional Intelligence*. Bloomsbury.

Harding, J. and **Meldon-Smith**, L. (2000) *How to Make Observations and Assessments* (2nd edn). Hodder & Stoughton.
Henderson, A. and **Tyrie**, J. (1991) Using adult resources, *Child Education*, December.
Hobart, C. and **Frankel**, J. (1995) *A Practical Guide to Activities for Young Children*. Stanley Thornes.
Houghton, D. and **McColgan**, M. (1995) *Working with Children*. Collins Educational.

Institute of Leisure and Amenity Management (1999) *Indoor Play Areas: Guidance on Safe Practice*. ILAM.

Kamen, T. (2000) *Psychology for Childhood Studies*. Hodder & Stoughton.
Kidscape (2001) *Keep Them Safe*. Kidscape.
Kirby, P. *et al.* (2003) *Building a Culture of Participation: Involving Children and Young People in Policy, Service Planning, Delivery and Evaluation – Handbook*. DfES.

Laishley, J. (1987) *Working with Young Children*. Edward Arnold.
Leach, P. (1994) *Children First*. Penguin.
Lee, V. and **Das Gupta**, P. (eds) (1995) *Children's Cognitive and Language Development*. Blackwell.
Lindenfield, G. (1995) *Self Esteem*. Thorsons.
Lindon, J. (2001) *Understanding Children's Play*. Nelson Thornes.
Lindon (2002) *What is Play?* Children's Play Information Service factsheet. National Children's Bureau.

Maddocks, J. (2002) *Playwork Training and Qualifications: Meeting the Daycare Standards*. SPRITO/SkillsActive Playwork Unit.
Masheder, M. (1989a) *Let's Co-operate*. Peace Education Project.
Masheder, M. (1989b) *Let's Play Together*. Green Print.
Matterson, E. (1989) *Play with a Purpose for the Under-Sevens*. Penguin.
Moon, A. (1992) Take care of yourself, *Child Education*, February.
Morris, J. and **Mort**, J. (1991) *Bright Ideas for Early Years: Learning Through Play*. Scholastic.
Mort, L. and **Morris**, J. (1989) *Bright Ideas for Early Years: Getting Started*. Scholastic.
Moyles, J. (ed.) (1994) *The Excellence of Play*. Open University Press.

National Playing Fields Association, Children's Play Council and Playlink (2000) *Best Play: What Play Provision Should do for Children*. NPFA.

O'Hagan, M. and **Smith**, M. (1993) *Special Issues in Child Care*. Bailliere Tindall.

Office of the Deputy Prime Minister (2003) *Developing Accessible Play Space: A Good Practice Guide*. ODPM.

Petrie, P. (1989) *Communicating with Children and Adults: Interpersonal Skills for Those Working with Babies and Children*. Hodder Arnold.

Play Wales and PlayEducation (2001) *The First Claim: A Framework for Playwork Quality Assessment*. Play Wales.

Roet, B. (1998) *The Confidence to be Yourself*. Piatkus.

RoSPA (Royal Society for the Prevention of Accidents) (2004a) Play Safety Information Sheet: *Information Sheet Number 16 – Legal Aspects of Safety on Children's Play Areas*. RoSPA.

RoSPA (2004b) Play Safety Information Sheet: *Information Sheet Number 22 – Design of Play Areas*. RoSPA.

RoSPA (2004c) Play Safety Information Sheet: *Information Sheet Number 25 – Risk assessment of Children's Play Areas*. RoSPA.

Royal College of Psychiatrists (2002) *Child Abuse and Neglect – the Emotional Effects. Factsheet 20, For Parents And Teachers*. Royal College of Psychiatrists.

Scottish Executive (2003) *Vulnerable Children and Young People*. HMSO.

Siraj-Blatchford, I. (1994) *The Early Years: Laying the Foundations for Racial Equality*. Trentham Books.

SkillsActive (2004a) *What can The Playwork Unit do for You?* The National Network of Playwork Education and Training.

SkillsActive (2004b) *National Occupational Standards NVQ/SVQ Level 3 in Playwork*. SkillsActive.

SkillsActive (2004c) *Playwork Training and Qualifications*. SkillsActive.

SPRITO (2002) *National Occupational Standards Playwork NVQ/SVQ Level 2*. SPRITO.

SPRITO/SkillsActive Playwork Unit (2001) *Recruitment, Training and Qualifications in Playwork – an Employer's Guide*. SPRITO/SkillsActive Playwork Unit.

SPRITO/SkillsActive Playwork Unit (2002) *Quality Training, Quality Play – the National Strategy for Playwork Education, Training and Qualifications 2002–2005*. SPRITO/SkillsActive Playwork Unit.

SureStart (2003a) *Managing Finance*, a 'Team Steps to Success' guide (Business Success for Childcare – SureStart). DfES.

SureStart (2003b) *Marketing your Childcare Business*, a 'Team Steps to Success' guide (Business Success for Childcare – SureStart). DfES.

SureStart (2003c) *Recruitment and Retention: A Good Practice Guide for Early Years, Childcare and Playwork Providers*. DfES.

Sylva, K. and **Lunt**, I. (1982) *Child Development: A First Course*. Basil Blackwell.

Tough, J. (1994) How young children develop and use language, in D. Fontana (ed.) *The Education of the Young Child*. Blackwell.

Train, A. (1996) *ADHD: How to Deal with Very Difficult Children*. Souvenir Press.

Wade, H. and **Badham**, B. (2003) *Hear by Right: Standards for the Active Involvement of Children and Young People*. National Youth Agency and Local Government Association.

Watkinson, A. (2003) *The Essential Guide for Competent Teaching Assistants*. David Fulton Publishers.

Whitehead, M. (1996) *The Development of Language and Literacy*. Hodder & Stoughton.

Wood, D. (1988) *How Children Think and Learn*. Blackwell.

Woolfson, R. (1989) *Understanding your Child: A Parents' Guide to Child Psychology*. Faber & Faber.

Woolfson, R. (1991) *Children with Special Needs: A Guide for Parents and Carers*. Faber & Faber.

Yardley, A. (1994) Understanding and encouraging children's play, in D. Fontana (ed.) *The Education of the Young Child*. Blackwell.

Yeo, A. and **Lovell**, T. (1998) *Sociology for Childhood Studies*. Hodder & Stoughton.

Index

abuse *see* child abuse
accidents 104, 110–11
achievement 58, 67
  and emotional well-being 145
  national framework 40–1
  see also competitiveness
acoustic conditions 31
active listening 161
activities
  for child development 58, 88
  encouraging risk taking 92
  for equal opportunity 206
  exploratory play 89
  imaginative play 90
  planning 74–5
adolescents, development 57, 60,
    62–3, 65, 67
adult resources 82
aggressive behaviour 171
annual leave 236
application forms 16–17
  see also job applications
argumentativeness 66, 67
art therapy, career 24
assertiveness 171, 179, 187
assertiveness techniques
  for children 129
  for playworkers 215
assessment 69–70
attention, from adults 177
attention span 62
attitudes 7–8, 34, 40, 160
auditory perception, activities 63
autocratic leadership 221

balance 59
balanced diet 142–4
ball games 88
basic disclosure 233
behaviour
  causing bullying 134
  goals and boundaries 58, 164–5
  modes for play 85
  negative 176–8, 195
    influences 172, 176
  of playworkers 157–8

  positive 170–1, 172–5
  social development 57
Best Play 246, 251
books 58, 68, 148, 179
boundaries 58, 85, 164–5
budgets 224–5
buildings, health and safety 96
bullying 133, 134

careers with children 4–5, 23–4, 24–9
carers 171, 181–8
challenge, degree of 68, 84, 92
change 151–3
Chartered Institute of Environmental
    Health 141
child abuse
  allegations 158
  definition 118
  response to evidence 124–6
  self-protection 128–9
  signs 122–3
  types 119
  vulnerability factors 123–4
child development 55–69, 200
child protection 117–18, 119–21,
    124–8, 158, 195, 214
childcare 41–2
childhood illness 100–2
childminding 24–5, 39
children
  as centre of play process 33
  decision making 43, 45, 48, 68, 92
  needs 34, 45–6, 54
  rights 34, 35–6, 37–9, 43, 44, 45,
    47, 157
  see also child abuse; child
    development; child protection
Children Act 1989 37–8, 200, 232
Children Act 2004 38–9
Children (Scotland) Act 1995 36
Children and Young People's Plan
    (CYPP) 39
children's centres 41–2
Children's Commissioner 38, 39
children's nursing, career 25
Children's Rights Alliance for England
    45, 46

children's trusts 41
Children's and Young People's Unit 48
closed questions 161
co-operation 34, 57, 168, 169, 178–9
    in networks 257
co-ordination 59, 60
code of conduct 159
cognitive development 61–3
collage 89
communication
    with children 65–6, 160, 161–3
    with other staff 194–5
    with parents and carers 182, 183,
        184–6
    in playwork 32
    social development 57
communication play 86
communication skills, development
        63–4
community organisations 41–2
competitiveness 57, 58, 62, 67, 168–9
    see also achievement
concentration 62
conditions of service 21
confidence, growth 67
confidentiality 70, 126–7, 182, 212, 214,
        232
conflict
    between children 178–80
    between staff 198–9, 243
    staff and parents/carers 187
consistency, for behaviour 175, 177
consultation
    with children 43, 48, 54, 80, 93, 143,
        256
    on service development 255–8
consumable resources 81, 82, 83
continuing professional development
        217–18, 244–6
contract of employment 192, 234–5, 243
cooking 89
coping strategies, for risky situations
        130–4
corporal punishment 158
courses see qualifications; training
covering letters 17
creative play 33, 62, 86, 148
creative process 32
creativity, activities 63
Criminal Justice and Court Services Act
        2000 234
Criminal Records Bureau 233
critical thinking, for children 130

cultural diversity 30, 82, 143, 203–4,
        206, 209
curiosity, stimulation 63
curriculum vitae (CV) 17–18, 19

Data Protection Act 1998 127, 202,
        212–13
day care 39, 41–2
Day Care and Childminding (National
        Standards) (England) Regulation
        2003 96, 200–2, 232
decision making, with children 43, 45,
        48, 68, 163
deep play 86
delegation, of tasks 240
democratic leadership 222
diet, healthy eating 142–4
disability
    and communication 162–3
    discrimination legislation 202
    and emergency procedures 107
    encouraging independence 43
    models of 204–5
    and play 53
    see also special needs
Disability Discrimination Act 1995 202,
        233, 254
disciplinary procedures 243
discipline 68
disclosure
    for employment 14, 118, 233–4
    of child abuse 125–6
discrimination 45, 202
diversionary tactics 175, 177
diversity 30, 82, 143, 203–4, 206, 209
dolls 90
dramatic play 86, 148
drawing 89
dressing-up 90
duties see playworkers, role

Education (School Premises) Regulations
        1999 96
effort, praise for 68
emergency procedures 107
emotional abuse 119, 122
emotional development 66–8
emotional intelligence 145–6
emotional well-being
    of child 137–8, 144–53, 159–60
    of playworkers 215
emotions see emotional well-being;
        feelings

empathy, development 66, 67
employees, health and safety 95
employment
  contract 192, 234–5, 243
  disclosure 14
  information sources 15
  job applications 16–22
  opportunities 14–15
  rights 234–6, 243
Employment Act 2002 243
Employment Rights Act 1996 233, 243
empowerment, through play 33
encouragement 61, 67, 68, 160, 174,
    177
ending play sessions 93
enhanced disclosure 14, 118, 234
entry requirements 12–13
environments *see* play environment; play
    settings
equality of opportunity 34, 43, 70, 82,
    202–6
equipment
  first aid 106–7
  health and safety 97–8
  maintenance 81
  for physical play 88
escorting children 115
evaluation
  play provision 76–7, 249–53
  in playwork 32
  staff 216–17, 241
event sampling 71
Every Child Matters: Change for
    Children 39–41
everyday routines 60
exploratory play 86, 87, 89–90

failure, sense of 66, 67
families, relationships with 157
fantasy play 86
feedback, from service users 253
feelings
  expression 147–8, 177
  see also emotional well-being
financial resources 82
fine motor skills 58–9, 60, 88
fire safety 108
first aid 104–6, 106–7
Five Year Strategy for Children and
    Learners 42
flexibility, in play environment 30–1,
    75–6, 80
floors 31, 100

food safety 140–2
Food Safety Act 1990 141
Food Safety Regulation 2002 141
freedom of choice, in play 33, 34, 43,
    80, 83

games 57, 62, 88
gender issues 204
Getting Serious About Play 251
goals 58, 164–5
grievance procedures 199, 243
gross motor skills 58, 59, 60
ground rules 165, 177
group activities, size 84
group dynamics 222–3

hand-eye co-ordination 59
hand washing 99
hazards 109–10
health 40, 137–44
health and safety 31, 32, 82, 92, 95–115
    see also safety
Health and Safety at Work Act 1974 96
healthcare plans 103
healthy eating 140–1, 142–4
healthy lifestyles 139–40
heating 31
holistic approach, observation 70
hospital play, career 25–6
hours of work 5, 236
hygiene 97–8, 99, 107, 141

illness 100–2
imaginative play 62, 66, 68, 86, 87, 90–1
inclusion 80, 207–9
independence, encouraging 43, 58,
    163–4
indirect bullying 133
individual needs 43, 159–60, 163
individuality 33, 67
induction, staff 244–5
information packs 261
information sharing 184–5, 195–6, 210,
    212
intellectual development 61–3
interpersonal emotions 147
interpersonal skills 161
intervention process 32, 80, 84
interview technique 20
interviews, for jobs 19–21, 231–2
Investors in People 246

jealousy 168

jigsaw puzzles 88
job adverts 14–15, 226
job applications 16–22, 227–9
job descriptions 230
job interviews 19–21, 231–2
job loss, notice 236
job offers 22, 232
job rotation 239

keeping calm 175, 177
Keepsafe Code 132

laissez-faire leadership 221
language development 57, 63–6
language use, adult communication 186,
    194–5
leadership 221–2
learning, through play 53
legislation 37, 95–7, 117–18, 202, 232–4
    children's awareness of 47
lighting 31
listening
    to children 43, 160, 161–2
    to colleagues 197–8
literacy skills 62, 64–6
local authorities 39, 41, 200
locomotor play 86

management, of play settings 220–6,
    237–46
Management of Health and Safety at
    Work Regulations 96, 254
market research 256
mastery play 86
materials, for play 81
media, impact on behaviour 172
medical needs 102, 103–4
medication 102–3
mentoring 241–2
miniature worlds 90
missing children 108
model making 89
monitoring, of staff 241
mood descriptors, in play 86
morality, development 62
motivation, of staff 239
motor skills 58–9, 60, 88
movement observation 71
music 89

name calling 133
National Daycare Standards 9
national framework for children's
    services 39–41

National Minimum Wage 236
needs
    children's 45–6
    individual 159–60
    of parents 184
    for play 34, 54
    provision for 58, 60–1, 63, 65, 65–6,
        67–8, 78–9, 79–80
neglect 119, 123
    see also child abuse
negotiation, of behaviour policies 164–5
negotiation skills, children 129
networking 257
non-participant observation 71
notice, termination of employment 236
nursery nursing, career 26
NVQ courses 13

object play 87
objectives, of play provision 76–7, 251
observation
    encouraging in children 63
    of children's play 32, 69–71
older children, development 57, 59–60,
        61–2, 64–5, 67
open door policies 183
open questions 161–2
organisational development 246
organisational process 32
outdoor play 88
    safety 98–9, 112
outings 108, 113–15

paid leave 236
painting 89
parents/carers 171, 181–8
participant observation 71
participation
    of child in groups 43
    in play by playworkers 63, 80, 84
partnerships, with parents and carers
        182
passive behaviour 171
pay see salary; statutory pay
peer approval 57
person specifications 231
personal development objectives 217
personal emotions 147
personal qualities 7
personality see emotional development
physical abuse 119, 122
physical bullying 133

physical development 58–61
physical play 87–8, 148
physical punishment 158
planning
　activities 74–5
　play space 79–82
play
　behavioural modes for 85
　children's need for 34, 54
　children's right to 44
　definitions 52–3
　imaginative 62, 68, 86, 87, 90–1
　importance 53
　mood descriptors 86
　process 32
　types 86–7
　VITAL opportunities 78–9
play areas
　safety 111–12
　see also play environment
play cues 84
play cycle 84
play environment 30–2, 33, 77–8,
　　79–82, 84, 177
　health and safety 97, 98–9, 110–12
　see also play settings
play frames 85
play opportunities, for child
　　development 58, 60, 63, 68, 88
Play Partnerships 258
play services
　development 253, 256–8
　evaluation 76–7, 249–53
play sessions, ending 93
play settings 5
　management 220–6, 237–46
　and parents 183–4, 188
　policies and procedures 49
　resources 81–3
　structure and organisation 194, 216
　transition to 152–3
　types 220
　see also play environment
play spaces 77–8, 83
play therapy, career 26
playgrounds
　safety 98–9, 112
　see also outdoor play; play areas
playwork
　assumptions and values 33–4
　principles 34–5
　processes 32
　promotion of services 258–60

Playwork Induction Standard 9–10
Playwork Principles 34–5
Playwork Quality Assurance Schemes
　　246
playworkers
　career 4–5, 23–4
　as role models 56, 140
　reflective practice 214–17
　role 3–4, 6–7, 44, 191–2
　　accidents 104
　　child protection 120–1
　　health promotion 138
　　injuries 104
　　planning activities 74–5
　　play environment 35
　　relationships with children 156
　　sick children 101–2
　　special needs 171
　　transitions 153
Police Act 1997 (Part V) 233, 234
police check see disclosure
policies
　behaviour 164–5, 173
　child protection 128
　conflict 180
　equal opportunities 203
　health 138
　health and safety 96, 97
　open door 183
　play provision 255
　play settings 49, 156
　record keeping 70
portfolios
　of child's progress 69–70
　professional 18–19, 217
positive attitudes 40
possessiveness 67
Practical Quality Assurance System for
　　Small Organisations 246
praise see encouragement
PRICELESS (mnemonic) 45
principles, of playwork 34–5
probationary period 235
procedures
　for child protection issues 119–20
　disciplinary 243
　for escorting children 115
　grievance 199, 243
　for play settings 49
　promoting health 138
professional development 217–18,
　　244–6
professional portfolios 18–19, 217

promotion, of playwork and services 258–61

Protection of Children Act 1999 118, 232, 234

punishment 158
   see also sanctions

puppets 58, 90

qualifications
   in food hygiene 141
   playworkers 8, 9–14
   other careers 24, 25, 26, 27, 28

qualitative evaluation 250

quantitative evaluation 250

Race Relations Act 1976 202, 233

reading skills 64–6

record keeping
   accidents 104
   children 43, 69–70, 209–13
   job applications 21

recruitment 226–36

Redundancy Pay 236

references 18, 19, 232

reflective practice 214–17

registration, of attendance 108

relationships
   with children 32, 155–7, 160, 166–70
   with parents and carers 181–4
   between staff 190–1

Reporting of Injuries, Diseases and Dangerous Occurrences Regulations 1985 104

resources, for play 81–3

responsibilities of staff 238
   see also playworkers, role

rewards 174–5

rights
   children 34, 35–6, 37–9, 44, 47, 157
   employment 234–6, 243
   individual 202
   policies reflecting 43
   respecting others' 45
   to safety 32, 33

risk assessment 109–10

risk-taking 91–2, 130

role
   of management 220–1
   of playworkers *see* playworkers, role

role models
   for behaviour 166–7, 172
   equal opportunity 206
   for health 140, 144

playworkers as 56, 140
   in social development 56, 57

role play 87, 90
   in development 57, 68, 130, 148, 204

rotas, for tasks 239

rough and tumble play 87

rules 68, 165, 175

safety 63
   around play setting 93, 100
   during play 32, 60, 110–12
   in national framework 40
   on outings 114–15
   right to in play 32, 33
   teaching dangers 130
   see also health and safety

salary 15–16, 236

sanctions 135, 176, 178
   see also punishment

sand play 89

schools, childcare 42

security, in record-keeping 212

self-esteem
   developing 129, 148–50, 167
   of playworkers 214

self-evaluation, playworkers 216–17

self-help skills 58

Sex Discrimination Act 1975 202, 233

sexual abuse 119, 122–3

sexual activity 158

sharing 58

shortlists 231

shouting (adults) 158

sick pay 236

signs
   of abuse 122–3
   of bullying 134
   of illness 101
   of inclusion 208
   of staff tensions 223

skills
   interpersonal 161
   leadership 222
   management 221
   of playworkers 7–8
   practising 60

SkillsActive Playwork Unit 254

smacking 158

SNVQ courses 13

social development 56–8

social play 68–9, 87

social work, career 27

socialisation 167

socio-dramatic play 87
SPECIAL (mnemonic) 166
special needs 61, 171
　　see also disability
SPICE (mnemonic) 55–6
sport 57
SPRITO 254
staff 82
　　allegations of abuse 125
　　communication 194–5
　　information sharing 195–6, 210, 212
　　mentoring 241
　　recruitment 226–36
　　relationships between 190–1
　　relationships with parents/carers
　　　　181–4
　　retaining 237
　　supervision 242
　　support for 197–8
　　training/development 244–6
　　　　see also qualifications
　　see also playworkers; teamwork
staff appraisals 242
staff development 244
staff meetings 196, 238
standard disclosure 233–4
statutory pay 236
stock maintenance 81, 82, 83
storage areas 97
stories 58, 68, 148, 179
supervision
　　children on outings 114–15
　　of staff 242
support
　　for children 131, 133–5
　　for colleagues 197–8
　　for play 83–4
swimming 88
symbolic play 87

tactile activities 63
taking turns 58, 66, 84, 168
target child observation 71
teaching, career 27–8
teaching assistant, career 28
team development 223
team meetings 196, 238
teamwork 193–9, 222–3
　　see also playworkers; staff
TEAMWORK (mnemonic) 193

temperament *see* emotional
　　development
Ten Year Childcare Strategy 42
tidying up 31, 58, 93
time management 215–16
time-out strategy 175
time sampling 71
toilet facilities 99
toy safety 98
trail observation 71
training 9–14, 217–18, 244–6
transitions, coping with 151–3
turn taking 58, 66, 84, 168

UN Convention on the Rights of the
　　Child 35–6, 44, 48, 157
unfair dismissal 236

values, in playwork 33
verbal abuse 158
verbal bullying 133
videos 179
views, listening to 43, 93, 160, 161–2,
　　197–8
visitors 108
visual aids 82–3
visual perception 63
VITAL (mnemonic) 78–9, 251
voluntary organisations 41, 200
voluntary work 8–9, 9

water play 89
whole-body co-ordination 59
work environment 96
work experience 8–9
working hours 5, 236
Working Together to Safeguard Children
　　117–18
Workplace (Health, Safety and Welfare)
　　Regulations 1992 96
writing skills 64–6
written statement of employment
　　234–5, 243

young children, development 57, 59,
　　61, 64, 66
young people *see* adolescents; children;
　　older children
youth and community work 28